Family and Property
in Sung China

Family and Property in Sung China

Yüan Ts'ai's *Precepts for Social Life*

TRANSLATED, WITH ANNOTATIONS AND
INTRODUCTION, BY
Patricia Buckley Ebrey

PRINCETON UNIVERSITY PRESS

Copyright © 1984 by Princeton University Press
Published by Princeton University Press,
41 William Street, Princeton, New Jersey 08540
In the United Kingdom:
Princeton University Press, Guildford, Surrey

All Rights Reserved
Library of Congress Cataloging in Publication Data
will be found on the last printed page of this book
ISBN 0-691-05426-6

The preparation of this volume was made possible by a grant from the
Translation Program of the National Endowment for the Humanities,
an independent federal agency

This book has been composed in Monophoto Bembo
by Asco Trade Typesetting Ltd, Hong Kong

Clothbound editions of Princeton University Press books
are printed on acid-free paper, and binding materials are
chosen for strength and durability.

Printed in the United States of America
by Princeton University Press
Princeton, New Jersey

CONTENTS

Contents

PREFACE

This book is in two parts. Part One is an essay in which I address general questions about the upper class of traditional China. I do this by exploring conceptions of family life and property as elements in the culture of the upper class, elements singled out because of their importance in shaping the behavior that sustained upper class status. Thus this book differs from most studies of the upper class, which concern political or economic behavior, as well as most studies of Chinese culture and intellectual traditions, which concentrate on issues chosen for their philosophical or artistic importance. Here, instead, I examine the elements of culture that were important in the routine decisions of everyday life.

Part Two is a translation of a manual of advice addressed to family heads on the subject of how to handle their responsibilities toward their families' material, moral, and social life. Titled *Precepts for Social Life*, it was written by Yüan Ts'ai in the twelfth century in a style so lucid that twentieth-century readers should have no difficulty understanding the concerns and ideas expressed in it. Some readers may wish to read the translation first, before considering my analysis of it in Part One.

Preparation of this book was greatly aided by a grant from the Translation Program of the National Endowment for the Humanities. In addition, the Research Board of the University of Illinois provided me with funds for assistance in the collation of the editions of Yüan Ts'ai's book and for the preparation of the final manuscript. Joyce Liu and Mary Hoffman ably aided me in these tasks. Burr Nelson helped me get the manuscript on a word processor and cheerfully came to my aid whenever technology failed me.

I must also thank those who have read the manuscript in whole or in part and offered advice and criticism. They include Lloyd Eastman, William Hennessey, Ronald Toby, and Howard Wechsler at the University of Illinois, as well as Robert Hymes of Columbia University, Brian McKnight of the University of Hawaii, and James Watson of the University of Pittsburgh. Without their encouragement, I would not have been as bold in the formulation of my views here. In addition, James Liu of Princeton University carefully reviewed the translation and kept me from making many errors. Whatever accuracy I have attained in the translation owes much to his suggestions and corrections. None of these scholars should of course be held in any way responsible for errors that remain.

ABBREVIATIONS

CCFC (1564)	*Ch'ü-chou fu-chih*, 1564 ed.
CCFC (1622)	*Ch'ü-chou fu-chih*, 1622 ed.
CF	*Chia fan*, by Ssu-ma Kuang
CHSC	Chung-hua shu-chü, Peking
CHTK	*Chou-hsien t'i-kang* (anonymous)
CMC	*Ming-kung sh'u-p'an ch'ing-ming chi*
CPTC	The *Chih-pu-tsu chai ts'ung-shu* ed. of the *Precepts*★
CSL	*Chin-ssu lu*, by Chu Hsi and Lü Tsu-ch'ien
CTTL	*Chieh-tzu t'ung-lu*, by Liu Ch'ing-chih
CTWC	*Chu Tzu wen-chi*, by Chu Hsi
CWKCC	*Chu Wen-kung ch'üan-chi*, by Chu Hsi
HH	*Hsiao-hsüeh*, by Chu Hsi
HTHSTCC	*Hou-ts'un hsien-sheng ta-ch'üan chi*, by Liu K'o-chuang
ICC	*I-chien chih*, by Hung Mai
KCTS	*Ko-chih ts'ung-shu* ed. of the *Precepts*★
PCMS	*Po-chia ming-shu* ed. of the *Precepts*★
PYT	*Pao-yen t'ang pi-chi*, *hui-chi* ed. of the *Precepts*★
SCSC	Shih-chieh shu-chü, Taipei
SHT	*Sung hsing-t'ung*, by Tou I
SK	*Ssu-k'u ch'üan-shu chen-pen* ed. of the *Precepts*★
SKCP	*Ssu-k'u ch'üan-shu chen-pen* series, facsimile copies published by the Commercial press, Shanghai, 1934 and continued by Commercial Press, Taipei, 1972–
SMCC	*Ssu-ma Wen-cheng kung ch'uan-chia chi*, by Ssu-ma Kuang

SMSSI	*Ssu-ma shih shu-i*, by Ssu-ma Kuang
SPTK	*Ssu-pu ts'ung-k'an* series, published by Commercial Press, Shanghai, 1919–1939
SS	*Sung shih*, by T'o T'o, et al.
SYHA	*Sung-Yüan hsüeh-an*, by Huang Tsung-hsi
TSCC	*Ts'ung-shu chi-ch'eng* series, published by Commercial Press, Shanghai, 1935–1939
YCL	*Yu-ch'un lu* ed. of the *Precepts*★
YSCH	*Yen-shih chia-hsün*, by Yen Chih-t'ui
1179 ed.	*KCTS, PCMS, PYT*, and *YCL*
1190 ed.	*CPTC*

Full bibliographical information is provided in Appendix A (which includes the editions of the *Precepts* marked by an asterisk above) or in the Sources Cited. Citation of classical texts, which often vary in their internal arrangement, has usually been to chapter and section, followed by a page citation to an English translation. If a translated passage then is given, it is still my own unless it is marked "from. . . ." The published translation cited is useful for seeing the context of the passage and does not always indicate that I have interpreted the passage the same way.

Class, Culture, Family, and Property

CHAPTER I

Introduction

In late imperial China (Sung through Ch'ing dynasties, A.D. 960–1911), the major social distinction routinely evoked was between *shih-ta-fu* (literati and officials) and everyone else. In social life, all the gradations of rank, wealth, and refinement that distinguished *shih-ta-fu* as individuals tended to be blurred. High officials could have brothers who were scholars, artists, estate managers, or lazy dilettantes. Men from these families, whatever their own choice of occupation, freely interacted, visiting each other and marrying each other's sisters.

The empirical evidence that officials, intellectuals, and other men of significance came from a single stratum has been provided by modern scholarly studies of their social backgrounds.[1] But people of the time were also well aware

---

[1] For the Yüan, Ming, and Ch'ing periods several recent studies have shown the varied activities of the group I am calling *shih-ta-fu*. See, in particular, Hilary Beattie, *Land and Lineage in China*; John W. Dardess, "Confucianism, Local Reform, and Centralization in Late Yüan Chekiang, 1342–1359"; Jerry Dennerline, *The Chia-ting Loyalists*; and James Polachek, "Gentry Hegemony." The classic works on the composition of the elite of this period, Ping-ti Ho's *Ladder of Success in Imperial China* and Chung-li Chang's *The Chinese Gentry*, are both now over twenty years old and reflect the concerns with measuring social mobility of that time. They contain, however, a great deal of other valuable information, and their demonstration that few officials came from families in which all immediate male ancestors had also been officials can be read the other way: the social group from which officials came also included teachers, estate managers, art collectors, and wastrels.

of the existence of the *shih-ta-fu* as a class of people. In occasional writing this term was used often and casually, as though its meaning were obvious. In Sung dynasty (960–1279) works, *"shih-ta-fu"* was used to refer to the category of people who owned, borrowed, read, or wrote books, who performed classical rituals, who aspired to office, and who paid visits to high officials and other powerful people.[2] In these historical sources, no rigid line separated *shih-ta-fu* from others. The qualifications for *shih-ta-fu* status were fuzzy. The most important was identification with the Confucian tradition of scholarship and public service; this identification in turn presupposed education, leisure, and freedom from the need to perform manual labor. Since no legal benefits accompanied the status, no one tried to set up unambiguous markers, or prevent the sons of peasants or merchants from learning to act like and associate with *shih-ta-fu*. Yet this fluidity did not undermine the significance of

---

For the Sung, the classic work on the composition of the elite is E. A. Kracke's "Region, Family and Individual in the Chinese Examination System." Recent scholarship has taken a much broader view of elite status, largely consistent with my view of the *shih-ta-fu*, though other scholars have chosen different terms and different criteria for selecting their unit of study (i.e. "political elite," "professional elite," "local elite," and so on). Particularly worth noting are Robert Hartwell's "Demographic, Political, and Social Transformations of China, 750–1550," and several recent dissertations and conference papers, including Robert Hymes, "Prominence and Power in Sung China: The Local Elite of Fu-chou, Chiang-hsi," John Chaffee, "Education and Examinations in Sung Society (960–1279)," and Richard Davis, "'Protection,' Imperial Favor, and Family Fortunes in Sung China." In addition to these works in English, detailed studies of the social background of officials have been done in considerable quantity by Japanese scholars, especially Aoyama Sadao and Ihara Hiroshi (see the articles listed in Sources Cited).

[2] For examples of all these usages, see Yeh Meng-te, *Shih-lin yen-yü*, 1, p. 6; 2, p. 13; 3, p. 23; Wang Ming-ch'ing, *Hui-chu hou-lu*, 4, p. 410; 7, pp. 548, 549; Chou Pi-ta, *Erh-lao t'ang tsa-chih*, 3, p. 50; Chu Yü, *P'ing-chou k'o-t'an*, 1, pp. 7, 10–11; *CTWC* 1, p. 22.

being a *shih-ta-fu*; even in relating humorous anecdotes Sung writers regularly indicated whether the person in question belonged to the *shih-ta-fu*.[3]

If labels are needed, the *shih-ta-fu* can be thought of as a social class in Joseph Schumpeter's sense. Schumpeter distinguishes classes that are the analytic constructs of the observer, sets of people arbitrarily selected according to some attribute (as in landlord class, educated class, mercantile class) and the classes that exist in society. These social classes are visible to observers because "class members behave toward one another in a fashion characteristically different from their conduct toward members of other classes." This occurs in part because "social intercourse within class barriers is promoted by the similarity of manners and habits of life, of things that are evaluated in a positive and negative sense, that arouse interest. In intercourse across class borders, differences on all these points repel and inhibit sympathy."[4] Social classes of this sort are not economic classes, nor are they necessarily rigid or closed.

Modern scholars' conceptions of the *shih-ta-fu* of late imperial China often seem a collection of contradictory images. Poets and painters are easily idealized. Chinese, Japanese, and Westerners alike are attracted to the human personality that shines through the writing of great poets, especially the

---

[3] Good examples of this effort to "place" people are seen throughout Hung Mai's *ICC*. Someone could be identified as *shih-ta-fu* by a statement that he was an official, or was attempting to become one, or was related to one. Or he could simply be called a *shih* or a *shih-jen*. For instance, in one case a five-year-old child who got trapped while playing was identified as the child of a *shih-ta-fu* family (*ICC chia* 12, p. 104). Those who were not *shih-ta-fu* could be termed "villagers," "commoners," "merchants," "rich people," and so on. Four successive stories in one chapter deal respectively with a *shih-jen*, a commoner family, a rich family, and the author's wife's uncle (*ICC chia* 16, pp. 140–41).

[4] *Imperialism, Social Classes: Two Essays*, pp. 105, 107, 109.

T'ang (618–906) and Sung masters.[5] Likewise, through their creative works, the literati painters of the Sung through Ch'ing (1644–1911) dynasties are seen as sensitive to beauty and truth and as essentially good, caring people.[6] By contrast, the political and economic activities of the *shih-ta-fu* have not been made to seem uniformly appealing. One image is of the corrupt official, merely venal or utterly vicious. Another is of the greedy, aggressive landowner who was always on the lookout for ways to squeeze more from his tenants or take over the lands of peasants with small holdings. Chinese social and political critics have decried these members of their society for centuries, but the potency of these images owes much to the writings of modern social critics, like Ch'ü T'ung-tsu, who have used them to unveil the exploitation inherent in the traditional class system.[7] Still, there has been a countervailing force tempering these images in the work of institutional historians. Scholars like E. A. Kracke, James Liu, and Ray Huang, even if aware of the inadequacies of the bureaucratic system, have generally been impressed with the commitment of a core of important officials to fairness in recruitment, in the imposition of taxes, and in the administration of justice.[8]

Confucianism as an ideology for the ruling class has also evoked divergent reactions. Not surprisingly, intellectual historians like T'ang Chün-i and Wm. T. de Bary have seen

[5] The work of Arthur Waley has helped establish this view of poets. See, especially, *The Life and Times of Po Chü-i* and *Yüan Mei, Eighteenth Century Chinese Poet*.

[6] See, for instance, James Cahill, *Hills Beyond a River* and *Parting at the Shore*.

[7] See *Law and Society in Traditional China*, *Han Social Structure*, and *Local Government in China Under the Ch'ing*.

[8] E. A. Kracke, Jr., *Civil Service in Early Sung China*; James T. C. Liu, *Ou-yang Hsiu: An Eleventh-Century Neo-Confucianist*; Ray Huang, *1587, A Year of No Significance*.

it as an ennobling philosophy; to them study of the Classics and concern with current scholarly issues fostered a great sense of seriousness about personal moral improvement and social responsibility.[9] But others have seen Confucianism as a cover for preserving the current distribution of power. Etienne Balazs argued that the traditionalist character of Confucianism served those at the top of a hierarchical state: "strict adherence to orthodox doctrines was the surest defense against the pressures of other social groups."[10]

The contradictions in these diverse images of the *shih-ta-fu* have resulted in large part because scholars habitually treat the self-serving behavior of the *shih-ta-fu* as phenomena unrelated to their culture. They see admirable cultural values as motivating highly accomplished *shih-ta-fu* but no values at all behind the actions of the others, presumed to be acting on self-interest. In this book I try to overcome this polarized view by examining how *shih-ta-fu* thought about two subjects that are fundamental to self-interest: family and property. I use an anthropological concept of culture to show how decisions about the everyday activities essential to survival and social reproduction were based in a system of meaning intricately connected to high ideals. Indeed, I suspect that common understandings on these matters—ones so vital to preserving social status—allowed the "similarity in manners and habits of life" that gave *shih-ta-fu* of varying attainments a common identity.[11]

[9] See Wm. Theodore de Bary, ed., *Self and Society in Ming Thought, The Unfolding of Neo-Confucianism*, and *Neo-Confucian Orthodoxy and the Learning of the Heart-and-Mind.*

[10] *Chinese Civilization and Bureaucracy*, pp. 18–19. This theme of ideology versus practice is developed further in Balazs, *Political Theory and Administrative Reality in Traditional China.*

[11] This is only speculation since no one has ever studied in detail the manners and daily habits of either *shih-ta-fu* or other social groups. From anecdotes we know that people were quick to guess the social status of

The concept of culture has been so central to the discipline of anthropology that new directions of anthropological theory or research have led to continuing redefinitions of it. Here I use culture in its broadest sense, as the repertoire of ideation behind the social behavior of members of a group. The components of a culture include habits of thought and fundamental categories, as well as notions of what should be done, what is fun to do, and what is actually done. Some components of culture are fully articulated (self-consciously held) by virtually all members of the group, some are seldom thought about, and many are assumed to be fact and not ideas at all. Emotions are frequently involved. As A. L. Kroeber and Clyde Kluckhohn wrote, "the individual is seldom emotionally neutral to those sectors of his culture which touch him directly. Cultural patterns are *felt*, emotionally adhered to or rejected." [12]

Because culture must be communicated to exist, people in a society vary in how fully they share in a common culture. Cultural principles are conveyed through written and spoken word, physical signs, clothing and building designs, gestures and manners, myths and folktales, stories and proverbs, to mention only some of the more important ways. Even those with identical access to these symbols and ideas do not act identically; besides simple idiosyncrasies, people's actions depend on the political, economic, and even demographic opportunities they face. What culture provides them is a stock of notions and meanings useful in defining their situations and the alternatives open to them. [13]

travelers, presumably on the basis of dress, presence of attendants, way of speaking, and so on, but only rarely do anecdotes go into detail on these matters.

[12] *Culture: A Critical Review of Concepts and Definitions*, p. 308. Excellent discussions of the concept of culture are also found in Clifford Geertz, *The Interpretation of Cultures.*

[13] A good analysis of the systemic relationship between culture and

Introduction

There may appear to be a disciplinary contradiction in studying the "culture" of "classes." Culture as a concept has been refined by anthropologists who by and large have studied classless societies. Thus they have generally analyzed the culture of entire societies, not separate classes. Sociologists who have studied classes have been well aware of their cultural distinctiveness but until recently have usually concerned themselves only with the emblematic aspects of this distinctiveness or with the social and political ideology that a class uses to justify its position. Here I look at something smaller than a generalized "Chinese culture" but larger than those features of the upper class's culture that identified them or justified their status.

This understanding of "the culture of the *shih-ta-fu*" differs from that of many historians, who usually think of upper class culture in terms of how it differed from the culture of commoners. By contrast, I use the phrase "culture of the *shih-ta-fu*" to refer to the entire set of ideas and notions that motivated the behavior of *shih-ta-fu*. It is certainly true that identification with a set of classical ideals separated *shih-ta-fu* from commoners, and a variety of prejudices maintained this distance, "inhibiting sympathy" across class lines. But these ideals and attitudes by no means account for all of the behavior that sustained status as a *shih-ta-fu*. Notions underlying education of sons and preservation of family property may have been more important in this regard, and yet they need not have differed radically from the ideas of peasants. After all, much of the difference between the actions of *shih-ta-fu* and those of commoners was due to differences in economic or political opportunities, not differences in goals. If we are to comprehend the commonalities underlying the

concrete social and economic situations (referred to as context) is found in Stevan Harrell's *Ploughshare Village: Culture and Context in Taiwan*, esp. pp. 8–14.

diverse activities of *shih-ta-fu*, we must look at the whole range of ideas and conceptions they acted on, not limiting ourselves to the ones they thought set them above commoners or ignoring others as merely "Chinese."

In recent years, as the basic anthropological concept of culture has come to be widely understood and appreciated, historians have explicitly set out to analyze culture. That is, rather than start out to study values or ideology, they have purposely gone in search of the culture of the group or society in question. The way to do this—the sources and methods to use—are still being worked out. For better-documented periods, such as the nineteenth and twentieth centuries, American and European historians have tried to use letters, diaries, newspapers, and other sources written by or for relatively undistinguished people.[14] Such sources are less readily available for premodern China, but some do exist. Here I focus on a lengthy advice book, using it as the testimony of an informant. The book is the *Precepts for Social Life* (*Shih fan*) written by Yüan Ts'ai (fl. 1140–1195) in 1178, printed first in 1179, and reissued by the author in 1190.[15] It is translated in full in Part Two.

---

[14] This is seen especially in works on the history of the family. See, for instance, Herbert G. Gutman, *The Black Family in Slavery and Freedom, 1750–1925*; Lawrence Stone, *The Family, Sex and Marriage in England 1500–1800*; and Tamara K. Hareven, ed., *Family and Kin in Urban Communities, 1700–1930*.

[15] The translation of the title of Yüan Ts'ai's book perhaps deserves explanation. The title in Chinese is either *Shih fan* or *Yüan-shih shih fan*. The addition of the author's name to help specify a book was a very common informal modification of a title; thus *Yüan-shih shih fan* means nothing more than Mr. Yüan's *Shih fan* (and not the Yüan family *Shih fan* as some writers have assumed). The *shih* in *Shih fan* is a word with a broad range of meanings, from "generation" to "era" to "social world." I think its meaning here is "social life" or "social world" not only because of the content of the book but also because of the discussion of the title in the prefaces. Yüan Ts'ai reported that the original title was *Su hsün*, "Instructions for [Improving] the Popular Ethos," and that, to assert an

Yüan Ts'ai makes a good informant because of who he was and what he wrote. Anthropologists choose informants for their intelligence, their willingness to talk, and their knowledge of their own culture. A key point in anthropological analysis is that one talks to an informant to learn about his own culture, and what he and those in his group do, not what he *says* members of other groups do. His conceptions of other groups are elements of his culture and inform his interactions with them, but they are not a substitute for such people's own statements about themselves. Yüan Ts'ai was certainly knowledgeable about family life and property management, and he was exceptionally skillful in explaining what he knew. The *Precepts for Social Life* consists of three chapters: Getting Along with Relatives, Improving Personal Conduct, and Managing Family Affairs. Each chapter has about seventy brief essays on topics such as rearing children, arranging marriages, writing wills, disciplining servants, investing money, avoiding arguments, and attaining tranquillity. In them Yüan Ts'ai reported what people generally do and what he thought they should do. He justified his opinions not by citing authority but by analyzing the situations, thus revealing *how* he thought about them, not just what he thought.

Yüan Ts'ai's thoughts on all these subjects gain added significance from his background; he comes as close to being a "typical" or "representative" *shih-ta-fu* as anyone leaving written record. This can be seen by looking at Yüan Ts'ai's society and his place in it.

---

even wider applicability, Liu Chen changed it to *Shih fan*. Later a friend suggested that this was too immodest, implying as it did that one was offering rules for an entire society, as some of the Classics had. Clearly they did not take the title to mean rules for the generations of the Yüan family, a rather modest audience.

YÜAN TS'AI'S BACKGROUND AND AUDIENCE

In his preface Yüan Ts'ai made it clear that he was not addressing classicists or philosophers. He said their points were abstruse, beyond the reach even of diligent students, and too concerned with metaphysics. Instead, he was addressing a general public and to that end writing in a way simple enough, he said, even for villagers and women. From the content of his essays, however, Yüan Ts'ai evidently was speaking mostly to his peers: educated property owners, often referred to explicitly as *shih-ta-fu*.[16]

The Sung was one of the greatest ages of the *shih-ta-fu*. It is by now commonplace to call the Sung the beginning of China's modern period, drawing attention not only to the great expansion of commerce and urbanization but also to a shift in the style of the upper class.[17] The civil service examinations produced several times as many *chin-shih* (highest degree holders) in the Sung as they had in the T'ang, and by the twelfth century they had gained full recognition as the primary and most honorable means to gain office. Almost every prefecture still had eminent families, and nationally

[16] J. P. McDermott, "Land Tenure and Rural Control in the Liangche Region During the Southern Sung," repeatedly refers to the *Precepts* as Yüan Ts'ai's family instructions to his sons and uses the text as a source for conditions in Ch'ü-chou alone. I see no evidence for this view. In Liu Chen's preface he says Yüan Ts'ai decided to publish his book in the town of Le-ch'ing, where he was then magistrate, in order to "promote honesty in inter-personal relations and bring improvement to habits and customs." Yüan Ts'ai mostly reports what he saw as generally true, in Ch'ü-chou, the capital, Le-ch'ing, and anywhere else he knew of. When he saw a custom or attitude as special to an area, he would specify the place, as he did for areas of exorbitant interest rates (3.65). Otherwise he was not describing his own family or his own prefecture so much as people as he knew them.

[17] A good introduction to the Sung is E. A. Kracke's essay, "Sung Society, Change Within Tradition." For current western scholarship on the period, a useful collection is John Winthrop Haeger, ed., *Crisis and Prosperity in Sung China*.

famous men usually were scions of them, yet the Sung was not so aristocratic as the T'ang. In the T'ang dynasty rich families tried to marry their sons to daughters of "famous families," especially the Lis, Lus, Ts'uis, Chengs, and Wangs. In the Sung, the cliche was that they sought top-placed examination candidates as husbands for their daughters.[18]

The Sung is also a period in which the effectiveness of civil officials in government was at its height. Competition between factions of officials was more crucial than either imperial whim or military force in determining policy. The examination system undoubtedly helped to inspire a deeper commitment to education and learning on the part of the *shih-ta-fu* in the Sung than had been typical in earlier dynasties. Probably even more important was a succession of great scholars who brought traditional learning—classical, historical, and philosophical—to new heights. Fan Chung-yen (989–1052), Ou-yang Hsiu (1007–1072), Ssu-ma Kuang (1019–1086), and Su Shih (1036–1101) provided inspiring models to their less talented contemporaries.[19] Moreover, the great political controversies of the eleventh and twelfth centuries—Wang An-shih's New Policies and the reaction to them—forced even minor local officials and examination candidates to think about national policies. The loss of north China in 1126 kept this concern for politics very high among the educated. Because of all these factors,

[18] On the aristocratic system of the T'ang, see David Johnson, *The Medieval Chinese Oligarchy*, Patricia Ebrey, *The Aristocratic Families of Early Imperial China*, and Denis Twitchett, "The Composition of the T'ang Ruling Class." For the transition to the Sung system, see Hartwell, "Transformations of China" and David Johnson, "The Last Years of a Great Clan." On the development of the examination system, see Chaffee, "Education and Examinations."

[19] On these men, see James T. C. Liu's "An Early Sung Reformer: Fan Chung-yen," his *Ou-yang Hsiu*, and the long biography of Su Shih by George C. Hatch in Herbert Franke, ed., *Sung Biographies*, vol. 3, 900–968.

the Sung was the classical age of the *shih-ta-fu*, the period when their civility, learning, respect for merit, and conscientious political administration were at their height.

During the Sung there were, of course, differences in style and attitude among the *shih-ta-fu* from generation to generation and region to region. Therefore, to understand which group Yüan Ts'ai can be thought to have represented and to have addressed, we must look more closely at his time and place. The prefecture Yüan Ts'ai came from, Ch'ü-chou, was neither the most advanced nor the least developed in this age. But it was part of the southeast—today's Kiangsu, Chekiang, Anhwei, Fukien, and Kiangsi—the region that witnessed a dramatic rise in population and economic importance during the Sung. Even during the Northern Sung (960–1126), with its capital at K'ai-feng in Honan, scholars and officials were as likely as not to have come from this region and to have lived in a milieu of merchants, manufacturers, and estates planted in highly productive rice.[20] After the loss of the north and the retreat of the court south of the Yangtze River in 1127, the cultural dominance of the south was to be expected, and the richness of its resources made possible a period of splendor. The fame of its capital, Hangchow, as a "Heavenly" city survives today.[21]

Within this southeastern region, Ch'ü-chou, well inland in the western part of the Sung circuit of Che-tung, was not a literary or philosophical center, and none of the one or two hundred most famous Sung men came from Ch'ü-chou.[22] Nevertheless, the area cannot be classified as backwater. The

---

[20] See Kracke, "Region, Family and Individual in the Chinese Examination System."

[21] See Jacques Gernet, *Daily Life in China on the Eve of the Mongol Invasion, 1250–1276*, esp. pp. 22–58.

[22] Based on Franke's *Sung Biographies*, which includes no biographies of men from Ch'ü-chou.

prefecture was founded in the early T'ang (621), and in the early Sung (981) its population had increased enough so that one of its four counties was divided in two to make five counties all together.[23] In the census of the Ch'ung-ning period (1102–1107), it was reported to have 117,903 households and was therefore probably over half a million in population.[24] Its capital, Hsin-an, where Yüan Ts'ai lived, was on the river linking present-day Hunan and Kiangsi with the national capital at Hangchow.[25] The outlying counties were more mountainous and undoubtedly less prosperous.[26]

Most important in asserting that Ch'ü-chou was not a cultural backwater is the success of its *shih-ta-fu* in the examinations. Two Ming gazetteers dated 1564 and 1622 provide full lists of all the *chin-shih* of the area in the Sung, the later one adding a list of families or kin groups who produced *chin-shih* in successive generations.[27] According to these lists, the prefecture as a whole produced 597 *chin-shih* during the Sung, or an average of two a year.[28] Since Ch'ü-chou contained only from about half a percent to one percent of the registered population of the country (about half a percent during the Northern Sung and one percent during the

[23] CCFC (1564) 1/2b–7a.
[24] SS 88, p. 2177. The individual figure given is 228,858, but these statistics are well known to be underestimates. On Sung population statistics, see Ping-ti Ho, "An Estimate of the Total Population of Sung-Chin China."
[25] See the map in Yoshinobu Shiba, *Commerce and Society in Sung China*, p. 43.
[26] For the variations in the economic conditions in the prefectures of Liangche in the Southern Sung, see McDermott, "Land Tenure and Rural Control." McDermott classified Ch'ü-chou as one of the least developed areas of Liangche, but this is, of course, in comparison with areas like Su-chou and Hangchow, not areas in other circuits further inland.
[27] CCFC (1564) 11/1a–18a; CCFC (1622) 11/40a–59a.
[28] Chaffee (p. 382) comes up with 609 *chin-shih* using a different set of gazetteers (p.351).

Southern Sung, 1127–1279), to produce about one and a half percent of the Sung *chin-shih* was a little above average.[29] In this it was typical of the prefectures of Che-tung.[30]

Ch'ü-chou was also not lacking in eminent and established families.[31] The 1622 gazetteer lists all the families of the prefecture who produced at least three *chin-shih* sometime during the Sung, Yüan, or Ming dynasties. The compilers must have had access to genealogies or other sources showing exact kinship connections because they often divided men of the same surname from the same county into several kin groups. If we take those that produced at least one of their *chin-shih* in the Sung (and of course at least two more either in the Sung or later), there were fifty-eight "established" families in the prefecture during the Sung, just over half of whom lived in the prefectural capital. These families produced 282 *chin-shih* during the Sung, or nearly half the total for the prefecture. If we take a much narrower definition of prominent family and look at only those who produced five or more *chin-shih* during the Sung, there were twenty-four "leading" families that altogether produced 233 *chin-shih*, approximately forty percent of the total. Since Yüan Ts'ai was the first to obtain the *chin-shih* in his family and was followed by only two later relatives, his family was not one of these twenty-four leading ones but was one of the fifty-eight established ones.

[29] According to the statistics given in the *Wen-hsien t'ung-k'ao*, 32, pp. 304–307, there were about 40,000 *chin-shih* in the Sung. This figure is approximate since figures for the last twelve examinations are missing.

[30] See Chaffee, "Education and Examinations," pp. 382–91.

[31] Here I am using "families" in the loose sense of family lines or kin groups. These lines or groups seem to be the constituent units of the upper class, yet their size and degree of cohesion are scarcely to be guessed at. (Cf. Hartwell, "Transformations of China," p. 380.) Although it would be desirable to follow James Watson's advice on use of kinship terminology for historical kin units ("Chinese Kinship Reconsidered: Anthropological Perspectives on Historical Research"), precision is not possible in this case.

In one of his essays Yüan Ts'ai advised his audience to think of the changes in the eminent families of their town during the previous twenty years as evidence of the instability of glory. Indeed, in Ch'ü-chou a dozen or more of the fifty-eight families were prominent only during the Northern or the Southern Sung. But the persistence of eminence is at least as striking. The Chiang family in K'ai-hua started early and remained strong. They produced thirteen *chin-shih* from 997 to 1223.[32] The "Kuan-t'ang" Hsü family was prominent early and later declined. They produced their first *chin-shih* in 985; two of this man's sons, one grandson, three great-grandsons, one fourth-, one fifth-, and two sixth-generation grandsons succeeded him, the last passing the examination in 1196.[33] By contrast, the Lous were late starters. Their first *chin-shih* was 1079; the next, his grandson, came in 1103; then there was a gap of over a century until 1226, but then successors came quickly: 1234, two in 1238, 1256, 1259, 1265, and two in 1268.[34] By far the largest number of individuals to be classified as one kin group were the Maos of Chiang-shan county who produced thirty *chin-shih* between 1038 and 1268 (indeed half of all those from their county).[35] The Maos may have been a long-established kin group, for few of their *chin-shih* are listed as close relatives of each other. Nevertheless, they were considered one group, as opposed to the Chengs (considered to be five), the Chiangs (three), the Hsüs (nine), and the Chaos (imperial family and others, three).[36]

[32] *CCFC* (1622) 11/58a–59a.
[33] *CCFC* (1622) 11/40a–b.
[34] *CCFC* (1622) 11/41a–b.
[35] *CCFC* (1622) 11/49a–50a.
[36] Since the gazetteer was compiled in the late Ming, it is possible that the divisions of people with a particular surname into several kin groups reflects realities of that time, not ones that date back to the Sung. Thus it could be that an even smaller number of active "families" dominated

Yüan Ts'ai must have been acquainted with many members of these established families in his home prefecture, and they most likely provided the bases for many of his comments. But his social network was wider than Ch'ü-chou; during his official career he would have become acquainted with *shih-ta-fu* from all over south China. His government service took him both to the capital and to a series of provincial cities. In the 1150s he was a student at the National University (*ta hsüeh*) in the capital, Hangchow. Enrolling at the university made it easier to pass the examinations for the *chin-shih*, since one could bypass the prefectural tests. It was thus a popular place for young men from wealthy families; Yang Wan-li (1127–1206), in fact, said it was a place suitable only for those with sufficient income.[37] We can probably assume, therefore, that by this time Yüan Ts'ai's family was already comfortable.

Yüan Ts'ai undoubtedly left the capital after passing the examinations for the *chin-shih* degree in 1163. Thereafter he served in several prefectures and seems to have spent much of his time writing books. While serving as a magistrate in Cheng-ho county in Fukien, he wrote two books, *Miscellaneous Notes from Cheng-ho* (*Cheng-ho tsa-chih*) and *A Little Book for Magistrates* (*Hsien-ling hsiao-lu*),[38] neither of which survives. While in Cheng-ho he also introduced revised policies on salt sales to deal with the prevalence of illegal privately produced salt.[39] In 1178 he became magistrate of Le-ch'ing, a flourishing commercial and cultural center on the coast of Chekiang. During his five years in that

---

degree-holding in Sung times if several of the Ming kin groups were then considered single groups.

[37] *Ch'eng-chai chi*, 64/9b–10a. See also Thomas H. C. Lee, "Life in the Schools of Sung China," p. 57.

[38] Wang Ch'i, *Hsü wen-hsien t'ung-k'ao*, 177/2b.

[39] *CWKCC* 29/7b–8b.

city, Yüan Ts'ai acted as compiler of a ten-chapter gazetteer of the county.[40] He also associated with members of the leading local families, including Liu Chen, author of the preface for the *Precepts* (completed in Le-ch'ing), and Cheng Po-ying, one of the leading classicists of the region.[41]

Altogether Yüan Ts'ai served as magistrate of four counties, the last Wu-yüan in southern Anhwei. He was there in 1190 when he reprinted the *Precepts* and was still there in 1192 when the poet Yang Wan-li wrote a memorial recommending him for promotion. According to Yang, Yüan Ts'ai had quickly recognized the disarray into which the judicial system of the county had fallen, and by notifying his superiors of the abuses of justice he managed to bring an end to false accusations.[42]

Yüan Ts'ai's last post was in the capital, as director of the Public Attention Drum Bureau. This post, which involved handling complaints from the public, was regularly given to magistrates who had distinguished themselves.[43] Since this post is probably the one Yüan Ts'ai received on leaving Wu-yüan, and since he probably held it no more than four or five years, he must have either died or retired from office in the mid-1190s.

If Yüan Ts'ai lived a decade or more after retirement, in 1205 he would have seen his second son and a cousin follow his lead in attaining the *chin-shih*.[44] Whether or not he lived that long, we do know that he found the time before, during, or after serving in office to write several more books, none of

[40] *Chih-chai shu-lu chieh-t'i*, 8, p. 253.

[41] See the prefaces to the *Precepts* in Part Two. Yüan Ts'ai had met Liu Chen while they were fellow students at the National University. On the intellectual life in Le-ch'ing, see Winston Wan Lo, *The Life and Thought of Yeh Shih*, pp. 43–44.

[42] *Ch'eng-chai chi*, 70/7a–8b.

[43] *SS* 161, p. 3782.

[44] *CCFC* (1564) 11/14b–15a; *CCFC* (1622) 11/42b.

which survives. The bibliography chapter of the Sung history lists a book not previously mentioned: *The Master Who Sobs and Sighs (Hsi-hsü tzu)*.[45] The Ming gazetteers of Ch'ü-chou list four further ones: *The Three Essentials for Supervising Clerks (Yüeh-shih san-yao)*, *A Proposal for Revival through Managing Strength (Ching-ch'üan chung-hsing ts'e)*, *Unsophisticated Discussions of the Thousand Concerns (Ch'ien-lü pi-shuo)*, and *Quick Methods of Land Measurement [for Tax Assessment] (Ching-chieh chieh-fa)*.[46] Although it is impossible to know much about the content of Yüan Ts'ai's eight books merely from their titles, it would seem that three or four of them were aimed at magistrates, perhaps belonging to the genre of guides for magistrates and prefects that offer a mixture of practical advice and moral encouragement.[47] It also appears quite likely that two or more of them concerned ways in which the central government could improve its capacity to fend off the Jurchens who had seized north China. If so, Yüan Ts'ai was not indifferent to the overriding concern of political thinkers of the twelfth century.[48]

Despite Yüan Ts'ai's thirty years in office and eight books, he was not an active member of the philosophical or literary circles of his day, at least not those that have left records. Yüan Ts'ai was a contemporary of the philosophers Chu Hsi (1130–1200), Lü Tsu-ch'ien (1137–1181), Ch'en Fu-liang (1141–1207), and Ch'en Liang (1143–1194), and the poets Lu Yu (1125–1210), Yang Wan-li (1127–1206), and Fan Ch'eng-ta (1120–1193). Scores of their lesser contemporaries

[45] *SS* 205, p. 5211.

[46] *CCFC* (1564) 10/11b–12a; *CCFC* (1622) 12/2b. It could be that some of these are different titles for the works written at Cheng-ho.

[47] See chap. 7, pp. 160–61 for a translation of two items from one such guide.

[48] See Hoyt Tillman, *Utilitarian Confucianism*, esp. pp. 23–67 and 169–89.

also left collected writings filled with letters, epitaphs, and eulogies addressed to their friends and acquaintances. Yet reference to Yüan Ts'ai is remarkably scarce.[49] The *Sung Yüan hsüeh-an*, a seventeenth-century collection of biographical notices of Sung scholars and thinkers arranged to show their teacher-disciple ties, omitted Yüan Ts'ai. The supplement, which did include him, could find no way to link him to a known scholar except through the fact that Yang Wan-li had discussed him in his memorial.[50] From the *Precepts for Social Life*, it is difficult to imagine that Yüan Ts'ai was a recluse, and indeed his education and his service as a magistrate would preclude that possibility. But it does appear that his contact with those who have left literary collections—primarily philosophers and poets—was slight.

CULTURE, PHILOSOPHY, AND INTELLECTUAL HISTORY

Yüan Ts'ai's indifference toward philosophical controversies and incompetence in the writing of poetry I consider among his major assets as an "informant" for the *shih-ta-fu* as a social class. I would guess that considerably less than twenty percent of those men who considered themselves as belonging to the category *shih-ta-fu* actually became officials.[51] Moreover,

[49] The *Sung-jen ch'uan-chi tzu-liao so-yin*, ed. Ch'ang P'i-te et al., which indexes epitaphs, elegies, notices of appointment, and many other biographical materials, found none for Yüan Ts'ai. Nor, according to Wang Te-i's *Sung hui-yao chi-kao jen-ming so-yin*, is Yüan Ts'ai among the thousands of Sung officials mentioned in the *Sung hui-yao chi-kao*. In Chu Hsi's collected works there is a letter that refers in passing to Yüan Ts'ai's salt sales while he was magistrate of Cheng-ho (*CWKCC* 29/7b–8b). This is the only reference to Yüan Ts'ai in the collected works of several of his contemporaries indexed in Saeki's *Chūgoku zuihitsu zaccho sakuin* and *Sōdai bunshū sakuin*.

[50] *Sung Yüan hsüeh-an pu-i*, by Wang Tzu-ts'ai, 44/83a–98b.

[51] According to Chaffee's analysis, during the Southern Sung about three percent of the adult men took the prefectural tests for entry into the

of those who became officials, only a small fraction have had their names preserved in any biographical record.[52] Again, the number who had strong literary or philosophical ambitions—who sought out the best teachers and were ready to subordinate their other interests and the needs of their families to perfecting their art or moral cultivation—cannot have constituted more than a few percent of the entire *shih-ta-fu* stratum. Although Yüan Ts'ai did hold office and did write books, he remained sympathetic to the large fraction of the *shih-ta-fu* who were not especially ambitious or successful in politics, art, or scholarship. There were other spokesmen for this group who recorded the stories and anecdotes they enjoyed. But Yüan Ts'ai went further than anyone else in laying out the principles underlying much of their daily life. His willingness to write on these subjects may well reflect the shift in the concerns of the elite toward securing their local social position that has been reported by Robert Hartwell and Robert Hymes.[53]

In making these arguments I am explicitly rejecting the common view of intellectual historians that the treatises of leading thinkers provide the surest evidence of the values and ideology of a society. My reasons for rejecting this view are best explained through a critique of the methodological premises in Thomas Metzger's widely praised *Escape from Predicament* (1977).[54]

---

civil service (some 200,000 men each time), but only about one percent of those who took the test passed ("Education and Examinations," pp. 59–60). Since anyone who tried the examinations had had a classical education, the ratio of educated men to officials was clearly very large.

[52] The number of officials whose names have been preserved would be less than 22,000, the total number of individuals who could be traced by the meticulous editors of the *Sung-jen ch'uan-chi tzu-liao so-yin.*

[53] Hartwell, "Transformations of China," pp. 405–425; Hymes, "Prominence and Power," pp. 179–89.

[54] For the critical reception of this book, see the symposium devoted to

Metzger's stated goal is almost the same as mine, to discover the "shared cultural orientations" of the "educated class." These, he says, "cannot be understood without analyzing the counterpoint of ideas traditionally studied by intellectual historians."[55] By this he means Neo-Confucianism of the inner-directed sort exemplified by Chu Hsi (1130–1200) and Wang Yang-ming (1472–1529). He admits that there were other "patterns of thought," which he briefly lists. There were those who emphasized Confucian ethics without pursuing metaphysics; others had a semi-legalist interest in political achievements; yet others went in more individualistic and egalitarian directions. Buddhism and Taoism had adherents, as did textual scholarship and art. Finally there was the culture of commoners, in which prime importance was placed on establishing a family, managing it, and maintaining it through industriousness and frugality.[56] Metzger goes on, however, to conclude, "having raised the problem of distinguishing Neo-Confucianism from other, partly overlapping trends, . . . we still have no reason to challenge the widely held view of Chinese scholars that Neo-Confucianism dominated not just the intellectual world but even the society of late imperial China."[57] Later he admits that "much political behavior was based on the realistic pursuit of material interests by men lacking much sincere commitment to Confucian principles."[58] Yet he still believes Neo-Confucian values shaped their behavior. "Certainly unscrupulous Chinese—the majority of the Chinese population, according to Chu Hsi—were still 'cul-

---

it published in the *Journal of Asian Studies* 39 (February 1980) by Guy Alitto et al.

[55] *Escape from Predicament*, p. 13.
[56] Ibid., pp. 52–53.
[57] Ibid., p. 54.
[58] Ibid., p. 167.

turally conditioned.'" [59] To solve the "puzzle of the relation between their culture and their behavior" he suggests that action characterized by ties of cooperation depended largely on shared values. "If the realistic pursuit of self-interest brushing aside moral injunctions can be said to characterize violent conflict and vertical class relations of exploitation, horizontal ties of organizational coordination between peers in a particular social class depend more on shared cosmological ethical beliefs." [60]

From the perspective offered in this book, there are three basic fallacies in the efforts of Metzger and others to use the writings of Chu Hsi to discover the "shared cultural orientations" of the whole educated class. The first might be called the "fallacy of the power of formal education." Metzger seems to assume that once a boy studied the Classics and the commentaries of Chu Hsi, his mind became a blank except for the perceptions and claims expressed in these books and the realistic pursuit of material interest. Forgotten were the teachings of his mother and nursemaid, the songs and proverbs he had heard, the novels and poems he read outside school, the conversations he had had with shopkeepers, priests, and doctors. Surely such facets of his education helped shape his culture.

The second fallacy is the assumption that the most important things thought, felt, or assumed were expressed in philosophical writings. This assumption ignores the well-known existence of different levels of discourse and different genres of literature. Some emotions and perceptions were regularly expressed in poetry but rarely in any other written medium. Some observations about human nature were considered the subject matter of novelists and playwrights, not philosophers. Some observations about proper behavior could be

[59] Ibid., p. 168.
[60] Ibid.

addressed to one's sons in "family instructions" but not to one's contemporaries in letters. Some thoughts, perhaps especially about "material interests," may have been widely discussed but considered unseemly to put down in writing of any form at all. By what right, then, can we say that the kinds of thoughts expressed in philosophical writings were more influential in determining a person's behavior than the thoughts expressed in poetry and other genres?

The third fallacy is that the "realistic pursuit of material interest" is an action divorced from "shared cultural orientations." As social psychologists have adequately demonstrated, no one acts automatically in response to external stimuli; people must always interpret them.[61] How they interpret them depends on the symbols, values, and ideas they have in their heads and that they largely share with those around them. It may seem "obvious" that people want wealth and property for themselves and their families and that this is the goal of the "realistic pursuit of material interest." But wealth and property have been conceived in widely divergent fashions; the very size of the field of comparative law on real property demonstrates this adequately. Needless to say, what people mean by "the family" is at least as diverse. Not only are there differences in how wide a group is thought of, how agnatic or cognatic it is in organization, and the role of each individual in it; but also the basic conceptions of the kind of unit a family is, what it is a subunit of, and what it is or is not comparable to, all vary considerably.

Above all, no study of culture can ignore the realm considered "realistic." Marshall Sahlins, in *Culture and Practical Reason*, notes that it is "common in anthropological knowledge that the 'rational' and 'objective' scheme of any given

[61] For an overview of this work, see Robert F. Berkhofer, Jr., *A Behavioral Approach to Historical Analysis*, pp. 27–45 and passim.

group is never the only one possible." Therefore it is falla-
cious to see "the practical interest as an intrinsic and self-
explanatory condition."[62] To put this another way, the
efforts of educated Chinese to feed and clothe themselves
were just as much shaped by cultural categories and orientations as anyone else's. Even if their patterns of behavior
were in violation of the moral imperatives articulated by
Chu Hsi or Wang Yang-ming, that does not make them
somehow merely natural or selfish. Just because Chu Hsi saw
most of his contemporaries as motivated by mindless selfishness does not mean that we have to look at them the same
way. In all likelihood, they set for themselves more accessible
goals than Chu Hsi's sagehood; if we are to understand their
behavior we must know *their* goals, notions, and cultural
orientations, not just Chu Hsi's. To do otherwise would be
much like interpreting the culture of well-educated people in
America today strictly in terms of the categories and perceptions of philosophical giants from Plato to Kant and
Wittgenstein.

Adherents of intellectual history as the key to the values
and principles of a society might well counter with the
following argument: Even if philosophers did not discuss all
topics or articulate all thoughts common in their culture,
they did articulate the key or core ones, the ones from which
most of the rest of the culture can be logically or analogically
derived. In this view, the general mentality of the upper class
would be an elementary version of the philosophy, simpli-
fied and less subtle, the way a high-school knowledge of
mathematics may be derived from the mathematics known
and taught by the leading mathematicians. But this is at best a
hypothesis. Testing it requires comparing the thinking of

[62] *Culture and Practical Reason*, pp. 168, 206.

ordinary educated men with that of the philosophers, which is one of the tasks I propose to do here.

THE PRECEPTS FOR SOCIAL LIFE
AS A SOURCE FOR CULTURAL ANALYSIS

In using the information an informant supplies to construct a model of his culture, anthropologists usually start with words and images. How are phenomena categorized? What things are sacred or spiritual? How do people conceive of "father," "ruler," "teacher," "servant," and any other social categories they routinely use? Anthropologists also ask informants for their explanations of their practices, customs, and beliefs (Why do you always kill a chicken in that rite? Why do daughters-in-law argue with their husbands' mothers?); but they have learned to recognize informants' conscious models—their explanations and rationalizations— as precisely that, parts of their culture, but not necessarily a very good anthropological model of what is being expressed or accomplished by the behavior in question. Often, to a sensitive outsider, it becomes clear that other things are also going on.[63]

The way in which I try to adapt these methods in my analysis of the *Precepts for Social Life* is to pick apart Yüan Ts'ai's words and statements as finely as possible. My first goal is to reconstruct his particular world view, explicit and implicit. I try to see exactly how he analyzed and divided subjects and the connections and causalities he assumed or posited. When his own explanations for phenomena seem inadequate, I try to probe further in what he wrote or in

[63] On participants' models and observers' models, see Claude Levi-Strauss, "Social Structure," and Barbara E. Ward, "Varieties of the Conscious Model: The Fishermen of South China."

related sources for explanations of the social and cultural system he described.

Thus although my overall goal is to understand the culture of the *shih-ta-fu* of the age, I try first to understand Yüan Ts'ai's own mental world. If I am to conclude that certain attitudes or assumptions were systematically related to each other, I want to know for sure that they coexisted in the thoughts of at least one man. Moreover, I do not want to dismiss as irrelevant aspects of Yüan Ts'ai's thought that appear at first glance to be unrepresentative. Although he may have held some peculiar views, our sources for what was typical are so spotty that hasty judgments are unwarranted.

Be this as it may, Yüan Ts'ai's interest for us is as an informant, not as an original thinker; therefore after I have done justice to his attitudes toward a subject, I usually try to assess how widely they were shared. Assessing representativeness requires a variety of methods, depending largely on the degree to which Yüan Ts'ai was conscious of the meanings he expressed. His terminology and basic modes of dividing things into categories were most likely acquired from those around him; moreover, communication with his audience would be difficult if he "spoke a different language." Thus one can posit a priori that he was typical in these regards. At a slightly higher level of consciousness were his assumptions about regularities in human behavior and motivation. When he assumed, for instance, that people would pursue certain goals or respond to kindness or mistreatment in certain ways, without giving any argument to that effect, it can probably be concluded that he saw no dispute on these issues; they were "facts," not opinions.

At a yet higher level of consciousness were Yüan Ts'ai's observations of how people in fact behaved. His tone was not one of caricature, and he seems usually to have assumed that his audience would recognize the situations he described. To

substantiate the representativeness of his perceptions of how
people act, I often cite evidence that others saw the same
phenomena. Since observations of how other people act are
one of the major bases on which people orient their own
behavior, understanding these perceptions is vital to any
analysis of culture or behavior.

At the highest level of consciousness are Yüan Ts'ai's
strategies for solving problems. These are significant because
many of the actions *shih-ta-fu* took to preserve or enhance
their family's social and economic position were done consciously, with careful planning. But not everyone made the
same choices, and Yüan Ts'ai clearly believed he had some
new ideas to offer. For instance, Yüan Ts'ai's advice on
resolving interpersonal disputes among family members
seems to have been based, not on the common view of the
time, but on his own reflections about what he saw and heard
around him. His descriptions of the attitude and behavior of
his contemporaries reveal points of tension in the family
system of the period, but his solutions were not necessarily
widely followed. By contrast, his advice on the use and
transmission of family property seems to have been an integral part of the culture of the *shih-ta-fu* of the time, even if
slightly off-center in the direction of prudence. It is entirely
consistent with the law of the period and matches in many
particulars the attitudes of Sung judges.

Because of all of these considerations, I try to deal simultaneously with three questions in the chapters that follow:
First, what did Yüan Ts'ai think? Second, in what ways did
he consciously differ from established authorities on the
subjects he wrote on, especially ones in the classical tradition?
Third, which elements in Yüan Ts'ai's ideas and notions did
he share with his peers? In the last chapter I return again to the
issue of the culture of the *shih-ta-fu* and its relation to the
teachings of the Neo-Confucian philosophers.

CHAPTER 2

The Family in the Classical Tradition

The meaning of any literary work can be fully uncovered only by comparing it with other works on similar or related subjects written by the author's predecessors or contemporaries. Did the author echo or subtly refute the ideas in earlier works? Did he write in an established genre? If so, did he push it in any new directions? If not, what were the ideas or sensibilities that he felt could be adequately expressed only in a new mode? These questions are highly relevant to a full understanding of the *Precepts for Social Life* because in his mode of presentation and in many of his ideas, Yüan Ts'ai broke with the established genre of advice on family ethics and rituals. To understand what Yüan Ts'ai wanted to say about the family it is therefore necessary to know the classical tradition on this subject.

In the Classics, the family was central to both political and ethical thought. The personal relations appropriate in the family (filial piety, parental concern, brotherly deference and guidance) were noble ones, ones on which all other social relations could be based. Almost never were evil sentiments attributed to the family context. Indeed, *jen* (benevolence or humanity), the supreme virtue of Confucians, was said to be rooted in filial piety.[1] In many texts, the overall goal was the well-ordered state, with well-ordered families seen as a necessary stage in achieving this goal. The *Great Learning*

[1] *Analects*, 1:2 (Waley, trans., p. 83).

contains one of the most famous expressions of this principle: "The ancients who wished to manifest bright virtue throughout the realm first brought order to their states. Those who wished to bring order to their states first regulated their families. Those who wished to regulate their families first cultivated themselves." [2] This intermediate position for the family in the scheme of things did not, however, undermine its actual importance. Before one could hope to be of service to community, state, or humanity, one had to fulfill obligations at home.

There are, of course, differences between what the Classics said and what Sung scholars chose to emphasize in them. In this chapter I deal primarily with the Sung scholars, especially two groups referred to as the classicists and the philosophers. By classicists I mean men who studied the Classics as the repository of moral truths, who as a whole were relatively unconcerned with metaphysics but often quite involved in issues of statecraft. I use Ssu-ma Kuang (1019–1086) to represent this group of scholars. His major writings on family life were his ten-chapter *Precepts for Family Life* (*Chia fan*), an essay on "Miscellaneous Forms to Follow in Managing the Family" (*Chü-chia tsa-i*, also called *Su-shui chia-i*, referred to here as "Family Forms"), and epitaphs. By philosophers I am referring specifically to scholars who identified with the Ch'eng-Chu tradition of Neo-Confucianism, that is, Ch'eng I (1033–1107), Ch'eng Hao (1032–1085), Chang Tsai (1020–1077), Chu Hsi (1130–1200), and their many students. [3] Most examples will be taken from the writings of Chu Hsi. His ideas about family matters are best found in his *Elementary Learning* (*Hsiao-hsüeh*), *Reflections on Things at Hand* (*Chin-ssu lu*), and epitaphs.

[2] *Ta hsüeh*, 4 (Legge, trans., *Classics* 1, p. 357).
[3] This group is also called the *tao hsüeh* scholars. See Hoyt Tillman, *Utilitarian Confucianism*, pp. 30–67.

At the broadest level of generalization, the difference between the classicists and the philosophers is that the former retained the classical belief in the centrality of life at home, but the latter did not. Probably influenced to some extent by Buddhism, scholars in the Ch'eng-Chu tradition were much more concerned with internal purity and service to the broader community than with actual family life. The famous "Western Inscription" of Chang Tsai opens with the statement that "Heaven is my father and Earth is my mother" and later adds that "all people are my brothers." In the use of family relations as metaphors for wider, and by implication more noble, social and ethical attitudes, actual family life is downgraded.[4]

In the Classics and the writings of classicists and philosophers, family matters were treated as three distinguishable but interrelated subjects: interpersonal ethics (*jen-lun*), the family as an economic and political unit (*chia*), and ancestors and descent lines (*tsu* and *tsung*).

INTERPERSONAL ETHICS

According to the Classics, achieving a properly ordered family required appropriate relations between parents and children, husband and wife, and elder and younger brothers. These relations (three of the Five Cardinal Relations) were assumed to be fixed and enduring. One of Confucius' most famous sayings concerns the "rectification of names": "A ruler should be a ruler and a subject a subject; a father should be a father and a son a son."[5] Implicit in this is the assumption that there is a true, enduring way to be a father, a way that holds in all situations. Thus from the time of the Classics,

[4] On this shift, see also Rolf Trauzettel, "Sung Patriotism as a First Step Toward Chinese Nationalism," pp. 201–203.

[5] *Analects*, 12:11 (Waley, trans., p. 166).

most discussions of family relations did not specify circumstances or conditions. The filial piety of a son for his father does not change as he grows older, marries, takes office, has children, or lives apart. The deference and respect of a younger brother for his elder is supposed to be just as constant. It is in large part because of the unconditional nature of these obligations that the didactic literature on family relations in later generations so often dwelled on self-sacrifice. The stepson or unappreciated daughter-in-law could not abandon faithful service no matter what the consequences.[6]

As a "fundamentalist," Ssu-ma Kuang always checked first to see what the Classics had to say on any topic.[7] He did not try to record everything said in the Classics, nor did he bring out every discrepancy in them; but he seldom argued for stances that had no classical authority. Thus in regard to interpersonal ethics he stressed the duties and appropriate deference and respect each person owed to those in defined kinship relationships to him. He related behavior not simply to seniority and sex but also to narrower roles such as wife, uncle, mother's brother, and so on. A younger brother had a permanent, unchanging relationship to his elder brother, as did a wife to her husband and a nephew to his uncle. In discussing cases where the deference and submission of the junior was not matched by fairness and kindness from the senior, Ssu-ma Kuang advocated greater submission to the point of extreme self-abnegation, saying that in these cases one had a special opportunity to display one's filial piety or fraternal submission.[8]

The only significant accommodation Ssu-ma Kuang

[6] Good examples of anecdotes of exemplary individuals drawn from the whole range of earlier historical and didactic literature are found in *CF*.

[7] On "fundamentalism," see Wm. Theodore de Bary, "Some Common Tendencies in Neo-Confucianism," p. 34.

[8] See, for example, *CF* 5, pp. 569, 573–74; 7, pp. 623–24.

made to changed circumstances was his treatment of the parents' relations to sons of different ages. The disappearance centuries earlier of primogeniture and the establishment of the practice of equal inheritance for brothers had changed general attitudes about the relations between elder and younger brothers. So long as property was eventually to be divided equally among them, it became common to feel that they should also benefit equally from the property before it was divided. Classical authority for this view was almost nonexistent, nor had later writers explicitly advocated it. Ssu-ma Kuang tried his best to find passages in the Classics that would justify it. Out of context he quoted a saying in the *Analects* that those who were good at running families "entirely share equally what they have." To this he added, "Even if food is not enough to fill the belly and clothes are too few to cover the body, no one will fell resentful. For, what produces resentment is partiality and selfishness which leads to some having plenty and others little." [9] He also quoted the case of a kind of bird that to ensure equal treatment of each of its progeny dealt with them from oldest to youngest in the morning and from youngest to oldest in the evening. To those who insisted that a father should favor his worthy sons and place at a lower level his unworthy ones, Ssu-ma Kuang replied, "It would be fine if in fact those he favored were worthy and those he set lower were incompetent. But men mired in their personal preferences often favor the incompetent and place lower the worthy. Disaster results from this." [10]

Chu Hsi did not adopt Ssu-ma Kuang's solution to this problem, even though generally his discussion of family ethics in the *Elementary Learning* closely followed Ssu-ma Kuang's. Moreover, whereas in his funerary inscriptions

[9] *CF* 1, p. 484.
[10] *CF* 3, p. 504.

Ssu-ma Kuang regularly praised men for being equitable in their distribution of family assets, Chu Hsi would praise men for following *li* (rules of ritual and decorum), which always implied drawing distinctions based on status.[11]

In the Classics, and even more so in the writings of later scholars, a father's primary responsibility toward his sons was to educate them properly. Yen Chih-t'ui's (531−591+) famous "family instructions" stressed the importance of this, as did most other works in this genre.[12] To Ssu-ma Kuang, laziness, indulgence, and the lack of ability to forego pleasures were major moral and social evils that fathers could prevent through proper education. He wrote, "Men who love their sons often say, 'The boy is too young to know better. Let's wait until he is older to teach him.'" This was like letting the bird out of the cage and then trying to catch it.[13] In his "Family Forms" Ssu-ma Kuang gave a schedule for study, modified from the "Patterns for Domestic Life" (*Nei tse*) in the *Record of Ritual* (*Li chi*). He stressed the age at which the various Classics should be recited and when the histories, commentaries, and philosophers could be introduced.[14]

If a father's duty to his son was to educate him and curb his inclinations toward self-indulgence, a son's duty toward his father was respect, obedience, and attention to matters of form. True filial feelings were always said to be more important than physical care or specific practices, but a great many words were expended in describing exactly which sorts of practices would be best. The classic on this subject was the "Patterns for Domestic Life," from which Ssu-ma Kuang and Chu Hsi each quoted dozens of times. In this brief

[11] See, for example, *CTWC* 17, pp. 576−77.
[12] *YSCH* 1, pp. 3−8 (Teng, trans., pp. 3−8); *CTTL*, passim.
[13] *CF* 3, p. 497.
[14] *SMSSI* 4, p. 45.

text sons and their wives were given a great many injunctions. For instance, they were told to get up early, dress properly, call on their parents, be constantly concerned for the parents' comfort, and show themselves eager to please them. They should wait on them at meals and only eat what their parents leave. In their parents' presence they should never sneeze, cough, yawn, stretch, scratch, or slouch. Men and women should stay as separate as possible, women not concerned with business or government ("outside matters") nor men with household chores ("inside matters"). Anything that had to be passed between a man and a woman should be put on a tray so that their hands need not touch, and there should be separate wells and privies for the men's and women's quarters. When parents do wrong, children should try to admonish them gently but cease if they are unsuccessful. Sons should divorce wives their parents do not like. Wives should consider nothing as their personal property.[15]

Ssu-ma Kuang's "Family Forms" was largely an updated version of this set of rules. Below are some of his revisions:

> A son must tell his parents before he goes out, and personally report his return. When he receives his own guests, he should not seat them in the main hall, but in a study or side room. He should not use the eastern steps to the main hall, nor mount or dismount in front of the main hall. In nothing should he place himself on a par with his father.
>
> When parents are indisposed, sons and daughters-in-law should remain close at hand, unless good reasons keep them away. They should personally prepare, taste, and serve the medicine for their parents. When a parent is ill, the son should be sorrowful; he should neither fool

---

[15] *Li chi*, "Nei-ts'e" (Legge, trans., I, pp. 449–79).

around nor go to parties. He should disregard all business affairs and devote himself solely to getting the best doctor, filling the prescription, and preparing the medicine....

Junior members of the family who are seated should rise immediately when a senior passes by. When they meet a senior on the road, they should dismount from their horses....

If a young family member has returned from afar, and he meets more than three of his elders at the same time, he first bows twice to them, then after making polite inquiries he bows three times and stops.[16]

To summarize, in the Classics and the writing of Sung classicists and philosophers, interpersonal relations among family members were ethical in nature, defined by exact genealogical connection, unconditional, and permanent. Rules of conduct were vital to perfecting these ethical relations but were not an end in themselves. Concerning interpersonal ethics, the only significant difference between Chu Hsi and Ssu-ma Kuang lay in Ssu-ma Kuang's attempt to sanctify equal treatment by parents of all their sons.

THE FAMILY AS A CORPORATE UNIT

Correct interpersonal ethics and ritual form were not all that counted in family matters; writers from classical times on had also discussed the *chia*: the family that continues through time, owns property, preserves a reputation, and needs to be managed. The *chia* was a corporate body, not merely a nexus of interpersonal relations. It lay in the realm of political economy, authority, responsibility, and the production and control of resources.

[16] *SMSSI* 4, p. 42–44.

The notion of the *chia* as a unit of political economy goes back to the Classics. As Mencius remarked, "Everyone says, 'The realm (*t'ien-hsia*), the state (*kuo*), and the family (*chia*).'"[17] These units were generally paired with the Son of Heaven, feudal lords or kings, and the ministers and great officers (*ch'ing-ta-fu*), or sometimes the lower officers (*shih*). In these types of discussions commoners were not generally seen as having *chia*, only bodies to preserve or parents and children to support.[18] The Classics assumed that every gentleman has a personal commitment to preserve and continue his family, one comparable to the commitment of a ruler to his state. In both cases, this commitment was seen as a duty to ancestors.[19]

The idea that one must preserve what he inherits from his forbears was argued at length in the *Classic of Filial Piety*. In this primer, the filial piety of the Son of Heaven, the feudal lords, the ministers and high officers, the *shih*, and the common people were presented as scaled up or scaled down versions of each other. The feudal lords avoid arrogance in order not to imperil their high positions and exercise restraint in order to retain their wealth. "If they retain their wealth and rank they will later be able to protect their altars to the soil and grain and keep their people in peace. This is the filial piety of the feudal lords." The ministers and high officers follow the established rules in every word and action, thus

[17] *Mencius*, 4A:5 (Lau, trans., p. 120).

[18] See, for example, *Mencius*, 4A:3, "If the Son of Heaven is not benevolent, he cannot preserve the realm; if the feudal lords are not benevolent, they cannot preserve their altars to the soil and grain; if the ministers and high officers are not benevolent, they cannot preserve their ancestral temples; if the *shih* and commoners are not benevolent, they cannot preserve their bodies intact" (Lau, trans., p. 119). In a similar fashion, Mo Tzu discusses "families overturning families" as analogous to states attacking other states. See Burton Watson, trans., *The Basic Writings of Mo Tzu*, p. 39.

[19] See, for example, *Li chi*, "Ch'ü li" (Legge, trans., I, p. 107).

offending no one and giving no cause for complaint. "When these three conditions are fulfilled they are able to preserve their ancestral altars. This is the filial piety of the ministers and high officers." The *shih* love their parents and are loyal and obedient to their superiors so that they will be "able to preserve their offices and salaries and maintain the continuity of the sacrifices to their ancestors. This is the filial piety of the *shih*." The common people "follow the laws of nature to utilize the earth to full advantage. They are cautious in their actions and frugal in their expenditures in order to support their parents. This is the filial piety of the common man." [20]

Although the Classics implied that the *chia* was a unit of political economy and that a source of income was indispensable to its survival,[21] these texts do not provide sanction for attempts to enhance the family's material base. Mencius, in talking to a king, said, "If Your Majesty asks, 'How can I benefit my state,' the great officers will say, 'How can I benefit my *chia*,' and the *shih* and commoners will say, 'How can I benefit myself.'" [22] This moral position posed a problem for men in the Han and later. In the classical period family property or income was held largely on political tenures; preserving it required no more than conscientious service. It could not be freely sold or given away, nor was it ordinarily divided among sons. In the Han and later, property was regularly divided among sons and could be permanently lost through sale to outsiders. Preserving the *chia* required some involvement in financial matters. One would either have to hope that moral actions would bring material

[20] *Hsiao ching*, 2–6 (Makra, trans., pp. 5–13).

[21] Hsün Tzu took this relationship as so obvious that it could be used as a metaphor for more abstract ideas. Benevolence, propriety, and ceremony, he said, have the same sort of beneficial relation to human beings as goods, money, and grain do to a family (*chia*). *Hsün Tzu*, "Ta lüeh" (SCSC ed., p. 338).

[22] *Mencius*, 1A:1 (Lau, trans., p. 49).

rewards or to look on efforts to attain or regain material sufficiency as justified if oriented toward the *chia* rather than toward personal comfort.

Not all classicists in the Sung agreed on this issue. Ssu-ma Kuang felt uncomfortable encouraging efforts to increase or enhance family property. He recognized the importance of preserving the *chia* but preferred to stress ethical rather than material means. Fathers or grandfathers who plan for their posterity by leaving them "fields that run from path to path, houses and shops which extend from one neighborhood to the next, storehouses filled with grain, and gold and silk in boxes" will find that the sons have been corrupted:

> What took a man several decades of hard work to accumulate his sons can dissipate through extravagance in a year. In fact they will laugh at the stupidity of their fathers and grandfathers who did not know how to enjoy themselves. They will also resent their stinginess without being grateful for the hard work they performed. At first they will secretly pilfer to satisfy their desires. When that is not enough they will take on debts, waiting for their fathers' deaths to repay. Their only fear is that their fathers may live a long time. The worst of the lot give no medicines when their fathers are ill, some even secretly giving poisons. Thus what was supposed to benefit later generations nurtures their depravity and brings personal ruin.[23]

Ssu-ma Kuang concluded by asking for moderation. "The resources for producing life are certainly something people must have. But do not seek too much beyond this, for surplus generally proves a burden."[24] He let a hypothetical critic ask, "Did the sages then care not at all if their descendants had

[23] *CF* 2, pp. 487–88.
[24] *CF* 2, p. 489.

nothing to live on?" His answer was no, to the contrary the ancient sages Shun, Hou Chi, Wen Wang, and so on left their descendants dynasties by establishing merit and accumulating virtue, so one should concentrate on those tasks. He insisted that the truly worthy would not starve, and riches were best kept out of the hands of the immoral.[25] In other words, those concerned with the fate of their descendants should concentrate on forming their characters.

In epitaphs for his own relatives, however, Ssu-ma Kuang was not so disdainful of efforts to assure a family's economic security. The Ssu-ma family was a complex one that had remained undivided for generations; several dozen people shared the same "stove." For centuries such families had been admired as the ideal expression of familial principles, but their management posed unusual difficulties. Efforts to achieve financial security seem to have been considered more praiseworthy in these families than in ordinary ones, probably because one's own descendants were never the only ones to benefit. Ssu-ma Kuang wrote that his family always had a head (*chang*) but this head could delegate management to a more junior man. One man made eight attempts to pass the civil service examinations, then "gave up any thought of personal advancement in office, and devoted himself entirely to managing the family" (*chih-chia*). "The number of people eating was very large but the fields and gardens were few. Mr. Ssu-ma did everything in his power to manage the food and clothes to supply them, being entirely equitable and showing no favoritism."[26] Another of the early managers of the family was especially praised for building up its financial assets. He never held office, nor studied for it, but was given charge of family matters from an early age. "Morning to night he would labor, never neglecting any effort, taking

[25] *CF* 2, pp. 489–90.
[26] *SMCC* 79, p. 982.

charge of the agriculture and animal husbandry until we became prosperous. But he never engaged in trickery or secondary occupations [trade and industry]. He distributed the income to the 'six relations,' giving any surplus to the local villagers, but keeping nothing for himself." This manager's early death at age thirty-two was said to have ended the family's financial improvement.[27]

Another Sung classicist who justified concern with the financial basis of family survival was Yeh Meng-te (1077–1148). From an official family in Wu county in Su-chou, he had a successful political career and gained note as a classical scholar and poet. He wrote two "family instructions," one on general ethical matters and the other on managing the means of livelihood (*chih-sheng*).[28] Much of his advice was close to Ssu-ma Kuang's. For instance, he stressed the importance of study as a means of improving character and told his sons to read from three to five chapters of a book every day. He also worried about the possibility of sons becoming vulgar and wasting their time drinking, gambling, or otherwise amusing themselves. He noted that anyone who did this for several years invariably would end up ruining himself and his family.

In his family instructions on managing livelihood, Yeh made the explicit argument that it is morally acceptable to concern oneself with the means of subsistence:

> What makes a person a person is life and that's all. If a person does not take care of his livelihood, he is making his life bitter and thwarting it. What can he live on? The ancient sages all took care of the people's livelihood— Yü managed the waters, Chi planted crops, Kao clari-

[27] *SMCC* 77, p. 954.
[28] *Shih-lin chia-hsün* and *Shih-lin chih-sheng chia-hsün yao-lüeh*.

fied the laws.[29] This they did because the common people's livelihood needed urgent attention; they did not purposely neglect their own livelihood. Some say, "The sages did not take care of their own livelihood; they only cared for the people's livelihood." It is true the sages saved those about to fall into wells and also wore themselves to the bone to aid the world, but this is not all that they did.[30]

Yeh also pointed out that although Confucius' disciple Tzu Kung amassed a fortune, no one considered him on that account morally inferior to those who were poor.[31]

A third Sung classicist who wrote at length on the measures required to preserve a family's assets was Lu Chiu-shao (b. ca. 1138), an elder brother of the eminent thinker Lu Chiu-yüan (1140–1192). Like Ssu-ma Kuang, Lu Chiu-shao came from a complex family, undivided for several generations. In this eassy on "Regulating Expenditures in Family Management," he argued that controlling expenditures to keep them in line with income was the ancient way of ruling states and also the right way to manage a *chia*. One should find a middle way between lavishness and meagerness. "Complaints will then be avoided and one's sons and grandsons will be preserved." He suggested that those with sizable landholdings set aside thirty percent of their income for bad years and ten percent for ritual matters. The rest they should use economically for daily expenses. About thirty percent should be budgeted for miscellaneous expenses such as clothes, celebrations, tuition, medicine, visits to the sick or bereaved, and gifts. If they had any surplus after that, he

[29] Yü, Hou Chi, and Kao were "sage rulers," believed to have created Chinese civilization in remote antiquity.
[30] *Shih-lin chih-sheng chia-hsün yao-lüeh*, 1b–2a.
[31] Ibid., 2a–3b.

encouraged charity to poor neighbors, kinsmen, tenants, and travelers. But this was only for those with substantial estates; Lu warned those whose landed income was small "to keep entirely clear of all such matters as entertaining guests, visiting those in mourning or ill, seasonal gifts, and group feasts." He also said it was almost as bad to be overly charitable as to be overly stingy, which he clarified by noting that one could go and offer help at a funeral or entertain guests with philosophical conversations, so long as no assets were used up in the process.[32]

In contrast to the three men just discussed, the Ch'eng brothers and Chu Hsi were consistent in condemning the desire for wealth. One reason was their unwavering belief that selfishness and selfish desires (*ssu, ssu-hsin, yü, jen-yü*) were evil and must be supplanted by concern for the greater good (*kung*) and adherence to what is right (*i*).[33] In the *Reflections on Things at Hand*, Chu Hsi quoted Ch'eng Hao to the effect that only those with no selfish thoughts could be completely righteous.[34] He also quoted Ch'eng I as saying that in family relations most people let their emotions override *li* (ritual and rules); they also let kindness supplant righteousness (*i*). "Only resolute people do not sacrifice correct principles for the sake of their private (or selfish, *ssu*) loves."[35]

---

[32] *SYHA* 57, pp. 118–19. Two other Sung classicists who discussed the need for material resources and the methods for securing them are Chao Ting (1084–1147) and Ni Ssu (1174–1220). Chao Ting's *Chia-hsün pi-lu* gives a list of rules on family matters with special emphasis on not dividing the family property. Ni Ssu's *Ching-ch'u-t'ang tsa-chih* has essays on budgeting, planning for descendants, frugality, and so on.

[33] On the philosophy of the Ch'eng brothers and Chu Hsi, see Wing-tsit Chan, *A Source Book of Chinese Philosophy*, A. C. Graham, *Two Chinese Philosophers*, and Carson Chang, *The Development of Neo-Confucian Thought*.

[34] *CSL* 2, p. 49 (Chan, trans., pp. 53–54).

[35] *CSL* 6, p. 179 (Chan, trans., p. 173).

Undoubtedly some of Chu Hsi's contemporaries were confused about where filial piety and the son's duty to serve and nurture his parents ended and where absolute avoidance of selfishness began. What if his parents wanted him to become an official? What if he needed to consider advantage to gain the wherewithal to support his parents? Was not concern with his descendants to some extent a duty to his parents and grandparents? As seen above, there was ample classical precedence for these views. Chu Hsi, however, condemned them all by condemning what would have seemed the most innocent. This is seen in the following dialogue between Ch'eng I and a student, quoted by Chu Hsi in the *Reflections*:

> Question: "When a person whose family is poor and whose parents are old is taking the examinations in order to gain a government position, he cannot help worrying about whether he will succeed or fail. Is there a way to avoid such worry?"
>
> Master [Ch'eng] I-ch'uan answered: "The reason he worries is that his will has not overcome his physical passions (*ch'i*). If his will overcomes his passions, he will naturally be free from such worry. Someone whose family is poor and whose parents are old should become an official and earn his salary. But he should consider succeeding or failing a matter of fate (*ming*)."
>
> [Question]: "That's all right for one's self. Is it also for one's parents?"
>
> [Answer]: "Things done for oneself or for one's parents are alike. If one does not succeed, what can he do about his fate? Confucius said, 'Without knowing one's fate, it is impossible to be a superior man.' [36] If one does not know his fate he will try to escape from

[36] *Analects*, 20:3 (Waley, trans., p. 233).

difficulty and danger. Whenever there is gain or loss, he
will be moved. And whenever he sees a prospect for
gain, he will rush toward it. How can he be a superior
man?"[37]

In other words, whereas Ch'eng I and Chu Hsi condemned fatalism about one's moral capacity, they insisted on
it with regard to wealth and rank. A person could enjoy and
make the best use of whatever was freely given to him but
should not pursue material or social advantages, even in the
name of filial piety. Indeed, they condemned all planning
for the sake of getting better opportunities or maximizing
chances to achieve goals. Chu Hsi quoted Ch'eng I as saying
that profit did not mean only money but anything of advantage. "Whenever one seeks to make a task safe and
convenient for himself, he is motivated by the sense of
profit."[38]

Chu Hsi had none of Ssu-ma Kuang's mixed feelings
about men who advanced their family's financial status. In
his epitaphs for men, he praised them for such qualities as
adding nothing to the family property even though serving
in office, or never inquiring about resources while living at
home; he even praised one man for not mentioning anything
related to the family property in his testamentary instructions to his sons.[39] When praising men for their thrift, he
usually added that what was gained thereby was used to aid
poor relatives, especially ones unable to marry.[40]

Even classicists with doubts about efforts to enhance a
family's property agreed that what there was should be
managed properly. Managing a family was analogous to the
responsibility of a local (or even a central) governmental

[37] *CSL* 7, pp. 219–20 (Chan, trans., pp. 198–99).
[38] *CSL* 7, p. 215 (Chan, trans., p. 195).
[39] *CTWC* 17, p. 570; 16, p. 546; 17, p. 582.
[40] *CTWC* 16, p. 556.

official to organize and discipline his subordinates and supervise the handling of revenue and expenditures. Both the "Patterns for Domestic Life" and Ssu-ma Kuang's "Family Forms" recognized the need for sound management. According to Ssu-ma Kuang, a family head should prepare a budget to provide food and clothing for everyone and pay for weddings and funerals. His principle for household financial management was "to establish proper gradations in the affairs of all members of the family, yet at the same time to maintain equality (*chün-i*). Unnecessary expenses should be cut, extravagances prohibited, and savings set aside for the unexpected." [41]

One of the first principles of budgeting was frugality. Ssu-ma Kuang's instructions to his sons concentrated on this message, as did those of many other Sung literati. They urged frugality not merely because it was prudent but also because it was morally superior. That is, a luxurious standard of living not only dissipated property but was a sign of indulgence in selfish desires. As Ssu-ma Kuang explained to his sons, "With frugality desires are few. When a gentleman has few desires he is not a slave to things, and can follow the correct way. When an inferior man has few desires, then he can be careful of his body and economical in his expenses, keeping far from crime and bringing prosperity to his family." [42]

Management of a family also involved personnel management, which Ssu-ma Kuang believed should be based on the rules of ceremonial conduct (*li*). There should be clear lines of authority and clear rules and regulations. In the *Precepts for Family Life*, he said, "In managing a family (*chih-chia*), what is most important is *li*. And the separation of males and

[41] *SMSSI* 4, p. 41.
[42] *SMCC* 67, p. 840.

females is the chief element in *li*." [43] He then described what this meant (men and women do not sit together or pass things directly to one another, men avoid their brothers' wives, and so on). But rules and regulations covered many other matters besides male-female segregation. For instance, his "Family Forms" had many rules for managing servants:

> All the servants of the inner and outer quarters and all concubines rise at the first crow of the cock. After combing their hair, washing, and getting dressed, the male servants should dust and sweep the halls and front courtyard; the doorman and older servants should clear the middle courtyard; while the female servants should tidy up the living quarters, arrange the tables and chairs, and prepare for the toilet of the master and mistress.
>
> When the master and mistress have risen, the maids should make their beds, fold their clothes, and wait on them during their toilet. Afterwards they retire to prepare the food. If they have time, they should wash and sew clothes, always tending to the business of their master's household first, their own affairs last. When night falls, they should again make the beds and prepare the night-wear for the master and mistress.
>
> During the day all the servants and concubines provide their labor under the orders of the master. The female servants call their elder counterparts "older sister" if they are of the same rank (servants of several brothers, for instance); lower-ranking servants (those of sons, for instance) call higher-ranking ones "auntie." The food and clothing of lower-ranking servants should always be inferior to those of higher-ranking ones.

[43] *CF* I, p. 463.

All servants are expected to get along harmoniously. If a quarrel occurs, the master and mistress should scold the participants; if the quarrel does not stop, the wrong-doers should be beaten with a staff. The one who is in the wrong should be beaten more severely, and anyone who refuses to end a quarrel should be punished.[44]

Managing a family "by the book" through a set of assigned duties and specified rules of interaction based on status and roles was clearly advocated in the "Patterns of Domestic Life" and does seem to have been successfully imitated by some Sung families, especially large, undivided ones.[45] As a mode of organization it would seem quasi-military, with emphasis on form (appropriate salutes, bows, and other gestures of relative rank) and rule (women do not cross the middle gate; sons do not use the doors, chairs, and so on used by their fathers). Some sense of what family life was like when it was organized on the basis of *li* can be seen in Ssu-ma Kuang's praise for Chang Ch'eng-chih: "Being a serious person, even inside the house he was always properly attired. If his robe and hat were not in place he would not see his sons or grandsons. They might talk together till midnight, still he would not tell them to sit. The women's quarters were as formal as a government office, with rules for everything, major or minor."[46]

Chu Hsi paid much less attention than did Ssu-ma Kuang to the managerial tasks involved in heading a household, although he did quote Ssu-ma Kuang on this subject in his *Elementary Learning*.[47] As mentioned earlier, in epitaphs for men he considered it high praise to say they were oblivious to all matters of family economy. By contrast, in his seventeen

[44] *SMSSI* 4, p. 46.
[45] See John Dardess, "The Cheng Communal Family."
[46] *SMCC* 76, pp. 938–39.
[47] *HH* 5, pp. 104–105.

epitaphs for women, Chu Hsi extolled again and again the virtues Ssu-ma Kuang called for. One woman was praised because she had strict rules and regulations for everything, saw that everyone got up at daybreak and that no one kept private property or dared to do anything without the permission of the family head. She was also very frugal and personally did everything she demanded of others. Another woman was praised by Chu Hsi for being so careful in managing the family's finances that her husband never had to be troubled with mundane matters and could pursue higher goals. A woman whose father, husband, and husband's father all died in quick succession was praised for her highly competent managerial skills, knowing where every penny was and keeping the servants in line, thus preserving the estate that had to support her husband's brothers and sisters as well as herself and her sons.[48] It would seem that to Chu Hsi in the best of all possible worlds there would be a hereditary scholarly class given to frugal habits but free from any need to think about how to ward off starvation.[49] The next best seems to have been one in which those lucky enough to be born in comfort received good educations and were married to women who through frugal management and great attention to form would handle all material and managerial matters, thus freeing men for higher pursuits.

Chu Hsi's attitude toward the *chia* was much like his attitude toward the state. In the past many scholars, including Ssu-ma Kuang, had been able simultaneously to maintain an interest in ethics (in the finest virtues and their ideal expression) and in statecraft (the management of pressing affairs even when the ruler was less than a sage and laws and

---

[48] *CWKCC* 90/13a, 19b, 91/8a–9b.

[49] In the *Reflections* he quoted Chang Tsai's disapproval of the examination system and praise for hereditary ranks. *CSL* 7, p. 220 (Chan, trans., pp. 199–200).

institutions were far from perfect). By contrast, to Chu Hsi all affairs were ethical and all of life was an arena for moral effort. Thus he could not admire the founders of the Han or T'ang dynasties because, unlike the sage rulers Yao and Shun, their motives had been impure, tinged with selfishness. The peace and order they brought to the common people was a byproduct of their efforts, not their original, unvarying goal, and therefore not sufficient to make them worthy models. Men who claimed that times had changed and new institutions were needed for new situations were seen as blind to the universal principles that were much more important than the mutable details.[50] For Chu Hsi it was easy to view the family in an analogous way. Rather than being two separate subjects—the ethics of interpersonal relations and the strategies for managing the *chia*—almost anything that had to do with family matters was interpreted as a moral issue.

To summarize, the conception of the *chia* as the family in its political and economic senses dated from the Classics. After the end of feudal tenures this conception came into conflict with the classical condemnation of the pursuit of gain. To preserve and certainly to improve their family's financial base it became imperative for most men to take deliberate actions. Ssu-ma Kuang and other Sung classicists tried to reconcile the diverse demands of acting as guardians of their *chia* while avoiding the pursuit of gain. The Ch'eng brothers and Chu Hsi, however, resolved the tension by abandoning the notion of responsibility for the *chia* as an economic unit. The classical phrase *ch'i chia*, "to regulate the family," they explained as perfecting the interpersonal ethics of the members of one's household.[51]

---

[50] On this subject, see Chang, *The Development of Neo-Confucian Thought*, pp. 309–331.

[51] See chap. 6 of the *Reflections* (CSL 6, Chan, trans., pp. 171–82).

ANCESTORS AND LINEAGES

So far family matters have been discussed in terms of dyadic interpersonal relations between kinsmen and in terms of the management of the human and material resources needed for a group of relatives to survive and reproduce themselves. The last subject to be discussed revolves around a different nexus of terms and ideas. The key terms are patrilineal ancestor (*tsu*) and patrilineal descent line (*tsung*) and descent group (*tsu*). This is the realm of religious piety, ritual, genealogy, and charity.

Yüan Ts'ai made very little mention of ancestral rites, duty to ancestors, or duty to kinsmen with common patrilineal ancestors. Most Sung classicists, however, wrote at length on these subjects, attributing to them greater moral urgency than concern with the *chia*. Therefore, in order to understand what failed to interest Yüan Ts'ai, a brief discussion of these topics is necessary.[52]

An aristocratic ancestral cult was already well established in high antiquity.[53] Confucius and Mencius assumed that gentlemen would offer periodic sacrifices to their ancestors and bury their dead with due solemnity. The *Record of Ritual* provides abundant detail on all of the rites performed, usually outlining the gradations appropriate to different ranks from the Son of Heaven down to lower officers and commoners. By the Han even commoners seem to have made regular offerings to their patrilineal ancestors at home, graves, or shrines, and such offerings were integral parts of ceremonies such as cappings, weddings, and funerals. From

[52] A fuller discussion of these subjects is found in Patricia Ebrey, "Conceptions of the Family in the Sung Dynasty" and "The Early Stages of the Development of Kin Group Organization."

[53] For general discussions of the ancient ancestral cult, see Henri Maspero, *China in Antiquity*, pp. 73–75, 103–110, 122–25, and Marcel Granet, *The Religion of the Chinese People*, pp. 80–90.

the late Han through the T'ang, concern with family rituals was the major distinguishing feature of classicists (differentiating them from Buddhists and Taoists). Books describing in detail the steps to be performed in each ritual were regularly published; both Ssu-ma Kuang and Chu Hsi compiled such manuals.[54] In the Sung all *shih-ta-fu* took some interest in their ancestry and performed ancestral rites. Classicists such as Ssu-ma Kuang encouraged punctilious and solemn performance of these rites, largely because doing so promoted appropriate ethical relations and led to orderly family life.

In the ancient period the ancestral cult was intimately tied to the kinship organization of the aristocrats.[55] In the idealized descriptions of the ritual texts, descent lines (*tsung*) were formed of those with common descent from a patrilineal ancestor.[56] The main line of descent (first son of first son, and so on) had claim to ritual headship of the descent line. Collateral lines regularly split off to form their own "small *tsung*" while the main line would continue. Succession to the headship of a descent line generally meant succession to political office, often endowed with land according to the quasi-feudal system of the time. This kinship system was already in decline by the time of Confucius and disappeared completely when feudal tenures were ended in the late classical era. The term *tsung*, however, retained other mean-

---

[54] Ssu-ma Kuang's book is the *Ssu-ma shih shu-i* (*SMSSI*). Chu Hsi wrote a *Chia-li*, the preface to which survives in his collected works. An extant *Chia-li* is often attributed to Chu Hsi, but scholars have disputed his authorship of it.

[55] How the kinship system operated in practice (as opposed to how the ritual texts said it should operate) is not very well known. See Maspero, *China in Antiquity*, pp. 73–75, and M. V. Kryukov, "Hsing and Shih: On the Problem of Clan Name and Patronymic in Ancient China."

[56] The main source on the *tsung* system is the "Ta chuan" chapter of the *Li chi*. See Legge, trans., II, pp. 60–67.

ings. It was a general word for the body of agnatic kinsmen (much like *tsu*) and the preferred term when the topic under discussion was ancestral rites or other rituals. When patrilineal kinsmen lived in the same area, however distant their kinship link, they could be referred to as *tsung-jen*, men of the same descent line. In the Sung, the spread of the practice of ancestral worship at graves at the Ch'ing-ming festival may well have added to the likelihood that local groups of agnates would gain a sense of group identity.[57]

Classicists and philosophers generally promoted strengthening and purifying the ties among agnatic relatives. Fan Chung-yen (989–1052) took the unprecedented step of endowing a "charitable estate," the income from which would benefit all those descended from his great-great-grandfather and provide the corporate base for an enduring social unit.[58] Other classicists like Ou-yang Hsiu (1007–1072) and Su Hsün (1009–1066) encouraged the compilation of genealogies in the belief that knowledge of common ancestry would make relatives treat each other in a more appropriate fashion.[59] Some philosophers even advocated, as a type of "restorationism," revival of the ancient *tsung* system. This seems particularly to have appealed to those who saw concern with the *chia* and with descendants as selfish but who could not escape recognizing that the Classics extolled kinship connections. In the *Reflections on Things at Hand*, Chu Hsi quoted at considerable length Ch'eng I's proposal that the ancient *tsung* system be reestablished, with ancestral property kept together, ancestral temples erected, monthly meetings held, and transmission of *tsung* headship

[57] See Ebrey, "The Early Stages of the Development of Kin Group Organization."

[58] See Denis Twitchett, "The Fan Clan's Charitable Estate" and "Documents of Clan Administration, 1."

[59] Su Hsün, *Chia-yu chi*, 13, pp. 125–34; Ou-yang Hsiu, *Ou-yang Hsiu ch'üan-chi*, 21, pp. 510–23.

decided on a strictly lineal basis. To him this was a "principle of Heaven." "It is comparable to a tree needing a main trunk coming straight up from the root but also having branches." [60]

All of the ideas and beliefs described above come from the classical tradition, from the Classics themselves and the writings of Sung classicists and philosophers. Yüan Ts'ai was certainly aware of this tradition; when he asserted something contrary to the Classics and the teachings of the classicists, it can generally be assumed he did it knowingly.

Other genres of Sung literature did not serve this purpose for Yüan Ts'ai and are of interest here mainly as evidence for the prevalence of ideas and assumptions comparable to Yüan Ts'ai's. The two most significant genres in this regard are legal writings and belle-lettres. In the chapters that follow, comparisons with material from these sources will be introduced regularly.

Judicial decisions are the main source for the tradition of legal thinking on family matters and property as it existed in the Sung. Over 150 decisions on cases involving family and property law written in the twelfth and thirteenth centuries survive in the *Collection of Famous Judicial Decisions* (*Ming-kung shu-p'an ch'ing-ming chi*). The main authors of these decisions were active in the period 1220–1260. They include Ts'ai Hang (1193–1259), Liu K'o-chuang (1187–1269), Fan Ying-ling (*chin-shih*, 1205), Weng Fu (*chin-shih*, 1222), and Hu Ying (*chin-shih*, 1232). A separate set of judicial decisions, on a wider range of topics, survives in the collected works of Huang Kan (1152–1221).[61]

Although these writings are too late to have influenced Yüan Ts'ai, they are our best evidence of the tradition of legal

[60] *CSL* 9, pp. 254–58 (Chan, trans., pp. 227–32).
[61] *Mien-chai chi*, chap. 32–33.

thinking about family and property that evolved slowly over the centuries. As a property owner and family head, Yüan Ts'ai had to be familiar with the basic rules of buying and selling land, and as a magistrate he needed to know the statutes and the interpretations that had accumulated by his time. Certainly some changes in statutes and interpretations were made between the Northern and Southern Sung, but these probably lagged behind common attitudes, for in the cases of major differences (such as the assignments of portions to daughters), Yüan Ts'ai anticipated the thirteenth-century view.

The concepts of family relations found in legal texts differ in many particulars from those elaborated by classicists. In Sung law relatives were distinguished not exclusively by the genealogical links between them but also by the property link: Did they "live together with common property" (*t'ung-chü kung-ts'ai*, or for short, *t'ung-chü*)? Did they have rights to control the property (*chu, kuan*)? Were they coparceners (*ying-fen jen*)?[62] Their merits could also be judged in terms of their contributions to the family property. Were they careful and conscientious as managers? Did they consult others before making major decisions? Or did they waste assets and dissipate property? Another major difference between classical ideals and Sung legal thinking concerned the rights and duties of family heads. In the classical period, holding land depended in theory at least on the favor of the ruler, and it could not be disposed of at will. With free buying and selling of land from the third century B.C. on, a whole new land tenure system developed. Land was generally held as "family property," but not all family members had equal rights to dispose of it. The family head who was a father had much more latitude in selling land than one who

[62] Coparceners were those entitled to a share of the property at its next division. They are discussed in Part One, chap. 5.

was a brother or uncle, but even he was limited in his freedom to give property away without receiving fair value in return, since his sons could seek restitution after his death. These rights and responsibilities toward common property altered the relations between co-resident relatives, especially brothers, from the model espoused in the Classics.

Literature does not represent so coherent a tradition as legal writing. In certain literary genres—poetry and epitaphs, especially—family relations could be discussed or described but generally only in a positive way. Although Sung poetry may be justly famous for an expansion of its subject matter to topics of daily life, intimate glimpses of family life are happy or poignant; disgust at wastrel sons or squabbling brothers was not a poetic topic. Likewise, epitaphs and elegies are an excellent source for basic facts of family arrangements, ancestry, and marriage; but they are not the best ones for the emotional texture of intrafamily relations, since an author said only good or neutral things of the dead and often said them in highly standardized ways.

Anecdotes are the genre of literature that presents the most rounded view of familial relations. Anecdotes record what happened to a particular person at a particular place. The truth of the events cannot be denied, but the author is not challenging any established beliefs about what should happen or about the essential principles of society and its units. Such anecdotes were written in great quantity in the late T'ang and Sung, and Yüan Ts'ai had undoubtedly read some of them.[63] Once he quoted the anecdote of one of his "elders" who turns out to be Chu Yü (ca. 1075–1119), author of the *P'ing-chou k'o-t'an* ("*Chats at P'ing-chou*"). This

---

[63] To get an overview of this genre of literature, see the bibliographical notices in Yves Hervouet, ed., *A Sung Bibliography*, pp. 279–349. Particularly worth reading is George Hatch's analysis of Su Shih's *Chih-lin* in the *Bibliography*, pp. 280–88.

book contains other anecdotes that echo Yüan Ts'ai's concerns, dealing with the rise and fall of families, the purchase
of concubines and its analogy to "purchasing" talented sons-
in-law, the divorce and remarriage of sisters, bossy wives and
mothers-in-law, and so on.[64]

The most prolific author of anecdotes among Yüan Ts'ai's
contemporaries was Hung Mai (1128–1208). Hung Mai
must have recorded every story he heard, and he apparently
heard a great many. Although only about half of his *I-chien
chih* survives, this portion contains well over 2,000 stories.
These deal with people in all walks of life: petty tradesmen,
beggars, prostitutes, high officials, farmers, children, wives,
concubines, and servants. Very often the stories concern
dreams, spirits, retribution, prophecies, or some other supra-
mundane event. But the world in which these phenomena
occur seems to be a very mundane one, one that matches
Yüan Ts'ai's in many regards.[65]

Proverbs and aphorisms often deal with subjects similar to
anecdotes but without details of person and place. Like Yüan
Ts'ai's *Precepts*, they present generalizations about how
people do in fact behave; but unlike the *Precepts*, they do not
explain why they do so or what can be done about it.
Proverbs, as common or "vulgar" sayings, need not have
originated among the *shih-ta-fu*, though they have been
preserved largely because *shih-ta-fu* cited them to underline
some point. A collection of aphorisms that often echo Yüan
Ts'ai's observations and advice is the *Sheng-hsin tsa-yen*, written in 1160 by Li Pang-hsien. Below are a few examples.

> If you are filial to your parents, your sons will be
> filial.

[64] See the anecdote by Chu Yü translated in Part One, chap. 3, pp. 79–80.
[65] On Hung Mai and his *I-chien chih*, see Chang Fu-jui, "Le *Yi-kien tche*
et la Société des Song."

Unless you work diligently in youth, you will certainly suffer in old age; unless you apply yourself in youth, you will have no ease in old age.

Only when there is discord in the family do filial sons appear; only when their is disorder in the state do loyal ministers appear.[66]

Other aphoristic sayings were less serious in their approach to human affairs. Good examples are the *Tsa tsuan* of Wang Ch'i (ca. 1020–1092) and Su Shih (1036–1101). These dictums employ humorous plays on words to comment on human frailties and their regularities. Below are three examples from Su Shih's book.

Fear others knowing—
A banished person who sneaks back
Someone buying stolen goods
Someone who hides a spy
Someone who stashes away money and goods while
    living jointly with his brothers
Someone selling a horse with flaws
Someone leaving a relative's house to flee
    punishment

Finally contented—
A monk or nun who returns to the laity
Palace ladies who are discharged
A son whose mourning for both his parents is over
A prisoner who is released
An "unworthy son" who suddenly has no seniors
A favored concubine who gets to be the only one
    to accompany the master to a post

Cannot be altered by persuasion—

[66] *Sheng-hsin tsa-yen*, 2a, 23b, 11b.

Those who take sulphuric medicines
A fellow sick from wine
An addicted gambler
Those who curse each other when drunk
A husband and wife who fight about a maid[67]

These clever sayings are similar to anecdotes in their attitude of accepting people and situations—the unworthy son, the gambler, the couple who argue, the purchased concubine whose asserted origins should not be believed, sons-in-law who support their wives' families, matchmakers who exaggerate, good wives with inferior husbands. These people all exist and must be dealt with as they are, not as we would rather have them be.

These sorts of situations and characters also appear in the vernacular short stories that first appeared in the Sung. But these fictional stories have generally been interpreted by modern scholars as an expression of the interest, beliefs, and world view of the commoners in the large cities, not those of the *shih-ta-fu*.[68] That many *shih-ta-fu* perceived and discussed human relations in similar ways is, however, evident from their use of proverbs, sayings, and jokes, as well as the recording of anecdotes. That Yüan Ts'ai shared these views and attitudes becomes evident in the chapters that follow.

[67] *Tsa tsuan*, 3, pp. 22–25. On this genre of literature, see the entries by I. E. Tsiperovitch in Hervouet's *Sung Bibliography*, pp. 347–49.
[68] See H. F. Schurmann, "On Social Themes in Sung Tales," and Jaroslav Prusek, *Chinese History and Literature: Collection of Studies*, esp. pp. 467–94. A scholar who takes a different approach is Robert Hegel, who, in dealing with much later fiction, argues convincingly that it was addressed to literati, even though much of its content seems at odds with their political and philosophical writings. See his book, *The Novel in Seventeenth-Century China*, pp. 1–65.

CHAPTER 3

Social Life and Ultimate Values

Before comparing Yüan Ts'ai's ideas and assumptions about the family and its property with those of the classicists and philosophers just described, it is necessary to examine Yüan Ts'ai's larger set of values. Yüan Ts'ai was not, by inclination, an abstract, speculative, or systematic thinker; he did not try to decide which of men's many goals was most important in an ultimate scheme of values. Yet, running through his text are assumptions about what it means to be a good person, about human nature and human proclivities, and about the moral rationality of the universe. As will be seen below, these ideas are distinctively Chinese, but within that sphere they are often closer to what has been thought of as popular mentality than they are to Neo-Confucian metaphysics.[1]

As expressed in the title of his book, Yüan Ts'ai was concerned with the social world, *shih*, the world of men. He saw around him foolishness, cruelty, unpleasantness, and insensitivity, which he thought could be reduced or eliminated. In suggesting how men could or should overcome these evils, Yüan Ts'ai related his advice to goals he thought his audience would share: achieving social harmony, avoid-

[1] In the last chapter, Neo-Confucian views on the family were described at some length because they are especially pertinent to evaluating the *Precepts for Social Life* and because they are not discussed in any detail in Western language sources. Neo-Confucian ethics and metaphysics are less crucial to understanding Yüan Ts'ai and are already described at length in many works, so they will be only briefly touched on here. For more detail, see the works cited in chap. 2, n. 33.

ing disputes and lawsuits, saving trouble, making money, protecting themselves and their property from danger, and above all preserving the family as a corporate, property-owning unit.

On the whole, Yüan Ts'ai tried to argue his points from common sense and self-evident truths. Naturally, what was common sense or self-evident to him was culture-bound, and many of the ideas can be traced in some form to the Confucian and Taoist Classics. He included only four quotations directly attributed to early sages: two to Confucius and one each to Lao Tzu and Mencius. Several times he cited the sage, referring usually to Confucius. Once he quoted from the *Book of Songs* and another time from the *Book of Documents*. Once also he cited by name Ssu-ma Kuang. At times he brought up unidentified "ancients," among them the authors of the *Tso chuan, Chan kuo ts'e, Hsün Tzu, Chuang Tzu, Shih chi, Han shu, Fa yen,* and *Wen hsüan.* More often, though, his quotations did not have even this much authority; he cited proverbs, popular sayings, what is said, what *shih-ta-fu* say, what people say, what his elders said, and so on.

Although it is interesting and useful to note the canonical sources of Yüan Ts'ai's beliefs and values, that does not explain them. Yüan Ts'ai did not write this book as a moral tract to inculcate a particular school's ethics and beliefs, starting with the doctrines and looking for ways to prove them. His quotations were ones that sprang to mind—like proverbs—when he was trying to make a point. Probably he left so many unidentified because he did not remember where they came from.

THE PRINCIPLES OF HEAVEN

Yüan Ts'ai had a deep belief in rationality: not only were there principles on which human affairs operate, but these could be comprehended by men, and comprehending them would solve many of the problems men faced. He spoke often of the "person of discernment" (*yu-shih chih jen*) or the "person of wide discernment" (*yu-yüan-shih chih jen*). These men were asked "to think about" (*ssu*), "to ponder" (*sheng*), and "to examine" (*ch'a*) the principles he pointed out. These principles were referred to as *li*, or as *t'ien-li*, "the principles of Heaven," and were seen to underlay human behavior and impersonal causation.

Although a belief in rationality was fundamental even to classical Confucianism, the term *li* was not used extensively as the term for principle until it was developed by Neo-Taoists and Buddhists after the fall of the Han. In the Sung *li* was developed as a major philosophical concept. Northern Sung thinkers and essayists like Ou-yang Hsiu (1007–1072) used it to speak of the principles underlying human and natural phenomena that could be understood through study and reflection.[2] *Li* also became one of the fundamental concepts of the metaphysics of Neo-Confucianism formulated by the Ch'eng brothers and Chu Hsi. Ch'eng I and Ch'eng Hao gave "principle" greater metaphysical force than Ou-yang Hsiu had. These *li* were not merely the patterns inherent in things but the truth underlying what exists and what happens; they were therefore ultimately more important than the things or events themselves.[3]

Since Yüan Ts'ai also used the term *t'ien-li*, it is likely that he was at least indirectly influenced by the writings of the Ch'eng brothers. Yüan Ts'ai used *t'ien-li*, however, much as Ou-yang Hsiu used *li*; the addition of *t'ien* suggested a broader scope—a principle that was universal, not limited to one group of things—but did not in Yüan Ts'ai's mind make

[2] James T. C. Liu, *Ou-yang Hsiu*, p. 92.
[3] See Wing-tsit Chan's "Introduction" in *Reflections on Things at Hand*, pp. xvii–xxi.

li more important than people in their concrete activities. This usage of *li* is clear in the passage below. In discussing how differences in temperament lead to friction among relatives, he wrote:

> If everyone expects to get his own way, disputes will certainly result. If the disputes are not settled, they will be repeated two or three, even ten or more times. Feelings of discord start in this way, and sometimes people end up disliking each other for the rest of their lives. If people could awaken to the way this works (*li*), and older family members could understand the feelings of their juniors and not demand that they be the same as them, and juniors could look up to their seniors but not expect them to accept all their advice, then whenever actions need to be taken everyone would cooperate and obstinate disputes could be avoided (1.1 in the translation in Part Two).

Clearly in this case *li* is the principle underlying actual human interaction, not a higher truth or ideal inherent in true human nature.

One aspect of "the way things work" for Yüan Ts'ai was reward and punishment; Heaven's principles do not allow the bad to flourish. After discussing the strategies kinsmen use to profit at each other's expense when dividing the family assets, Yüan Ts'ai remarked, "If only people today would recognize that clever strategies cannot overcome the workings of Heaven (*t'ien-li*), the impulse to go to court would be checked" (1.27). Where evidence seemed to contradict the belief that good was rewarded and bad punished, Yüan Ts'ai asserted that retribution would come to the sons for the crimes of their fathers. He said at one point, "If you see other people succeed in their bad deeds, do not be jealous. Heaven is rejecting these people. Once their evils have piled up,

Heaven will destroy them, wreaking punishment either on them or on their descendants" (2.19).

A divine intelligence—the knowledge of the gods (*shen chih ts'ung-ming*)—was an agent in this process of reward and retribution, knowing of bad deeds, even ones concealed from human eyes. "When you do something that in your heart you know is wrong, whether or not other people know anything of it, the gods are aware of it" (2.15). Gods thus deserve respect. Yüan Ts'ai took to task skeptics and agnostics who did not believe in gods by citing a passage in the *Book of Songs* saying the gods must not be despised (2.15) and pointing out that even Confucius enjoined respect for gods and ghosts (2.17). Yüan Ts'ai also refered to a coordinating power, the Creator (*tsao-wu che*), who works along with the gods to bring about Heaven-ordained rewards and punishments. The Creator arranges early death for those who have had life too easy and success for those who have suffered and worked hard in their youth (2.6).

Yüan Ts'ai's belief in moral response as a principle of Heaven was a widely held one in his day. Indeed, in various forms it went back to the Classics. The *Book of Documents* contains the claim that "the way of Heaven is to bless the good and to punish the bad." [4] The idea that the merits or demerits of one's ancestors affect one's fortune is found in a commentary in the *I ching*: "The family which stores up virtue will have a surplus of blessings." [5] In popular thought, the belief in reward and retribution held even greater sway. Mo Tzu (fl. 479–438 B.C.) argued in favor of its utility. [6] Wang Ch'ung (A.D. 27–90+) argued at great length against the belief, since it seemed to imply that people deserved the circumstances in which they found themselves and to leave

[4] *Shang shu*, "T'ang-kao" (Legge, trans., *Classics* 3, p. 186).
[5] "Wen-yen" commentary to *Chou I*, "K'un" (Sung, trans., p. 20).
[6] See Burton Watson, trans., *The Basic Writings of Mo Tzu*, pp. 117–23.

little room for destiny—the arbitrary decrees of Heaven—a belief that also had a long tradition in Chinese thought.[7] After the Han, the Buddhist notion of karma strengthened the hold that the belief in moral response had on both the popular and the elite imagination.[8] Stories and anecdotes revealing how particular good or bad deeds were rewarded were a major literary genre. The great tenth-century collection of tales, the *T'ai-p'ing kuang-chi*, included thirty-three chapters of stories of "true incidents" of the consequences of good or evil deeds. The popular moral tract of Sung date, the "Book of Rewards and Punishments," was entirely devoted to this theme.[9]

Many Sung writers expressed ideas about divine responsiveness that are quite close to Yüan Ts'ai's. For instance, Chou Hui, in the *Ch'ing-po tsa-chih* (1192) remarked that the Creator will not allow long life to those born rich and high-ranking.[10] Hung Mai's *I-chien chih* recounts people praying to the gods and depicts people as punished by Heaven, sometimes through such agencies as lightning.[11]

Philosophers of Yüan Ts'ai's time held to more subtle views of causality and seldom directly evoked the concepts of rewards and punishments. Therefore the question arises: Was Yüan Ts'ai addressing *shih-ta-fu* in his references to rewards and retributon, or did he purposely evoke the thought that the gods were watching for the sake of simpler minds? In his preface Yüan Ts'ai said he was writing clearly enough even for farmers and women, but this, I think, was a way of deflecting criticism of his style of writing. If he admitted he

[7] See Alfred Forke, trans., *Lun-Heng*, esp. I, pp. 139–55.

[8] See Lien-sheng Yang, "The Concept of 'Pao' as a Basis for Social Relations in China."

[9] A translation of this tract is found in Patricia Ebrey, ed., *Chinese Civilization and Society*, pp. 71–74.

[10] *Ch'ing-po tsa-chih*, 7, p. 59.

[11] *ICC chia* 14, p. 121; *ting* 1, p. 541; 9, pp. 613–14.

was addressing the educated, he would have to justify his lack of "fundamentalism," his failure to prove his points by citing the Classics. By claiming to address the less educated, he could argue from common sense and self-interest, not from what the sages had said. Since many of his examples of reward or retribution concern activities clearly limited to the *shih-ta-fu* (such as passing the civil service examinations early only to get embroiled in factional disputes later on), he can hardly have been addressing only the ill-educated. Moreover, Yüan Ts'ai seems to have fully internalized the belief in moral response himself and referred to it in passing in essays that were not specifically on moral cultivation. For instance, in a discussion of local bullies, he said, "Anyone—official or commoner—who is so wicked will in due course be punished by Heaven even if he avoids suffering at the hands of men" (2.66). In discussing the incompetence of some magistrates, he wrote, "In such cases, the grievances the commoners suffer never get redressed. This is why so many of those who serve in office have no descendants" (2.68).[12]

Although Yüan Ts'ai believed in Heavenly reward and retribution, he did not make each person (in conjunction with his ancestors) fully responsible for his own situation. Several times he evoked the traditional concept of allotted shares. Wealth and rank, that is, social position, are allotted by Heaven and set from birth. Although through their own

---

[12] A further reason to believe that Yüan Ts'ai meant what he said about retribution is that his tone is much less calculating than truly popular works such as the "Book of Rewards and Punishments" or the "Table of Merits and Demerits." In these works, spirits are portrayed as mechanistically subtracting a specific number of days from a person's life span for offenses of varying gravity. Yüan Ts'ai made no such argument and indeed limited the scope of moral response, allowing also for fate. He did not say justice would be swift or obvious, just that it would triumph eventually, often through the common enough occurrence of one's grandsons reducing the family to poverty.

actions people can "ruin their families," neither "rushing around" nor morally correct behavior can be counted on to bring one glory. "In the world today, often the stupid enjoy great wealth while the intelligent dwell in poverty and obscurity. The reason is that their lot (*fen*) is fixed" (2.4). By this logic it is wrong to be too eager for gain; one should be conscientious and work hard but not expect an automatic reward. Such expectations show contempt for Heaven (2.7).

There is, of course, a basic contradiction between Yüan Ts'ai's view that Heaven allots wealth and rank in a way that cannot be fathomed but is not a reward for proper behavior and the view that Heaven wreaks punishment on evil people or their descendants (2.19). The dual conviction (or perhaps, to them, perception) that goodness brings rewards but that Heaven ordains certain fates for people against which their struggles are useless goes back at least to Confucius.[13] The way Yüan Ts'ai reduced the logical tension between moral response and arbitrary destiny was to apply each principle to different cases: Do not expect rewards for your own good deeds or strenuous efforts, but let Heaven punish those who are bad.

---

[13] Neither the early philosophers nor Yüan Ts'ai seem to have been concerned to demarcate the exact boundaries between the realms controlled by each. Donald Munro argues that in classical times destiny was seen as controlling only a small number of events, the most important of which was the date of one's death (*The Concept of Man in Early China*, pp. 87–88). Yüan Ts'ai also believed destiny had a major—often decisive—effect on wealth and rank, an idea that went back to Confucius and Mencius but that may well have become more powerful as the belief in social mobility based on merit gained acceptance. (People needed an explanation for failing to attain the position they thought they deserved.) Philosophers in Yüan Ts'ai's time shared his belief that destiny controlled ultimate success, the Ch'eng brothers and Chu Hsi arguing strongly that one should leave these matters to Heaven. See the passage from the *Reflections on Things at Hand* quoted in the preceding chapter.

SOCIAL ETHICS

Yüan Ts'ai's belief in Heavenly response was based on the assumption that actions were either good or bad and that both men and Heaven could distinguish between them. The good qualities Yüan Ts'ai expected to be rewarded were described in the traditional Confucian vocabulary. He talked of good faith (*chung*), trustworthiness (*hsin*), sincerity (*tu*), respectfulness (*ching*) (2.13), fairness (*kung-p'ing*), straightforwardness (*cheng-shih*) (2.17), forbearance (*jen*) (2.21), tolerance (*k'uan*) (1.4), and the willingness to correct oneself (2.14, 2.24). His major discourse on these virtues started with a quote from the *Analects* (2.13). The way that he described these virtues made them relatively accessible. Their attainment depended mostly on effort; anyone determined to do so could hope to master them:

> To secure your own advantage without harming anyone else when dealing with business matters and in crises to take care of yourself without hindering others is good faith. To fulfill promises to the last iota and to keep appointments to the dot is trustworthiness. To be cordial in your dealings and honest in your heart is sincerity. To behave with deference and to speak with humility is respectfulness. (2.13)

The vices Yüan Ts'ai most condemned were in part the opposite of these virtues, especially deceit and insincerity. But he also loathed envy, self-satisfaction, and disdain for the less fortunate. Although never calling for humility (except before the gods), he did hate arrogance (2.3, 2.12).

Despite his belief in Heavenly moral response, Yüan Ts'ai often failed to detect clear-cut right and wrong. In one place he said that "people are only rarely of one mind and their

judgments are seldom uniform" (2.30). One of his arguments against pursuing lawsuits was that each side was usually partly right and partly wrong and publicized "its
strengths while concealing its weaknesses" (2.65). Sung
writers outside of the Ch'eng-Chu tradition often expressed
similar pluralistic attitudes.[14]

This pluralism was related to Yüan Ts'ai's view of human
nature, which was fundamentally different from that of
Mencius or Chu Hsi. He did not see one truly human and
fully admirable set of instincts that every person possesses
underneath whatever he may have acquired through experience. Instead he saw considerable variety in people's
innate style or temperament, a situation to be accepted, not
condemned. Yüan Ts'ai's very first essay brought up this
theme: people are not all alike and cannot be expected to act
the same way in all situations; expecting them to do so only
leads to endless friction and ill will. Many of these differences
are what we would call differences in personality or temperament: "Some people are relaxed, others tense; some are
tough, others timid; some are serious, others light-hearted;
some are disciplined, others indulgent; some like calm, others
prefer excitement; some have narrow vision, others are farsighted" (1.1).

Yüan Ts'ai's strategies for dealing with such human
variety were to cultivate tolerance, forbearance, and forgiveness, traits he found in much too short a supply. The way to
master tolerance was through reflection and insight. People
who recognize innate personality differences, who can see
that people have strengths as well as shortcomings, who can
appreciate that whatever a person's failings, he or she is no
worse than others in the same role, such people can avoid
feeling resentment and anger (1.1, 1.3, 2.11). Yüan Ts'ai

[14] See Hoyt Tillman, *Utilitarian Confucianism*, p. 60, and Hatch, "Su
Shih," pp. 912–13.

stressed that tolerance is not the same as repressed anger. Repressed anger will eventually burst forth with flood-like force. Instead, anger should be avoided altogether by excusing lapses. "Do this by saying to yourself, 'He wasn't thinking,' 'He doesn't know any better,' 'He made a mistake,' 'He is narrow in his outlook,' or 'How much harm can this really do?'" (1.6). When resentment has developed, one should also be ready to take the first step to break the ice (1.7).

Tolerance was appropriate in cases of minor misdemeanors. Forbearance Yüan Ts'ai saw as needed when one had to deal with a malicious scoundrel. If the soundrel was a household member and did not "even do one thing right in one hundred," confronting him everyday could be extremely provoking (1.30). The only thing to do in such cases was to "deal with the scoundrel as a fact of life beyond [one's] control" (1.30). Forbearance was also needed by juniors who had to deal with unreasonable superiors and in cases of local bullies and gangs who subvert local government (1.5 and 2.38).

Yüan Ts'ai was of course not unique in calling for tolerance and forbearance. The power of yielding had been recognized since the early Taoists, and popular tales often recorded men who excelled at transforming others through turning the other cheek.[15] Yüan Ts'ai, however, was less positive in assessing forbearance: it would not so much solve problems as keep them from getting worse. This view of forbearance is also found in many "family instructions." For instance, a favorite paragon was Chang Kung-i, the head of a family in the early T'ang that had remained undivided for nine generations. The T'ang emperor Kao-tsung (r. 650–648), on a trip to Mt. T'ai, personally visited his house and asked the explanation for their "righteousness." Chang

---

[15] See the biography of Wang Lieh, *San-kuo chih*, 11, pp. 355–56.

"requested brush and paper and wrote the character 'forbearance' over a hundred times."[16]

Much of Yüan Ts'ai's advice on social behavior was based
on his perception of the widespread incidence of envy, resentment, and ill will. He perceived a general tendency to
differentiate manners according to a person's wealth and
status, to be deferential to the high-ranking and rude to the
lowly (2.3). He also saw people who were "envious of the
successful who have had things go their way" (2.5), who
were upset whenever they heard someone praised but "overjoyed at reports that someone has shortcomings" (2.12).

To avoid inciting either envy or disdain Yüan Ts'ai urged
maintaining a balance between familiarity and distance. One
should be pleasant and easygoing and not put on airs. On the
other hand, one should not be too casual or familiar. "At
banquets and parties where wine is served you should certainly sing and laugh and have a fully enjoyable time, but
beware of making fun of others, for you might hit someone's
sore spot and spark a quarrel" (2.36).

As Yüan Ts'ai saw things, social life was also marred by
too much preaching and backbiting. People who were not
perfectly virtuous had no right to criticize others, and even
those who were above reproach merely would provoke
resentment if they were too ready to point out others' faults
(2.14, 2.29). At the same time, Yüan Ts'ai advised people to
be unperturbed by criticism they received. If it was wide of
the mark, it should be ignored: "None of the sages and
worthies of antiquity, or the chief ministers of this dynasty,
or the current governors and magistrates have escaped from
gossip. So how can someone living in the countryside along
with the registered commoners?" (2.30).

Because of Yüan Ts'ai's view of the variability of human

[16] *Chiu T'ang shu*, 188, p. 4920. A longer version is in *CF* 1, pp. 478–79.

nature, he did not hold each person fully accountable for the behavior of others he dealt with. Early Confucians had stressed the transforming power of moral example and the ability of the good person to reform the bad. If carried to a logical extreme, this could easily lead to "blaming the victim," a problem Yüan Ts'ai recognized. He thought one could influence many people for the better—especially one's own children—but not everyone. The world was full of envious, greedy, deceitful, arrogant people who did not change because one treated them fairly and honestly. The world would be a better place if they would change and try to correct their faults, but neither advice nor example could be counted on to bring about that result (2.26, 2.27, 2.28, 2.38). If a family head were unlikely to be able to influence them, he would be well advised to protect himself and his family members from their harm (material and spiritual) and let Heaven punish them.

Taken together, Yüan Ts'ai's social ethics can hardly be called classically Confucian. Despite verbal similarity in the labels for many virtues, his underlying attitudes differed in many regards. He emphasized tolerance and compromise more than moral duty or righteousness and almost never spoke of *jen* ("benevolence") or *li* ("rules of ritual and decorum"). Even when he did use those terms he did not elevate them to supreme virtues or see them as transforming powers, as Confucian theorists regularly did. Furthermore, a fearful, negative tone pervades much of his discussion of social relations outside of the family. He described a social world in which people were constantly testifying to their respect or disrespect for each other. He found this painful but saw no way to change the entire system. All he could propose were preventive measures: Be polite to all those you have to deal with and avoid any occasion likely to be humiliating.

Few of Yüan Ts'ai's contemporaries explicitly expressed

the same views he did on social relations, but one who did share some of his fears was Lu Chiu-shao. Lu wrote that anyone who was not rich should avoid entertainment and gift-giving: "In this way he can avoid making requests to relatives and old friends, which invites blame, or making demands on old acquaintances, which causes resentment, or secretly taking out loans, which invites humiliation."[17] Yet even if writers were unwilling to advocate such negative attitudes, they often acknowledged them in anecdotes. For instance, in anecdotes people were often depicted as highly sensitive to slights. In one passage Yüan Ts'ai said most men whose neighbors scorned them in their youth because of their straitened circumstances would treat those former neighbors like enemies if they ever attained success themselves (2.63). Much the same sort of social world is depicted in the following anecdote recorded by Shao Po-wen (1057–1134).

> Sun Wen-i was from Yü-she in Mei-chou. When young his family was poor, so he needed to pawn a field in order to take the examinations in the capital. He was at the county offices on a legal matter when the constable, Li Chao-yen, made fun of him: "People like you don't often want to take the examinations in the capital." Wen-i passed the examinations in the third place and received an appointment as an assistant in the Court of Personnel Administration. When Li Chao-yen went for reassignment he saw Sun and was extremely afraid, thinking Sun would not have forgotten his comment. Sun made a point of assigning Li Chao-yen as magistrate of [Sun's home prefecture] Mei-chou.[18]

[17] *SYHA* 57, p. 119.
[18] *Ho-nan Shao-shih wen-chien ch'ien-lu,* 8, p. 53.

Thus in this case Li, having once made fun of Sun for having ambitions out of line with his financial status, expected Sun to hold a grudge against him. The anecdote was recorded, of course, only because this did not occur and Sun behaved with generosity.

PRESERVING THE FAMILY

Whatever value Yüan Ts'ai placed on honesty, sincerity, tolerance, forgiveness, and politeness as good in themselves and liable to reward from Heaven, he seldom failed to note that they would also contribute to social harmony and especially to the preservation of the family. Yüan Ts'ai took for granted that his audience would consider preservation and promotion of one's *chia* as an honorable aspiration. He never apologized for it or questioned whether greed entered into it. The importance that he attached to family preservation can be seen in the following quotations:

[Parents should not show arbitrary favoritism toward their sons or] they will make the older ones resentful and the younger ones spoiled, leading to the ruin of the *chia*. (1.19)

[When a brother, son, or nephew in a complex family always wants the largest share of something which is to be divided, quarrels will result] bringing the financial ruin of the *chia* estate. Thus, a desire for small gains brings about a major disaster. (1.22)

Fathers, brothers, and sons who live together will be a mixture of good and bad. If the ones who are quarrelsome, stingy, or wasteful of the family's estate die first, then the family's fortune will be difficult enough to determine. If the kindly, generous, diligent, and careful ones die first, then the *chia* will be beyond salvage. (1.41)

If you give a boy away while he is still in diapers and by chance he turns out to be unworthy, not only will he ruin the other *chia*, but that family will try to return him to yours, which regularly leads to lawsuits, and the ruin of your *chia* also. (1.43)

When [widows] can read and do arithmetic, and those they entrust with their affairs have enough to live on themselves and some sense of fairness and duty, then [the widow's] affairs will usually work out all right. When these conditions do not prevail, the usual result is the ruin of the *chia*. (1.53)

[Early engagements are unwise because the prospective bride or bridegroom may turn out undesirable on various grounds.] If you honor the agreement, preserving your *chia* will be difficult. But to renounce it is unethical (literally: thin in righteousness) and may lead to lawsuits. Be warned! (1.54)

As a general rule, among ten or more well-behaved sons and grandsons, there will be one who is unworthy. There are cases where the dozen good ones all suffer because of the single bad one, even to the point where the *chia* is ruined. The hundreds of stipulations in our laws can do nothing to prevent this; neither can the hundreds of plans laid by fathers and grandfathers. (1.62)

If your family property is in the middle range, you must start to worry early about all affairs.... [If you don't prepare for the funerals of your parents in advance], the only alternatives are provisionally selling land or houses or callously allowing the funeral and burial to fall below the ritual norm. (2.56)

People who drink without limit or eat meat without moderation, who love to have affairs with women or are given to chess playing will bankrupt their *chia* if it is a rich one or become thieves if it is a poor one. (2.59)

When the servant class bear children, they attribute them to the master. As a result people often raise stupid and vulgar offspring who end up ruining the *chia*. (3.21)

The terms "poor" and "frugal" indicate wisdom and virtue and are compliments. You should not be ashamed of them. If you understand this, you need not worry about ruining your *chia*. (3.69)

As can be seen from these quotations, Yüan Ts'ai saw "ruining the *chia*" as a major disaster, caused by personal failure on a par with failure to fulfill ethical or ritual obligations (*i* and *li*). Indeed, it was not much better than becoming a thief.

Yüan Ts'ai may have gone on at greater length about preserving the family than any other Sung writer, but his concern was certainly a common one. Anecdotes often describe the reasons for the rise and fall of families.[19] "Family instructions" were written largely to teach ways to "preserve the family."[20] They generally argued that this would depend on the character of the family members, but in asserting this, they would stress that the common view was that property or income from office was indispensable. Ssu-ma Kuang wrote that "all grandfathers want to benefit their

[19] For instance, Wang Ming-ch'ing (1127–1214+) in a series of anecdotes described the fortunes of many families, concluding that only some twenty-odd families had been able to retain high official status for several generations in a row (*Hui-chu ch'ien-lu*, 2, pp. 73–87). In a similar vein, Hung Mai recorded tales of families who were ruined. For instance, in one story a son of an official spent money with great abandon, discarding any clothes that were soiled rather than having them washed. When his father died, his stepmother made off with the remaining money and the son had to learn to live in near poverty, supporting himself as a tutor on 1,000 cash a month. In another story, a lawsuit over three feet of land led to the ruin of two families. *ICC ting* 6, pp. 583–84; *chia* 16, p. 137.

[20] For Sung family instructions, see *CTTL*, passim.

descendants," and so they try to accumulate property to leave them.[21] Lu Chiu-shao similarly wrote, "What human being does not love his *chia*, love his children and grandchildren, and love himself?" He thought their efforts usually ended up hurting them, however, because they conveyed the wrong set of values to their sons, their faces lighting up "whenever mention is made of fame or profit," but boredom showing itself "whenever mention is made of filial submission, fraternal respect, benevolence or moral duty." Lu Chiu-shao was not indifferent to the importance of property, however, for he advocated strict budgeting, even saying that if one could not save at least ten percent of one's income a year, his *chia* would be sure to be ruined.[22]

What most distinguished Yüan Ts'ai from classicists like Lu Chiu-shao and Ssu-ma Kuang was his unconcealed admiration for those who worked honestly and diligently to ensure their families' financial security. Whatever the importance of ethical strengths, he did not think one should ignore the need for productive property (*ch'an*) or wealth (*ts'ai*), or an occupation or other heritage that brought in income (*yeh*). "Men who establish their families (*ch'i chia*) not only produce riches (*ts'ai*) in abundance, but also day and night they make plans, worrying about how to avoid slipping back to hunger and cold. Sons who ruin their families (*p'o chia*) not only cause trouble and waste time, but also they boldly indulge themselves, saying there is nothing more to worry about" (2.51). To Yüan Ts'ai diligence and laziness were not mere differences in temperament, to be accepted or tolerated. Because they were so much tied up with the *chia*, they carried with them moral significance. In other words, indulgence, laziness, and irresponsibility were not merely unwise; they were as deserving of general condemnation as

[21] *CF* 2, p. 487.
[22] *SYHA* 57, p. 117.

unfilial behavior and other kinds of insubordination. Fathers could be as guilty of this as sons. "Some people living in our society ... give no thought to their descendants' need for something to rely on to protect them from hunger and cold; they give birth to numerous boys and girls and then treat them like strangers. They indulge in wine and women, gamble, and get up to no good, depleting their family property for the sake of momentary pleasures" (2.54)

Yüan Ts'ai placed so much value on the preservation of the *chia* that one cannot help wondering which was more important to him, being a good person or preserving the patrimony. At the same time, however, it is necessary to recognize that Yüan Ts'ai did not see these goals as conflicting: the good man benefited his *chia*, and those who succeeded in their efforts to preserve their *chia* were the ones who had always been honest and fair in their dealings.

In this chapter evidence has been cited to show that Yüan Ts'ai's contemporaries shared his beliefs in Heaven's principles of moral response, the variability of human nature, the need for tolerance, and the duty to preserve one's *chia* through prudent measures. Not only did other writers concur on particular attitudes; many seem to have accepted a very similar overall value system. Consider, for instance, the anecdote recorded by Chu Yü (ca. 1075–1119+).

> Su I of Ch'ang-chou reached the post of circuit intendant. His family was rich, but he was extremely stingy. Every time he bought land, he begrudged the fair value. He would go pale fighting over a single cash. He especially enjoyed taking advantage of other people's financial emergencies to get choice properties or goods at little expense. Once when he was buying a country retreat, the dithering back and forth with the seller was getting bitter. His son took him aside and

said, "Sir, you could give a little more for it. Then when I sell it someday I'll also get a better price for it."

His father was startled and came to his senses a little. The gentlemen-officials (*shih-ta-fu*) competed to spread the story.[23]

This anecdote assumes a belief in retribution (the sons would end up getting less if the father got more). Also it portrays a world populated with imperfect but not entirely evil people. The father who had enjoyed taking advantage of others was, after all, brought to his senses by his son. Yüan Ts'ai also would have "competed to spread" this story.

[23] *P'ing-chou k'o-t'an*, 3, pp. 44–45.

CHAPTER 4

The Harmony of Co-Residents

Yüan T'sai saw around him many families whose home life was unpleasant. Among co-residents (*t'ung-chü chih-jen*), he found frequent "loss of affection" (*shih-huan*), his term for what we would call dislike or ill will. With loss of affection people became irascible and argumentative; sometimes their every action irritated other members of their families. According to Yüan Ts'ai, some brothers would treat each other like enemies, some uncles and nephews would "fight with each other with more bitterness than strangers ever could" (1.28), and some parents would take arbitrary dislike to certain sons or grandsons. Yüan Ts'ai, like all those before him who wrote on family matters, saw no value in discord and concentrated all his powers of analysis on thinking of ways to eliminate it.

To understand Yüan Ts'ai's analysis of interpersonal relations within families, it is first necessary to look at the terms he used for relatives and the assumptions he made about categories of people.

CATEGORIES AND HIERARCHIES

In Chinese usage there are specific one-character terms for a large number of kinship positions: from elder brother and younger brother, to father's sister and mother's sister, to sister's son and brother's son, and so on. Moreover, by the use of two- or three-character terms, a great many other relationships can be referred to with considerable genealogical exactitude: wife's elder brother, father's father's younger brother, and so on. As discussed in Chapter 2, Ssu-ma Kuang often took advantage of these possibilities for exactitude in discussing the relatives who lived together. Yüan Ts'ai, by contrast, seldom did. Broader categories were sufficient for his purposes. He described the various components of a household by two-character terms mentioning key members. Thus the women in a family were referred to as *fu-nü,* "wives and daughters"; the senior men as *fu-hsiung,* "fathers and elder brothers"; the younger men and boys as *tzu-ti,* "sons and younger brothers"; the female menials as *pi-ch'ieh,* "maids and concubines"; the male menials as *nu-p'u,* "male slaves and male servants" (really meaning male bondservants); and so on.

Often the full meaning of these two-character compounds depended not so much on the specific referent of each of the terms but on what term it was used to contrast or complement. One contrast worth noting is that between the women in a family (wives and daughters) and the menial women attached to a family (maids and concubines). "Maids and concubines" was a rather vague category in Yüan Ts'ai's usage: at times it referred primarily to maids, to women who should not bear children for the master, and at other times primarily to concubines, who should. The distinction between maids and concubines does not seem to have been very important to him (even if it was to them). That between wives and concubines, however, was crucial. Yüan Ts'ai never grouped the two, seeing them as entirely separate elements of the household make-up. Wives dealt with mothers-in-law or parents-in-law (*ku* or *chiu-ku*), maids and concubines dealt with masters and mistresses (*chu* or *chu-mu*).

Yüan Ts'ai made only one distinction among families on

the basis of their organization. What I have translated as complex family (meaning a household with a collateral rather than a lineal head), Yüan Ts'ai referred to by listing its key male members: elder and younger brothers, sons and nephews (*hsiung-ti tzu-chih*), qualified by the fact that they pooled their resources (*t'ung-chü*). Such a household could of course also have included mothers or grandsons, but they were not its distinctive feature. Families that were not complex had no special terms. Thus Yüan Ts'ai saw no need to distinguish among what we call a nuclear family (parents and their children only), a stem family (parents, one married child, and grandchildren), and an extended family with the father still surviving (father, two or more married children, and grandchildren). To him these were simply ordinary families, structurally significant only in their lack of collateral extension in the senior generation of men. In this regard Yüan Ts'ai's distinction accords very closely with the legal thinking of the period.

The categories Yüan Ts'ai used to discuss the relations among co-residents reveal some of his most basic assumptions about the hierarchy of authority in the family. Like almost everyone else in the Chinese tradition, he took entirely for granted hierarchical authority based on age and sex. Although fathers and elder brothers were asked to try to imagine the needs and feelings of those subordinate to them, they were never told to give in to them. Sons and younger brothers were also told to consider the needs and feelings of their elders, but when they could not convince themselves that the fault was their own, all they could do was wait for Heaven's response. "The relationship of a son to his father or a younger brother to his elder brother is like that of a soldier to his officer, a clerk to the official above him, or a bondservant to his master: that is, they may not consider themselves peers who may dispute points whenever they please" (1.5). Between fathers and sons this relationship was unchanging and unconditional, just as it was to Ssu-ma Kuang.

Male-female relations were discussed in a different manner. Very little of Yüan Ts'ai's advice was directed to women themselves.[1] Most often Yüan Ts'ai discussed women in the context of how men should cope with them. In these essays he assumed an extreme dependency for women. They were dependent on men of both their natal families and their families of marriage. In one essay Yüan Ts'ai explained why women were generally better off when they are young than when they are old. They have strong ties to their fathers and brothers who can help them when they are young, but weaker ones to their brothers' sons, who may be the only surviving representatives of their natal family in their old age (1.60). This deficiency was not fully compensated by strong ties to sons and grandsons, for Yüan Ts'ai depicted widowed mothers as having little authority over their sons, despite some legal protections. When sons break the law or sell the family property, mothers have no avenues of recourse. "For women these are grave misfortunes, but what can they do about them? But wouldn't it be great if husbands and sons could only remember that their wives and mothers are helpless, and suddenly repent!" (1.52).

The only substantial responsibility Yüan Ts'ai gave to women was the rearing of young children. When children grow up spoiled, it is probably because mothers concealed their misdeeds from their fathers. Still the fathers were ultimately responsible since they should have known better than to listen so exclusively to their wives (1.12). Even the management of maids and concubines was not something Yüan Ts'ai would fully delegate to women. Their experience was

---

[1] An exception is a passage in which brides whose parents-in-law fail to appreciate them were told to be patient and wait for eventual justice (1.21).

too narrow for them to have good judgment; therefore, they were too easily pleased with a maid who flattered them and told them gossip about the other women in the household (1.36). They also often were too severe with their maids because of their tendencies to be "petty, quick-tempered, quarrelsome, obstinate, cruel, oppressive, and ignorant of the ancient and modern moral truths" (3.30).[2]

One reason Yüan Ts'ai may not have wished to see women have much authority in the affairs of the family is that he did not think they shared its views. Their relations to the other members of the family were not based on "natural relations" but on ones borrowed from their husbands (1.35). They were sympathetic and emotional, attached to their blood relatives without regard to current *chia* membership. Thus "if her husband's *chia* is wealthy but her mother's *chia* is poor, then she wants to take from her husband's *chia* assets to give to her mother's *chia*. . . . When her own sons and daughters are grown and married, if either her son's *chia* or her daughter's *chia* is wealthy while the other is poor, she wishes to take from the wealthy one to give to the poor one" (1.59).

Yüan Ts'ai's opinions of women may sound harsh, but they seem less so when compared with those of classicists and philosophers on the subject. Consider, for instance, the view of Liu K'ai (947–1000) quoted by Chu Hsi.

> In a family the brothers may all be quite dutiful but because their wives have entered the house, different surnames live together, leading to competition over small differences. Slowly the partiality the brothers hear each day will be stored up, until they turn their backs on each other, and divide the family. This calamity can be equal to an attack by robbers, and it is entirely

[2] An illustration of this is found in *ICC chia* 15, p. 130. A low official's wife, who had formerly been a prostitute, was so cruel to her maids that she killed several of them.

brought on by the wives. How many men have the firmness not to be affected by what their wives say?[3]

Although Yüan Ts'ai urged men to avoid adopting their wives' prejudices, he never likened their presence to an attack of robbers or anything else as calamitous.

FATHER—SON TENSIONS

To us it may seem obvious that families are emotion-charged arenas and thus likely scenes of bitterness and even cruelty, but this was not a common perception in Yüan Ts'ai's time. In fiction and humorous accounts, stereotypes of cruel mothers-in-law, unfair stepmothers, and bossy or jealous wives were abundant enough, as were accounts of the irresponsible (but often good-hearted) son. But little recognition was given to the problem of friction and dislike among apparently normal, responsible male relatives, especially fathers and sons and elder and younger brothers. These were the people who had to get along if the *chia* were to survive as a unit, and therefore within Yüan Ts'ai's value system antagonism among them was much more dangerous than friction among women or between a man and a woman (so long as it did not entangle other men or endanger the primary goals of the *chia* as a corporate body).

Yüan Ts'ai gave considerable thought to the problem of achieving harmony among co-residents. His analyses of it are among his most original and most perceptive essays, differing fundamentally with the teachings of the classicists. His general opinion was that one should reserve judgment in cases of family discord: moral inadequacy did indeed exist in plenty (the classicist diagnosis), but circumstances also played

[3] *CTTL* 6/5b and *HH* 5, pp. 119–20.

a part. In any society some individuals, such as novelists, are more perceptive than others about what goes on in interpersonal relations. Yüan Ts'ai seems to have been such a person. Although most of his contemporaries may not have seen as clearly as he did why friction develops between people, there seems little reason to doubt Yüan Ts'ai's analysis. I think it can be looked on as an explanation of the principles in operation among his peers, but ones they acted on unintentionally.[4]

In Yüan Ts'ai's view, tensions between fathers and sons were usually generated by the ways fathers attempted to keep their sons from becoming "unworthy sons." The term here translated as "unworthy" (*pu-hsiao*) literally means "not similar" and had been used in the Classics to describe sons who did not match their fathers in ability or moral character and therefore were unworthy of them. The "sage-rulers" of mythical antiquity, Yao and Shun, were said to have had *pu-hsiao* sons, which was the reason why they passed the throne to nonrelatives.[5] By late classical times the term had already become a cliche, a conventional term for sons of weak character whose fathers were disappointed in them. In T'ang

---

[4] Here I should admit that later evidence has influenced my thinking. Yüan Ts'ai's discussion of the interpersonal dynamics of families has much in common with modern sociological and anthropological analysis of "traditional" Chinese family life. Since Yüan Ts'ai can hardly have been influenced by these writings, the most plausible reason for the similarities in description is a similarity in the object described, that is, that the families of Yüan Ts'ai's contemporaries operated on many of the same principles still in evidence in the twentieth century. Even though most of his contemporaries were unaware of these principles, Yüan Ts'ai recognized them. For modern analyses of the interpersonal relations in Chinese families, see Martin Yang, *A Chinese Village*, pp. 45–85, Francis Hsü, *Under the Ancestor's Shadow*, pp. 54–130, 200–260, and Myron Cohen, *House United, House Divided*, pp. 57–225.

[5] *Mencius* 5A:2, 6 (Lau, trans., pp. 139–40, 144–45).

and Sung literary stories and Yüan plays, "unworthy sons" of this sort were a standard feature.[6] In Sung judicial decisions they were cited as the source of many problems, especially dissipation of the family property.[7] "Family Instructions" often provided advice on how to reform them.[8]

Those whom Yüan Ts'ai labeled "unworthy" ranged from lazy to vile. Self-indulgence, albeit not the most reprehensible trait, was still a major family problem because of its destructive effects and its widespread incidence. The most common reasons why sons failed to learn self-discipline, in Yüan Ts'ai's view, were that they were spoiled when young or had no occupation when grown. Like Ssu-ma Kuang, Yüan Ts'ai thought that the way to avoid spoiling a son was strictness from early childhood. A father should not give in to his son's every demand or tolerate his every action or make excuses for his misbehavior (1.12). Moreover, he should teach him to observe social distinctions based on age and rank and to know the difference between right and wrong (1.15).

Yüan Ts'ai dwelled at some length on the need for occupations. Those with inherited land could concentrate on

[6] See, for instance, the Yüan play, "The Mo-ho-lo Doll," in Crump, trans., *Chinese Theater in the Days of Kublai Khan*, pp. 311–92. In *ICC* unworthy sons are even sometimes seen as retribution for the father's past failure to repay a debt. See *ICC pu* 6, pp. 1604–5.

[7] See, for example, *CMC*, pp. 96–98, 323–26.

[8] A good example is the advice that Lo Ts'ung-yen (1072–1135) gave to his sons and nephews in *Lo Yü-chang hsien-sheng wen-chi*, 10, pp. 110–11. He described two exasperated fathers. The sons of the richer one gambled, drank, and hung around with local toughs. The sons of the other were insolent and disobedient. The fathers thought the sons were so unworthy that correcting them would require so much beating that they would end up seriously injured; but without correction they would ruin their patrimony and get into trouble with the law. The fathers were then introduced to a model father whose sons were perfect because they engaged in study and were corrected by being made to copy admonitory couplets instead of being beaten.

managing it, but others needed training or skills. Men who study the Classics might become officials, professors, tutors, or clerks, depending on their level of ability. Those without the talent for classical scholarship could become doctors, monks, farmers, or merchants and make their money in an honest and honorable way (2.58). Whatever their occupation, it was better than wasting their time in amusements, in the company of riffraff (1.13).[9] Thus in his approach to formal education, Yüan Ts'ai was more eclectic than Ssu-ma Kuang. (See above, chap. 2). Not only did he allow for education aimed at a variety of careers, but also he admitted the "usefulness of the useless" and the value of broad, miscellaneous reading of poetry, fiction, histories, books on Yin-Yang, divination, and so on (1.14).

In Yüan Ts'ai's observation, the temptations facing young men in rich families were very great, and he emphasized the need for experience to escape misjudgments (2.49).[10] Therefore Yüan Ts'ai disagreed with those contemporaries who would confine their young men to the house to keep them from going astray. "Once you relax these prohibitions, the passions will find a hole to break through and will be as irrepressible as a prairie fire" (2.50). A better strategy was to choose their friends and make them keep reasonable hours so that their experience would grow and they would learn to size up situations (2.50).

Even more dangerous than self-indulgence was willful

[9] By and large the *Precepts* seems to be addressed to the *shih-ta-fu*. Yüan Ts'ai would seem to imply that the son of a *shih-ta-fu* family without talent for book learning could learn a skill such as medicine or business without great loss of prestige to his family. Whether his own children would still be considered the social peers of *shih-ta-fu* is not clear.

[10] A literary story of the basically good man who lost all sense of proportion because of his passions is found in *Master Tung's Western Chamber Romance*, written by a contemporary of Yüan Ts'ai. See the translation by Li-li Ch'en.

and defiant behavior, something Yüan Ts'ai very much abhorred. Sons whose fathers had not taught them self-control and good manners would insult their seniors and bully their juniors (1.15). Especially bad were the sons and grandsons of high-ranking officials, who would take advantage of their elder's power to become local bullies. They would extort wine and food, force people to sell them goods but never pay for them, and act as brokers for local residents in their relations with the authorities, getting their taxes or service obligations excused or charges against them dismissed (1.39).

As Yüan Ts'ai reported it, most fathers responded to lazy and willful sons by scolding, rebuking, and berating them. The friction this created in family life did not seem to him at all commensurate with any improvement in the behavior of the sons. Several times Yüan Ts'ai argued that scolding does very little good; the incorrigible will not change anyway, and those who mildly accept the rebuking are probably not very bad and may end up becoming resentful. When efforts to raise good sons failed, the best course was to try to preserve the rest of the family from the harm an unworthy son could cause. He should not be given up for adoption (1.43), or married to a superior woman (1.56), or allowed to cheat his brothers out of property (1.62), or allowed to take office (1.40).

The major reason why scolding did so little good, according to Yüan Ts'ai, was the variability of human nature and the blindness of fathers. Often the flaws they saw in their sons were not ones they could realistically expect them to change, since "personalities cannot be made to conform" (1.1). Fathers should have tried instead to tolerate their sons' differences. Much of Yüan Ts'ai's plea for tolerance (discussed in the last chapter) was addressed to fathers. Scoldings were also ineffective because fathers scolded at the wrong time or picked on the wrong son. This irrationality starts with the nearly universal tendency to dote on babies and young children, at least until the next one comes along. Yüan Ts'ai saw this as instinctive: "the Creator has made such attachment a principle of nature, to ensure that the succession of births will continue uninterrupted" (1.11). As sons grow older, parents—just as unreasonably or emotionally—would take a dislike to one son or another (1.15). Indeed, fathers were especially likely to pick on their obedient sons rather than on their worthless ones because of the common tendency to "retreat when [one] runs into strength but becomes reckless when he encounters weakness' (1.3). Even when there was some basis for their partiality, it was unwise, since the son or grandson they loved best could turn out to be unfilial or die young, and they might have to depend on the one they mistreated (1.18). Yüan Ts'ai also thought fathers were easily biased against the sons of a first wife after they had remarried (1.21).

Considering the hierarchy of authority Yüan Ts'ai accepted, fathers had more they could do to improve their relations with their sons than sons had for improving relations with their fathers. Yüan Ts'ai reminded sons of how much they owed their parents for rearing them (1.11) and urged them to try to see things from their father's point of view. They should say to themselves, "Now I am someone's son, but one day I will probably be someone's father.... If I treat my son exactly the way my father treats me, then I will be able to hold up my head without shame" (1.2). But Yüan Ts'ai knew that such reflection was not always enough. If a father was clearly in the wrong and would not listen to respectful advice, and indeed offered twisted excuses, "the junior should listen even more submissively and not argue with him" (1.5). Elsewhere, he suggested that when parents were obviously partial to certain sons, the sons themselves should recognize the situation and modify their behavior: the despised ones yielding a little and the favored ones practicing self-restraint (1.19). If a son was resentful because his parents were giving more to a brother with special needs, he should try to overcome his resentment by reflecting that, if he were the needy one, he would be getting the help (1.17).

The most fundamental difference between Yüan Ts'ai and the classicists on father–son relations lay in their attitudes toward scolding. Yüan Ts'ai argued that there should be no fault-finding between fathers and sons (1.1), elaborating on a principle stated by Mencius. Ssu-ma Kuang, to the contrary, made it a point to challenge Mencius on this idea: "Mencius says 'Between fathers and sons there should be no fault-finding.' But if there is no fault-finding, isn't this a failure to remonstrate [with superiors] and to teach [ethical principles to inferiors]? How can this be acceptable?"[11]

If fathers and sons among Yüan Ts'ai's peers often got along as poorly as he described, why was Yüan Ts'ai nearly alone in trying to remedy the situation? The explanation may lie in the tremendous power of the concept of filial piety. Because of it few Sung men may have been able to bring themselves to the conclusion that fathers were sometimes at fault and that they should try to tolerate their sons' quirks while teaching them to distinguish right and wrong.

THE TENSIONS OF COMPLEX FAMILIES

Difficult as the relations between fathers and sons could be, Yüan Ts'ai saw them as based on instinctive love and obvious self-interest; the unpleasant feelings that developed were primarily resentment and disappointment. But between brothers living together Yüan Ts'ai saw hatred as an everyday occurrence.

[11] *SMCC* 73, p. 896.

Yüan Ts'ai never questioned the hierarchical basis of the elder brother–younger brother relationship, but he also never gave it the unconditional or enduring quality of the father–son relationship. In his discussions of the relations between brothers, Yüan Ts'ai could not conceal a belief that age, family composition, and living arrangements had much to do with the possibilities of any relationship, and he regularly specified circumstances: whether the father was still living, whether the brothers shared a common *chia*, whether one was rich and the other poor, whether they had divided their assets but shared a courtyard, and so on. Likewise, he considered the relationship between an uncle and a nephew to be quite different when they lived apart than when they lived together, and when the nephew's father was living and when he was not. It is surely not coincidental that all of these circumstances altered the legal relationship between men with respect to the property of the *chia*.

Because the competition among brothers for material goods was the source of so much tension, Yüan Ts'ai insisted that parents must make equal treatment of sons their basic policy in childrearing. If parents are generous to one son and stingy to another, they should not be surprised if the sons later quarrel over property (1.15). What we would call sibling rivalry he saw as very common. When parents are partial, "the beloved one becomes more outlandish in his desires and behavior day-by-day, and the neglected one is resentful. With time these feelings build up into deep hostility between the sons" (1.16).

Among adult brothers, scrupulous fairness in anything related to contributions or consumption was imperative. Yüan Ts'ai observed that no one could be indifferent when one of his co-residents was selfish and did not think of the common interest (1.22). If the selfish one tried to take a little extra for himself or take the largest share when something was being divided, he was, in essence, stealing from the others. The solution he saw as simple: "When individual funds are to be used, all use their individual funds; when common funds are to be used, all use the common funds. When there is something to be distributed to everyone, it is divided fairly, even if it is fruit or candy, worth only a few dozen coins" (1.22).

Unfortunately, the existence of both individual funds (*ssu-ts'ai*) and common funds (*chung-ts'ai*) could very much complicate matters, making what one brother considered fair seem not at all fair to the other. As will be discussed in more detail in the next chapter, a brother's individual funds could include earnings from public office, his wife's dowry, or businesses he built up on his own. Yüan Ts'ai noted that when the differences in brothers' individual fortunes were great, it led to jealousy, arrogance, and suspicion (1.24). Besides that, the rich one would always worry about being burdened by the poor one (1.27). Consequently, some efforts to even out the wealth between co-resident brothers seemed advisable to Yüan Ts'ai. Rich brothers should make gifts to their poorer ones without expecting gratitude (1.24). They should share the profits of their private businesses as acts of benevolence (1.25). They should also lend to co-residents capital to start businesses without expecting interest (1.26). A poor brother should also try to gain some perspective, thinking to himself: "Even if [my richer brother] really embezzled common property, he prospered because of his own hard work and management. How can all his profits be distributed? And what if it really was his own property? For me to try to get it then certainly would be shameful" (1.25).

Although Yüan Ts'ai advocated equality in the division of income among brothers, he did not propose democratic decision making, even as a means of preventing deceit and partiality. Rather he suggested a division of responsibility, with the elders making the major policy decisions and the younger ones carrying them out. With such a system, "the elders would certainly consult with the younger ones and the younger ones would do as their elders tell them" (1.23). This division of responsibilities does indeed seem to have been carried out by some Sung families, such as Ssu-ma Kuang's.[12]

Bad as relations between brothers could be, to Yüan Ts'ai those between uncles and nephews living together had even worse prospects, for uncles would "take advantage of the fact that their nephews have no parents to seize their assets, thinking up ploy after ploy to do them harm" (1.31). From surviving case law, Yüan Ts'ai's suspicion seems to have been well founded.[13] The tensions between uncles and nephews Yüan Ts'ai thought derived in part from those between brothers. "A man with several sons may love each and every one of them, yet treat his own brothers like enemies. Frequently the sons, adopting their father's attitudes, are rude to their paternal uncles" (1.32).

Many classicists idealized the "righteous house," the family that lived for decades or even generations without dividing, thus always having a collateral head.[14] Yüan Ts'ai, in another departure from the classicists, proposed resolving the tensions between uncles and nephews by division of the

[12] See *SMCC* 77, pp. 948–49, 952–54; 79, pp. 981–83.
[13] An uncle who seized all of his nephew's property figures in *CMC*, pp. 122–26, and one who forced his nephew to become a monk appears in *CMC*, pp. 242–47. A nephew who sold land he held in common with his uncle appears in *CMC*, pp. 320–23.
[14] See, for instance, the comments of Huang T'ing-chien (1045–1105) in *CTTL* 6/1a–4b. This sort of "righteous house" is also sometimes called a "communal family." The best known such family mostly postdates Yüan Ts'ai. It is the Cheng family of Chin-hua, a county not far from Ch'ü-chou. On its history and family rules, see John Dardess, "The Cheng Communal Family," and John Langlois, "Authority in Family Legislation."

large complex family. Once the major cause of their contention was removed, they might get along quite well, for the
friction caused by living together is what does the most
damage to love and mutual responsibility (1.28).[15]

WOMEN IN THE FAMILY

The type of structural tensions discussed above all concern
the group of men who had primary rights to the family
property: the coparceners of the *chia* and their sons. But often
living with these men were female relatives, especially unmarried daughters and widowed or divorced sisters who had
returned home. These people seldom seem to have been at
the center of internal family disputes, but they could lead to
conflict with outsiders, usually again about property. A
daughter's new family may think she was supposed to bring a
larger dowry (1.57); a widowed sister's husband's relatives
may claim that she had property they should inherit even
though they failed to provide for her support (1.61). Thus to
Yüan Ts'ai, relations with sisters' and daughters' families also
warranted a family head's prudent consideration.

Wives, of course, could also lead to disharmony in a
family, a perception Yüan Ts'ai shared with almost everyone
in the Chinese tradition who wrote on family matters. If

[15] One element in the uncle–orphaned nephew relationship that Yüan
Ts'ai curiously failed to mention is the deceased brother's widow. At least
half of the nephews whose property was being purloined by an uncle must
have had living mothers. It could well be that so long as nephews were old
enough to articulate their interests (perhaps about fifteen years old), the
general taboo on contact between a woman and her husband's brothers
focused the conflict on the two men. This would not be possible, however,
when the nephew was a young child. Yüan Ts'ai assumed the duty of a
man to care for his brother's widow and her children, but he never
discussed it or the frictions it could cause. From legal cases these would
seem to have been plentiful, for example, *CMC*, pp. 15–17, 32–41.

anything, Yüan Ts'ai downplayed the importance of this. He repeated the common warning that all but the most perceptive husbands would be unconsciously affected by their wives' biased opinions (Compare the comments of Liu K'ai earlier in this chapter.) The disasters this could cause, Yüan Ts'ai said, were too numerous to relate in full, but he mentioned brothers who would not adopt nephews or turn sons over to their brothers and ones who would let their parents go hungry or remain unburied rather than do more than another brother could or would do (1.35). A major reason why women cause these disputes was that they passed gossip, aided in this by their maids (1.36). Men could put an end to this by refusing to listen to gossip, to criticize others, or to pass on stories (1.33).

Since women could so easily disrupt the harmony of a family, Yüan Ts'ai thought selecting appropriate brides for one's sons was a major responsibility for a family head. He agreed with many of his contemporaries that spouses should match in family status, an attitude some authorities opposed.[16] Consequently Yüan Ts'ai criticized the common practice of childhood engagements because wealth and status can change in a few years and character cannot always be predicted (1.54).[17] Spouses who did not match in intelligence, character, and looks would get along very poorly; the

---

[16] Some Sung scholars advocated choosing brides from less prosperous families than those of their husbands so that they would be frugal and submissive. See *CTTL* 5/4a for the quotation from Hu Yüan (903–1059). Chu Hsi's *HH* 5, p. 116 also quoted Ssu-ma Kuang's opinion that a wife from a rich or high-ranking family would be highhanded with her husband and his parents. He also said that it would be embarrassing to become rich because of one's wife's assets or gain high rank because of her family's influence.

[17] Even prenatal engagements are mentioned in Sung sources. For an example, see *HTHSTCC* 158/11a.

resulting discord (or even divorce) was their parents' fault (1.56).[18] The matter was so important that one should not simply trust the matchmaker but had to check out everything carefully oneself (1.57). This, again, was a very common observation of Yüan Ts'ai's time.[19]

Yüan Ts'ai gave particular attention to the problem of marriages among cousins. He reported that it was common to "use a marriage connection to make a marriage connection" (1.58), so daughters often married into the homes of their father's sister or their mother's brother or sister.[20] Difficulties arose because "women of narrow vision" would use the closeness of the families as an excuse to skimp, and consequently the other family would take offense.[21] (Women seem to be the only relevant people in these marriage disputes.) The solution Yüan Ts'ai proposed was to omit no courtesies and to avoid criticizing the other party.

Remarriage by men after the death of their wives posed other problems. Such remarriage had been enjoined as a duty in the Classics,[22] but Sung men often seem to have had ambivalent feelings about it. Yüan Ts'ai argued, apparently reluctantly, that widowers generally had no choice but to

---

[18] For the case of a *chin-shih* marrying a peasant's daughter because of a prior agreement, see *SS* 459, p. 13471. In another instance, the husband's declining financial status after marriage caused problems. See *CMC*, pp. 433–35.

[19] The deceptions of matchmakers appear often in Sung and Yüan literature. See, for instance, "The Honest Clerk" in Hsien-yi Yang and Gladys Yang, trans., *The Courtesan's Jewel Box*, pp. 27–41, and "The Shrew" in H. C. Chang, trans., *Chinese Literature*, pp. 32–55.

[20] For some cases, see Patricia Ebrey, "Women in the Kinship System of the Southern Song Upper Class," pp. 126–27.

[21] There was a famous case of this sort of friction among Yüan Ts'ai's contemporaries. The poet Lu Yu (1125–1210) married his mother's brother's daughter, a childhood friend, but his mother forced him to divorce her within a year. See Michael Duke, *Lu You*, pp. 23–25.

[22] See *Li chi*, "Tseng Tzu wen" (Legge, trans., I, p. 316).

remarry because their "little boys and girls have no one to care for them; there is no one to manage the cooking, sewing, and other work of the women's quarters" (1.51). In much the same vein, Hung Mai recorded cases of men who promised on their wives' deathbeds that they would not remarry but who had to relent and remarry when it proved impossible to manage the household with a concubine as the mistress.[23] In Yüan Ts'ai's opinion, good second wives were harder to locate than good first ones. Widows with children would have divided affections, and young girls would not be happy if married to middle-aged men (1.51).

As can be seen here, Yüan Ts'ai took remarriage of widows almost for granted. He assumed that widowers would consider marrying widows and in other places talked of the problems of the children of widows who remarry (1.48, 1.50). Ch'eng I's condemnation of the remarriage of widows may be one of the best known precepts of Neo-Confucianism, but there is little evidence that many *shih-ta-fu* in the Sung agreed with him.[24]

Although this chapter is titled "The Harmony of Co-Residents," a major insight that Yüan Ts'ai offers about the family life of his peers is the prevalence of tension and conflict. This, in itself, is an important corrective to the view of the Chinese *shih-ta-fu* as so immersed in the values of filial piety and compliance with seniors that conflicts of the sort Yüan Ts'ai analyzed could not exist, at least not among relatively decent people. Behind the social and political

[23] See *ICC chia* 2, p. 11; 16, p. 143; *ting* 9, pp. 608–609. For a man who seemed embarrassed even to take a concubine, see *HTHSTCC* 161/10a.

[24] *HH* 5, p. 117. For evidence of the prevalence of remarriage in the Sung, see Ebrey, "Women in the Kinship System," pp. 120–24. Anecdotal evidence concerning remarriage is also abundant. See, for instance, *ICC san-jen* 2, pp. 1479–80, *ICC pu* 4, p. 1580, and *ICC pu* 10, pp. 1642–44. For later periods, see Ann Waltner, "Widows and Remarriage in Ming and Early Qing China."

behavior of *shih-ta-fu* must often have been emotional responses they learned at home—whether the supreme self-control Yüan Ts'ai wished to see sons acquire, or the willfulness he observed as all too common when fathers had failed to train their sons properly, or when brothers could not suppress their competition and resentment.

CHAPTER 5

The Transmission of Property

The transmission of property or other assets from one generation in a family to the next is essential if there is to be any stability in the membership of a social class. *Shih-ta-fu* in the Sung gave considerable attention to the issue of transmitting property, but they did not look on it as in any way related to the existence of their social stratum. Rather, what was at stake to them was the preservation of the *chia*.

In Sung statutes and judicial decisions the basic principles for transmission of family property are clearly stated. Yüan Ts'ai seldom referred to these specifically but seems to have taken them for granted, assuming his audience was well aware of them. His comments are in almost all cases consistent with what is known of interpretations of the law in his period.

FAMILY PROPERTY

Yüan Ts'ai used a variety of terms to evoke both the concept of "family" and that of "property." "Property" could be referred to as *ch'an*, "productive resource," generally meaning land but also including businesses and other immovable property. *Ch'an* could be contrasted with *ts'ai*, usually translated here as assets, wealth, or funds, and referring to money, valuables, and other movable property. These two were also used as a compound, *ts'ai-ch'an*, to refer to everything owned. (Sometimes *ts'ai* alone was used with this meaning.)

Another term with this broad meaning is *yeh*; in varying contexts it meant estate, business, or an occupation that produced an income (including scholarship). These forms of property could be described as "family" by adding *chia* (as in *chia-ch'an, chia-yeh*). The idea that they were inherited could be conveyed by describing them as "ancestral" (*tsu*) or "father's and grandfather's" (*fu-tsu*). A slightly different connotation was conveyed if the property was described as "group" (*chung*). Group, or common, property was property in which several men had rights, men referred to as "coparceners" (*ying-fen-jen*), that is, those who would get a share of the property if it were divided that day. Thus a man whose father was alive was never a coparcener. The concept of coparcener was used by Yüan Ts'ai almost always with reference to a complex family, one without a father as its head, with the coparceners brothers, cousins, or uncles and nephews.[1]

As Yüan Ts'ai discussed it, family property was the property of people who "live together" (*t'ung-chü*) before they divide and establish "separate assets" (*i-ts'ai*) (1.28). Often implicit was the idea that it should be used for family purposes and transmitted along family lines. But it should not be considered truly jointly owned by family members; in cases where there was a father as the family head, he for most purposes was the owner. That is, Yüan Ts'ai never questioned that a father could sell family property as he saw fit or use it to assist poor kinsmen or provide daughters with generous dowries. The corollary of this was that sons could not dispose of any part of the family property on their own, so long as their father was alive and serving as family head.

---

[1] On the legal principles involved in property and its transmission, see Ian Burns, "Private Law in Traditional China," and Shūzō Shiga, "Family Property and the Law of Inheritance in Traditional China."

Even after the father died, if the mother survived and the family remained intact, a son was not supposed to sell land without her permission (1.52). Where there was more than one surviving son, none could dispose of family property without the other's permission. Doing so Yüan Ts'ai called embezzlement or theft (1.25, 1.26).

To see the consistency of Yüan Ts'ai's general understanding of family property and that of Sung judges, compare a judgment written by Liu K'o-chuang:

> There are appropriate legal articles concerning the transfer of fields and houses. When the mother is alive, her signature should come first on the deed. If brothers have not yet divided the property, then they should write up the deed together. Never, when the mother is living with them and five brothers are alive, can one brother mortgage (*tien*) land on his own. . . . Wei Chün is unworthy (*pu-hsiao*); he drinks and gambles. To get spending money he took common landed property (*chung-fen t'ien-yeh*) and mortgaged it to Ch'ui Ju-li.[2]

Not everything owned by people who live together was family property; they could also have individual funds (*ssu-ts'ai*). As seen in the last chapter, these funds could be a source of many disputes. Yüan Ts'ai referred to individual property from wives' dowries, official salaries, and businesses built up without using capital from the family property (1.25, 1.26). The existence of such individual funds had no classical authority, and indeed the "Patterns for Domestic Life" forbade them in strong language, particularly stressing that daughters-in-law could have nothing of their own. Ssu-ma Kuang commented on this prohibition in his "Family Forms":

[2] *CMC*, pp. 323–24.

If a daughter-in-law has received gifts from others of food, clothing, fabrics, ornaments, or accessories, she should offer them to her husband's parents. If they accept the gifts, she should be as pleased as if she herself had been given the gifts again; if they return them to her, she should decline them. If, however, they insist that she take them, then she should put the gifts away, waiting for the day when they may have use for them. If she intends to give them as gifts to her own brothers, she must ask her parents-in-law for permission first.

Even a person's body belongs to his parents; since he does not even have exclusive control over his own body, how can he have full control over belongings? If father and son were each to own property and they borrowed from each other in times of need, then there would be cases of a son being rich while his parents were poor; or of the parents starving while their son eats his full—such would be the ultimate of unfilial and immoral behavior![3]

Despite the strength of Ssu-ma Kuang's language, the law recognized individual property, certainly in the case of dowries. In a judgment in the *Judicial Decisions* concerning a father's attempt to sell the land brought in as a dowry by his son's wife, Weng Fu stated: "It is not right to call this common-held land. According to the law, assets acquired from a wife's family are not within the bounds of division. Also, the law is that a wife controls her property (*ts'ai-ch'an*) along with her husband."[4]

Legal evidence of the exclusion of salary from family property is weaker, but the *Yüan tien-chang* quotes an "old rule," presumably either Sung or Chin, whereby property

[3] *SMSSI* 4, pp. 41–42.
[4] *CMC*, pp. 247–48.

obtained from office or military service is excluded from division.[5] Indirect evidence of its exclusion in practice is found in the great praise given to men who in fact contributed earnings from public office to the common pool. Even Ssu-ma Kuang wrote this way, for instance singling out the family of the early Sung minister Li Fang (925–996) as exemplary. Over two hundred people lived together, and "even the salaries of those who were officials were gathered into one treasury."[6]

Nevertheless, it must be admitted that Yüan Ts'ai went further than other Sung authors in allowing assets to be excluded from the family property. For he implied that businesses built up by family members without any help from the common estate became theirs alone. He contrasted property embezzled (and claimed as the wife's property) to property that was honestly held as private because the owners had "established[ed] themselves and set up prosperous businesses without making use of any inherited family resources" (1.25).

To Yüan Ts'ai common property and individual property differed in both their management and their transmission. Common property had to be divided among coparceners according to specified rules. Individual property a man held and passed to his own sons (that is, none went to his nephews, as it might have if he had pooled it with the common property). Common property was managed by the family head. It was possible (but not advisable) for fathers to be partial in their distribution to their sons for daily living expenses (1.16). Collateral heads could also be highhanded and unfair, but such cases "inevitably [give] rise to disputes" (1.23). Younger brothers and nephews had no right to control common property themselves unless the head delegated

[5] *Ta Yüan sheng-cheng kuo-ch'ao tien-chang*, 1, p. 389B.
[6] *CF* 1, p. 480.

such tasks to them. Individual property, by contrast, could be managed by its owner without consulting the family head.

HEIRS

For family property to be transmitted to the next generation requires heirs or successors. Yüan Ts'ai assumed knowledge of the law that all the sons of a man are heirs. Included were sons of wives and of concubines who lived in his house, legally adopted sons, and sons of "separately established concubines" if they were recognized as heirs. Deciding which claimants were indeed sons of the family head or legitimately adopted could become matters of contention, especially if the family's assets were substantial. According to Yüan Ts'ai, a family head had to be on the watch to prevent fraud but also to prevent unfair exclusion of certain heirs by others who did not want to share.

Adoption, to Yüan Ts'ai, was a commonplace event. Only a man who had become a bitter enemy of his brother would refuse to give him an extra son or refuse to select his extra son as heir over a more distant relation (1.35). Because adoptions were done as much as possible between close agnatic relatives, Yüan Ts'ai implied that the families of *shih-ta-fu* were as likely to give up sons as to adopt them. This was not merely a matter of duty to kinsmen but also one of self-interest, for as Yüan Ts'ai said, "Having too many sons is certainly something to worry about" (1.43). He insisted that a father had a responsibility to see that his sons acquired either property or the education for an occupation (2.58); if his means were modest, giving up one or two of his sons might make it possible for all of them to prosper.

Fear of having too many sons to provide for was not an attitude unique to Yüan Ts'ai. Ch'en Liang (1143–1194) recorded that his youngest brother was given away because of the family's financial straits.[7] In the *Judicial Decisions* a man was portrayed as anxious to have his brother adopt one of his sons because he had five. In another case a man from an official family sold his son to a peasant, much to the disgust of the judge.[8] Hung Mai recorded a case in which the spacing of the children, not merely their number, made them superfluous. In this instance a widower of over sixty with two grown sons contemplated infanticide when his concubine bore a son (a daughter apparently would have been no problem).[9]

According to Yüan Ts'ai, a family head who needed to adopt an heir had a variety of alternatives: he could choose a close or distant relative or a nonrelative; he could adopt an infant, child, or adult; he could look on adoption primarily as a ritual-contractual relationship (continuation of the ancestral rites in exchange for succession to the family property); or he could look on it as one of nurturing and maintenance (care of the adoptee in youth in exchange for care of the parents in old age). Wise choices between these alternatives depended on both circumstances and goals.

Yüan Ts'ai explicitly stated that the key difference in circumstances to be considered was the size of the potential inheritance. Poor people, with no land, had "no choice but to clothe, feed, and care for adopted sons from their infancy to create an emotional attachment between them" (1.42). That way they could depend on their adopted sons to pro-

---

[7] See Hoyt Tillman, *Utilitarian Confucianism*, pp. 71, 101.

[8] *CMC*, pp. 81–86, 99–100.

[9] To continue the anecdote, the man asked his younger son what to do: kill the child (literally, "not lift him"), give him away, or raise him to be a monk. The son said to keep him alive until the older brother returned from his studies. A letter was sent to him and he returned quickly. When presented with these choices he acted quickly, taking the baby and throwing him into a wine vat. This behavior was not generally approved, however, since the point of the story was the retribution that awaited the older brother. *ICC ting* 5, pp. 573–74.

vide for them in their declining years. Yüan Ts'ai implied that the need for an infant would override preference for close agnates (1.42) and suggested that when a child of a different surname was chosen both surnames should be retained (1.44). In the *Judicial Decisions*, adoptions of babies of other surnames (i.e. with no possible common patrilineal ancestor) was not encouraged or ordered posthumously, but it was upheld when done during the lifetime of the father.[10]

By contrast, rich people had to adopt adults, whose characters and abilities could be judged. For them, succession to the property was the key issue. Yüan Ts'ai did say that the spirits of one's ancestors would not be pleased with offerings from adopted heirs of other surnames (1.44) (one of only two references to ancestor worship); but he showed much more concern for finding someone who would not dissipate the property, an attitude he shared with Sung judges.[11] To avoid bankrupting the family, rich families needed young men who were "genial, honest, and possess self-control." With these qualities, the absence of a tie from childhood would not matter (1.42). Families also needed to be sure that any sons they gave up for adoption would not be returned (1.43). In

[10] *CMC*, pp. 14–16, 18–20. See also *SHT* 12/8b. On adoption of children of other surnames in later periods, see Ann Waltner, "The Adoption of Children in Ming and Early Ch'ing China."

[11] One judge stated that a man establishes an heir both to preserve intact the family property (*chia-yeh*) and to ensure that ancestors receive their offerings (*CMC*, p. 78). In a case where a man wanted to oust the distant relative adopted by his late brother and have him replaced by his own younger son, born after the brother's death, the judge did not attribute to him any concern with ancestral rites; rather he said he "couldn't bear to see the ancestral property divided with someone from a distant branch" (*CMC*, p. 60). The only significant difference between the *Judicial Decisions* and the *Precepts for Social Life* concerning adoption is that Yüan Ts'ai is entirely silent on the question of establishing posthumous heirs for one's brothers, sons, cousins, and nephews who die without male issue. From the *Judicial Decisions*, it would seem that this practice was a source of endless lawsuits.

the *Judicial Decisions* Hu Ying explicitly stated that "according to the law, if an adopted son or grandson dissipates the family property or proves incapable of service or support," he can be ousted.[12] As Yüan Ts'ai said, such ousters could lead to the ruin of both families (1.43).[13]

Since formal adoption conferred financial rights (status as coparcener), people not actually adopted might try to claim that they had been, especially if they had received foster care. A man who had heirs could, as a charitable act, feed, clothe, and educate an agnatic relative or a relative of his wife or mother, or a son of his wife by a former husband. But such a boy might "covet his benefactor's property" (1.48) and after his death claim to have been appointed an heir. The *Judicial Decisions* includes cases of this sort, indeed one in which the foster son succeeded in gaining the property.[14] The way to prevent this, in Yüan Ts'ai's view, was to have the situation entirely clear from the beginning, especially if the foster son was older than one's own sons (making the story of formal adoption more plausible). With the sons of a wife's previous husband, "whether the boys will be brought into the house and whether they will share in the household economy must be declared publicly and reported to the authorities" (1.48). In order to avoid raising the expectations of foster sons, they should not be addressed as though they were sons, nor share living quarters with the family's sons.[15]

[12] *CMC*, p. 123. The most frequent type of case, in surviving Sung customary law, was of widows who tried to expel sons adopted by their husbands and replace them with others. See, for instance, *CMC*, pp. 81–86, and *HTHSTCC* 192/11a–12a.

[13] A case of a boy given up for adoption causing trouble to his natal family is included in *CMC*, pp. 314–15.

[14] *CMC*, pp. 211–18.

[15] The wisdom of this advice is attested in the *Judicial Decisions*. In one case, a widow brought two sons with her when she remarried, and they took the name of her new husband. She later had a son by this man. After the husband died, the former husband's children controlled the property.

Part One

Next to adoption, the most serious concern with regard to heirs was the parentage of the sons of maids and concubines. Eight of Yüan Ts'ai's items concerned this matter, showing how important it was to him. He saw it as all too common for a maid who was expelled from a family to return on hearing of the master's death with a son she claimed the master fathered. This was especially disastrous if she had been sent away because she had gotten pregnant by someone else and out of delicacy the master had not publicly denounced her offense (1.46, 3.22). Even if the child was born while the maid was in the household, Yüan Ts'ai worried about actual parentage. Had the master taken every possible precaution with regard to her access to his sons and younger brothers or the male bondservants (3.24)? Yüan Ts'ai's strategy for preventing such access was very strict segregation of the men's and women's quarters, with servant boys used to carry messages between them (3.20). Yüan Ts'ai observed, however, that since wives generally did not get along with concubines, men would set them up in separate wings of the house or separate houses (3.24, 3.25). Yüan Ts'ai tried to discourage these practices by pointing out how impossible it was to be absolutely sure that the concubine was supervised every minute. When they were in separate wings, maids and concubines would "take turns keeping a lookout for each other," making it hard for the master to catch them in illicit acts (3.25). When a woman was set up in a separate house, the man assigned to guard her might be bribed to become the lookout for another lover (3.23). Also, when the woman was set up on her own, if she gave birth to a girl, she could quickly trade it for a baby boy whom the master would unwittingly raise as an heir (3.23).

When grown, the true son wanted them expelled. *CMC*, pp. 93–96. The opposite situation is found in *CMC*, pp. 147–50. There a son who came with an "invited-in" husband later caused trouble to his stepmother.

(110)

Yüan Ts'ai worried not only about true blood lines but also about the probable intelligence of the offspring of maids. "When the servant class bear children [whatever the actual parentage] they attribute them to the master. As a result people often raise stupid and vulgar offspring who end up ruining the family" (3.21). In large part this was because of the education they received. Thus when a man acknowledged that a maid's or concubine's son was his, he should personally see to the child's education. "If the boy is left with his mother and by imitating those around him becomes a lowly, uneducated sort of person and then later wants to join your family, the situation will be very troublesome" (1.46).

Yüan Ts'ai's suspicions about maids and concubines and the lengths to which they would go to deceive their masters on the whole matches the attitude expressed in fictional sources, from T'ang and Sung literary tales through the plays, short stories, and novels of the Yüan and Ming.[16] A few legal cases also dealt with this issue. In one case a maid and her baby son were ousted at the instigation of the wife but provided with support by the husband.[17] There is also a case in the *Judicial Decisions* concerning a man whose mother had been a maid in a well-to-do house and was later married to one of its tenants. On the death of the master, the son of the former maid tried to claim that his mother had been pregnant when she was married off and that therefore he was an heir. The judge dismissed the case, saying that the law requires clear evidence of parentage.[18] The emotions that inheritance disputes of these sorts could arouse are seen in an anecdote recorded by Chou Mi (1232–1308). An elderly rich

---

[16] By far the fullest portrayal of the maids and concubines and other women favored by one man is in the late Ming novel, *Chin P'ing Mei*, translated as *The Golden Lotus* by Clement Egerton.

[17] *CMC*, pp. 187–91.

[18] *CMC*, pp. 143–46.

man had in fact fathered a child by a maid in his old age. Afraid of what his wife and married sons would think, he quickly married off the maid to a soup peddler, regularly sending her money for the boy. When the father died, the former maid's neighbors encouraged her to send her son, by then a young man, to mourn the father and demand a share of the property. They said they would put up the money for a lawsuit over the inheritance if that proved necessary. When the boy arrived, the old mother wanted him driven away but the eldest son, perhaps by then knowing the story, said to do so would ruin the family. He introduced the youth to his "mother," brothers, and nephews and let him stay there for the mourning period. Moreover, he had the former maid's stipend continued. Her neighbors tried to sue anyway, much to the disgust of the prefect.[19] It was just this sort of situation that Yüan Ts'ai wanted to prevent.

DIVISION OF PROPERTY AMONG HEIRS

In the statutes on household property, there was no ambiguity about transmission of the property on the father's death if he had only one son (adopted or natural) and had already provided for his daughters' marriages. In such cases the property went to the son. If the son was an adult he took charge of it, needing the signature of his mother, however, if he wanted to sell land.[20] If he was a minor, his mother took charge of it as a trustee for him.[21] When a family had more than one son, it would someday be necessary to divide its property. As Yüan Ts'ai recognized, this could occur before the death of a father, at his death, or at any later time, even generations later.

[19] *Ch'i-tung yeh-yü*, 20, pp. 257–58.
[20] *CMC*, pp. 118–20, *Mien-chai chi*, 33/20a–24b.
[21] *CMC*, pp. 32–41, 249–53.

Yüan Ts'ai implied that the legal status of property divisions made during the father's lifetime was different from the status of postmortem divisions. A father could distribute the property as he pleased, on whatever grounds he wanted. Sons who felt cheated could not take him to court; they would have to wait until he died and then sue their brothers for a more equitable share.[22] "Lifetime" divisions could be initiated by the father because he was "old and tired of management" (1.62), or they could be requested by the sons because the family head was unfair in his distribution of food, clothes, and goods to the families of his sons. Yüan Ts'ai mentioned as common causes for such partiality the existence of both adopted and natural sons, or of sons by different mothers, or of orphaned grandsons; he also recognized the role of simple favoritism (1.62). Of course, the father was not always at fault. An "unworthy" son might seek his share early and the father decide to give it to him in the hope of saving the other sons from having to deal with him. Yüan Ts'ai recommended in such cases giving the unworthy son a share of the income but not transfering land to him, for these young men were the type to sell it to meet expenses and then return for another share when the rest of the property was divided (1.62).[23]

Yüan Ts'ai considered it wise for fathers who had not seen to the division during their lifetime to specify how it should

[22] Cf. *CMC*, pp. 211–18.

[23] A case of seeking a second division is recorded in *CMC*, pp. 102–106. A couple had two sons of their own after adopting a son. According to the judge, rather than encourage their harmony, they gave each son a share of the property, presumably so they could live apart. After the father died, the mother divided the remainder of the property equally among the three. The adopted son sold his and was now suing to rejoin the family of his brothers. The judge, suspecting that the mother had wanted to be rid of him, insisted that the family be reunited and the adopted son entitled to another share. Compare also *ICC pu* 5, pp. 1592–93.

be done in a will. Yet since the provisions in wills could be contested in court, all sorts of trouble would ensue if a man listened to a concubine or a second wife to favor some sons over others (1.63). The *Judicial Decisions* confirms both that men could specify how their estate should be handled in a will and that this could be appealed. In one case the judge refused to overturn the will, stating, "According to the law, three years after a division of property or ten years after the execution of a will, no accusations of unfairness will be dealt with." [24]

As Yüan Ts'ai recognized, division itself was a legal procedure. Among brothers it was to be on an equal basis, and if one brother died, his son or sons would get his share, divided equally among them. When only grandchildren of the original family head survived (i.e. cousins), the statute ordered that the division be "equal." [25] There seem to have been two interpetations of what this meant. Some took this to mean the shares for all cousins would be worth equal amounts. [26] Yüan Ts'ai interpreted it as *per stirpes* ("by lines") division. Thus if one brother had one son and one had four, when the family came to divide, the only son would get half and the sons with brothers would each get an eighth. As Yüan Ts'ai said, "only [the one] with no brothers will be well-to-do while those who have several brothers will gradually decline after the division" (1.27). With this system, some people had an interest in early division, others in a delayed one. For instance, Yüan Ts'ai noted that one brother might be married with several children, whereas the other had none. The "encumbered" brother was using up much more of the

[24] *CMC*, p. 237.
[25] *SHT* 12/2b.
[26] See Niida Noboru, *Chūgoku hōseishi kenkyū: Dorei nōdo hō, kazoku, sonraku hō*, pp. 430–34, Shiga Shūzō, *Chūgoku kazoku hō no genri*, pp. 259–60.

family income than he would get after the property was divided in two, prompting his brother to demand an early division (1.27).

Documents were necessary to record the division, and these were used to prove legal ownership in the same way as bills of sale. Samples of such documents have survived from Tun-huang and from Yüan and Ming encyclopedias.[27] Drawing lots was the standard practice for assigning shares, at least of land. Yüan Ts'ai warned, however, that this could be tampered with. Some men, in writing down the specifications of the pieces of property on the lots to be drawn, would divide plots to make their separate management uneconomical, hoping to buy out their coparceners (1.27). Some people also, instead of giving each coparcener a full list of the property to be divided showing each share, would give him a list only of what he was to get, leading to suspicion that some of the property had not yet been divided (3.56). Yüan Ts'ai argued that the best procedure was to have a complete listing of all property. Even individually held property should be listed in an appendix so that suspicions would not be aroused (3.56).

Because documents of division were legal documents of ownership, Yüan Ts'ai urged that they be prepared with all due care. The new boundaries had to be clearly specified, with reference to markers that would persist for generations, not ridges, trees, pits, or stones. One also had to get the documents officially sealed, not begrudging the heavy fees sometimes demanded by the government authorities. If no seals were obtained, a brother or nephew could claim the property on the pretext that no division had yet been made or on the grounds that it had been assigned to him in lost documents of division (3.59).

[27] For an example, see Patricia Ebrey, ed., *Chinese Civilization and Society*, pp. 66–67. See also Niida, *Tōsō hōritsu*, pp. 603–18.

WOMEN AND PROPERTY

Yüan Ts'ai's primary concern was with the preservation of the *chia*, which required transmission of property along a male line of descent. Women were largely outside of this process and, according to Yüan Ts'ai, did not even fully share in its ideology. In one passage he suggested that women looked on property very differently from men; they wanted financial equality not merely among the members of a *chia* but also among all the *chia* to which they had blood ties, including their mothers' and daughters' *chia* (1.59).

Despite the importance Yüan Ts'ai placed on preserving the *chia*, he took it as entirely consonant with the goals of the *chia* that some of its property be transmitted to the women who would leave it. He remarked that families of means should give their daughters substantial dowries (1.59) and noted that the size of the dowry was a major item of negotiation in marriage arrangements (1.57). Provision of a dowry he considered one of the largest expenses a family would ever have, on a par with the parents' funerals (2.56). Marriage of sons, by contrast, was not mentioned as an occasion of great expense. If a family did not set aside enough money, they would have to watch their daughter's humiliation in her new family. One indication of the size of a dowry that Yüan Ts'ai considered generous is the praise he gave to the practice of planting ten thousand pine trees on a daughter's birth, to be ready for her marriage (2.56).

In regard to dowries, Yüan Ts'ai seems to have been typical of his contemporaries. In a fictional tale written in the twelfth century, a man who had just married off his eldest daughter said it would take two or three years to accumulate enough money for a dowry for his second daughter. His "ghost wife" speeded this up by "discovering" fifty gold coins he had earlier owned.[28] In an anecdote in another Sung work, an official had to postpone for at least a year the marriage of his daughter, having used the dowry prepared for her for a charitable act.[29]

After marriage, the dowry became "wife's assets" (*ch'i-ts'ai*) and was not merged with the common fund of the family (1.25). Husbands undoubtedly often managed their wives' assets, since Yüan Ts'ai mentioned them selling land they called their wives' or claiming that their businesses were started with capital from their wives' assets. In a legal decision cited earlier Weng Fu referred to husbands and wives managing property together (note 4 above). Yüan Ts'ai, however, did not see "wife's assets" simply as the individual property of the husband, equivalent to earnings from public office. For he said that a danger for husbands in fraudulently listing common property as "wife's assets" is that, after their deaths, the widows could take the property with them when they remarried (1.26). Clearly he assumed that a widow would be able to take with her anything that was genuinely her dowry.[30]

To Yüan Ts'ai, property given to daughters as dowry was different from property transmitted to sons. First, he saw considerable leeway and variation in how much property was assigned to daughters. It should depend on how prosperous the family was and, apparently, on the value it attached to the proposed match. Yüan Ts'ai argued on the side of

[28] Wolfgang Bauer and Herbert Franke, trans., *The Golden Casket*, pp. 184–87.

[29] *Tung-hsüan pi-lu*, 12, p. 90.

[30] This view was not universal. Some Sung judges, most notably Huang Kan, thought dowry belonged to the sons of the marriage, even, in one interpretation, the sons born to other women (*Mien-chai chi*, 33/30b–32a, 34b–37a). On women's dowry and property rights, see Ebrey, "Women in the Kinship System," pp. 117–20.

(117)

generosity, in part because giving generous dowries created a bond of obligation. Daughters who received property would feel obligated to support their parents and managed their funerals if their brothers proved unworthy or died (1.59).

Yüan Ts'ai referred in one place to daughters who had a right to a portion of the family property (1.49). He could have been thinking of daughters whose fathers died before they were married and who, in Southern Sung customary law, would receive a portion of the family property equal to half that of a son, presumably to provide their dowry. He could also have had in mind orphaned daughters who had no brothers, even adopted ones. Such daughters were entitled to some share of the property, in varying proportions, depending on whether or not they were single, married, or "returned," and whether or not an heir was posthumously appointed by agnatic relatives.[31]

Besides her own property, a woman might also manage her husband's property. Yüan Ts'ai reported that a woman might handle her husband's family property because he was dull-witted or unworthy or because he died and left her a widow with young children to raise (1.53). In the former case she would merely be acting for her husband, "calculating the outlays and income of money and grain," while the husband, presumably, would sign any tax receipts, bills of sale, IOUs,

---

[31] In Southern Sung customary law orphaned daughters were entitled to shares of the property if their father died before they were married. If they had a brother or brothers they would receive a share half as large as a brother's. If they had no brothers (natural or adopted), they could receive all of the property on the grounds that the family line was extinguished. This would be true even if they were married, but in that case the state might confiscate part of it. If close agnatic relatives wanted to appoint a posthumous adopted heir to reestablish the family line, he would get one-quarter of the property and the unmarried daughter of daughters three-quarters. (If there were only married daughters, the state would get one-third and the daughters and heir would divide the remainder.) See *CMC*, pp. 108–113, 127–34, *HTHSTCC* 193/7a–b, 10a–17b.

and so on. In the latter case, as a widow with children, the woman would be legally authorized to act on their behalf. Yüan Ts'ai observed that such a woman faced great difficulties and needed a male relative from her natal family or her husband's family to depend on (1.53). The cases recorded in the *Judicial Decisions* show that widows' legal powers to manage their minor sons' inheritance were very limited, since they were not supposed to sell any land.[32]

Yüan Ts'ai also mentioned a further practice open to a widow with young children: she could "invite a husband" to help her manage her former husband's estate and raise his children (1.48). This alternative was clearly provided for in Sung law, though judges might place limits on it. One judge, for example, insisted that a wife and her new husband quit her former husband's property, since her sons were over thirty and hardly in need of supervision.[33] When husbands were "invited in" they might have children by a former wife whom Yüan Ts'ai said should be treated much like a wife's children by a former husband. That is, whether they were to be adopted fully or merely given foster care should be decided at the begining and reported to the authorities (1.48). Husbands who were "invited in" need to be distinguished from ordinary second husbands. When a woman married an ordinary second husband, she did not normally retain control over her former husband's assets.[34]

As mentioned in Chapter 1, how people conceive of "family" and "property" will shape their "realistic" efforts to assure their families' material security. Yüan Ts'ai's notion of the *chia*, of common and individual funds, and his ideas on

---

[32] Cf. *CMC*, pp. 32–41, 249–53, 331–34.

[33] *CMC*, pp. 455–64.

[34] In case law there seem to be some exceptions when a remarried widow could act as trustee for a son she brings with her. See *CMC*, pp. 165–68.

heirs and division of property all would have had implications for everyday economic behavior. For instance, if
Yüan Ts'ai had been more interested in the descent line and
less interested in the *chia*, he might have more strongly
preferred appointing a fraternal nephew as heir. But to Yüan
Ts'ai continuing the descent line was no more important
than continuing the *chia*, and so at least as crucial as prox-
imity of relationship was qualifications in talent and personality to manage the *chia*. Since in Yüan Ts'ai's time perhaps
from twenty to thirty percent of couples would have had no
surviving sons,[35] a system that allowed high-ranking families to choose adult heirs according to their talents certainly
must have aided the social stability of the elite. This large
fraction at least did not need to worry so much about unworthy sons.

Other aspects of Yüan Ts'ai's conceptions of family property and individual property would also have affected economic behavior. Yüan Ts'ai, like judges of his time, had deep
qualms about men's right to waste family property. Living
off the income may have been acceptable, but selling the land
to meet temporary needs was unfair to one's sons. Individual
funds were different; usually held as money, they should be
invested to bring the highest return in order to help offset the
effects of division of the family property. These business
strategies of conservation and investment will be discussed in
more detail in the next chapter.

[35] This accords with general demographic models and with some rough
statistics from China. Wolfram Eberhard, in *Social Mobility in Traditional
China*, p. 153, estimated that one-third of the men who reached age 15
never had sons in one large Kwangtung lineage.

CHAPTER 6

The Business of Managing a Family

Because the *chia* was a unit of political economy, not simply a group of relatives, its existence could be ended by the dispersal of its property. Consequently, to Yüan Ts'ai and to most classicists, managing the property of a *chia* was not a matter of petty details but a primary duty of the family head. Both the "Patterns for Domestic Life" in the *Li chi* and Ssu-ma Kuang's "Family Forms" recognized the need for sound management. As mentioned in Chapter 2, Ssu-ma Kuang stated that a family head had to see that each of the servants had assigned duties and carried them out successfully. He also had to prepare a budget that would cover both routine and extraordinary expenses and allow for savings.

Neither the Classics nor Ssu-ma Kuang's writings specified the practices a family head should follow in managing financial affairs. In fact, although some of Yüan Ts'ai's predecessors and contemporaries exhibited a general interest in these matters, none left anywhere near so detailed or fully argued an analysis. Perhaps the closest to it are the rules provided by Yeh Meng-te in his instructions on managing livelihood. Below are paraphrases of his key points:

(1) Be diligent, get up early, and avoid procrastination.
(2) Be frugal (the principal method of preserving a family).

(3) Be patient. Because you see a chance for a small profit you may lose sight of your larger goal.

(4) Get along with people and be willing to yield in order to avoid disputes.

(5) Buy good land when you get the chance. The profit is slight but it is long-lasting, and "no family without land ever became wealthy."

(6) Do not be stingy in entertaining and gift-giving.

(7) The family's women should dress plainly.

(8) Do not arrange marriages to families without family discipline.

(9) Be careful about remarrying after your wife's death and about siring children by concubines.

(10) It is essential to be impartial in managing a family, dividing income equally.

(11) As Yen Chih-t'ui said, if you have a surplus income, use it for annual expenses; if there is still a surplus, aid your relatives and friends. This is knowing when you have enough. For the richer you are, the less satisfied you are. Recognize how much income you have and stay within it. If it is too little, economize; if it is adequate, distribute some.[1]

These themes, which Yeh discussed only briefly, Yüan Ts'ai a generation later developed at considerable length.

Yüan Ts'ai's treatment of business-related subjects was sometimes technical, since he believed that a family manager had to know current business and legal practices. For instance, he had to be personally familiar with the land law and investment opportunities. Yet, as usual, Yüan Ts'ai stressed attitude above all. Running through all his discussions is the idea that a family manager had to think ahead. Three words

---

[1] *Shih-lin chih-sheng chia-hsün yao-lüeh*, 1b–4b.

that appear and reappear in discussions of business matters are *lü* (to worry about or make plans for), *fang* (to take precautions against), and *chin* (to be prudent, attentive, and careful). At one point he said, "The general rule . . . is to be careful of what is begun and to take precautions concerning how things may end" (3.21).

WEALTH AND INCOME

Yüan Ts'ai was open-minded about how and where one could acquire income. Despite classical injunctions to the contrary, he assumed one's goal in business was profit. He thought surplus funds should not be stored as gold or silver both because of the danger of theft and because in storage they produce no income. Rather, assets should be invested in land, loans, or business. Yüan Ts'ai remarked that an investor could double the worth of his assets in ten years with most businesses, and in as short as three years with a pawnbroking business (1.26).

On the whole, however, Yüan Ts'ai discouraged haste or acquisitiveness. He observed that many of his contemporaries wanted to get rich quickly when they saw others doing so. Not meeting the good luck of their models, they would resort to cheating. "If they sell rice, they add water to it; if they sell salt, they mix ashes with it; if they sell lacquer, they add oil to it; if they sell medicine, they substitute other things for it." To Yüan Ts'ai such activities were counterproductive: their perpetrators would end up in poverty because "men cannot win over Heaven" (3.72). Honesty and diligence would prove to be better strategies. "The goods must be genuine and they must be handled with respectful care, as if you wished to offer them to the gods. You also should not dare to covet great profits, but accept what the workings of Heaven produce" (3.72). This applied especially to those who had bought state monopoly rights for such enterprises as manufacture of wine (3.72).

Yüan Ts'ai gave specific advice on what must have been a common investment, loans of money. He advocated asking "reasonable" interest on loans, that is, from two to five percent per month. "Demanding this is not considered extortionate, and those who pay do not object" (3.65). The higher rates charged in some localities of ten percent or more per month he considered inhumane and sure to bring retribution. Yüan Ts'ai advised appraising applicants carefully before making loans. Loans to relatives and friends he did not consider sound investments; affection will turn into hostility and the loans will not be repaid (1.38). Loans should also not be made to chronic borrowers: "They are certainly unreliable people who from the start intend to default on their obligations" (3.67). Large loans of a hundred piculs of grain or a hundred strings of cash were also dangerous, since the borrower would probably never be able to repay (3.67). In large measure this was because those with a deficit one day were unlikely to have a surplus later (3.68).

To operate commercial enterprises, Yüan Ts'ai assumed that most *shih-ta-fu* would employ managers. He mentioned managers placed in charge of the family's storehouses who kept the financial records. Those selected for these positions had to be conscientious and obedient (3.47).

Rather than operate a business through a manager, Yüan Ts'ai said the family head could entrust the entire operation to an agent. Agents were given capital to invest, after which they acted on their own.[2] Yüan Ts'ai warned that the relationship between master and agent was a precarious one. In his observation people became agents because they needed money (they could "barely afford to keep themselves warm

[2] Yoshinobu Shiba, *Commerce and Society*, pp. 189–94, discusses both managers and agents.

and fed"). Remaining honest while handling someone else's money usually proved extremely difficult for the agent, as he was "within sight of overflowing wealth and goods." If the master was easygoing, the agent might begin to embezzle small amounts and eventually have to falsify the books to cover up for himself (3.47). Yüan Ts'ai's solution, of course, was for the master to be attentive to details from the start.

Although he approved of commercial investments, Yüan Ts'ai devoted more space to advice on buying land and gaining an income from it. This was undoubtedly due in considerable part to the legal and social complexities of land ownership and the frequency of disputes over ownership rights. Yüan Ts'ai made it a premise that "no house or field has a permanent owner. When you have money, you buy; when you lack it, you sell" (3.64). For the man interested in the welfare of his *chia* this truth was doubly significant: He wanted to buy land without causing great social friction or difficulties with the government, but he wanted to keep his heirs from selling it.

Legal complications and social frictions were built into Chinese laws of land tenure. There was a strong presumption that land should remain in a family or at least with long-term local residents; therefore when a man had to sell, he first had to offer the plot to relatives, then to neighbors.[3] If he had to sell it to outsiders, a revocable sale, *tien-mai*, or pawning of land, was better than a complete sale. When "pawning" or "mortgaging" land in this way, the seller received a sum of money and gave up use of his land to the buyer; but if he

[3] On Chinese property law, see H. F. Schurmann, "Traditional Property Concepts in China." Neighbors and close relatives had a prior option on any sale of land, including *tien* sale. The exact provisions of this law were changed several times during the Sung. In the original Sung code both relatives and direct neighbors had an option (*SHT* 13/6a). In much of the Southern Sung only neighbors who were agnatic mourning relatives had this right. See *CMC*, pp. 344–45, 202–203.

could later raise the money he could redeem it, under time limits set in the original contract. The new owner, meanwhile, was not a full owner, for he could not simply dispose of it as he wished, the previous owner having, in a sense, a lien on it.[4] Other complications of title concerned coparceners, the individuals who by rights were supposed to get a share of family property when it was eventually divided. If A bought a plot from B, and it later turned out that B had a brother C who claimed that their assets had not yet been fully divided, A might find that he had to make restitution to C (if he could not force B to do so).

Besides these complications of title were ones of legal registration. For purposes of tax collection the government kept registers showing the owners of every plot of land and the tax assessed on it. Whenever land changed hands, the deeds of sale were supposed to be seen by the magistrate or his subordinate, who would put the official seal on them, certifying that the transaction was in order and the new owner had registered with the government.[5] The problem, as Yüan Ts'ai observed it, was that to avoid fuss or to avoid having to pay bribes to the government clerks, some people would skip going to court, reassigning taxes, or getting seals. These people often would end up violating the laws on land transfers out of ignorance. "When the piece of property is sold over and over again, the lawsuit can drag on for years" (3.60). The situation was naturally even worse when fraud had been intended from the start.

[4] *Tien-mai* is translated here as partial sale, mortgage, or sale with the right of redemption. See Schurmann, "Traditional Property Concepts in China." Many examples of selling land with right of redemption are contained in *CMC*, for instance, pp. 159, 187–88. A pro-forma *tien* contract is found in the Yüan encyclopedia, *Hsin-pien shih-wen lei-yao ch'i-cha ch'ing-ch'ien*, 11, p. 747.

[5] On land tax registers, see Brian E. McKnight, *Village and Bureaucracy in Southern Sung China*, pp. 51–52.

Land taxes were assessed on the size and productivity of plots; in theory, at least, the tax on ten *mou* of good land should have been ten times that on one *mou* of good land; therefore it made no difference whether the land was registered under one or ten names as far as the total tax was concerned. Labor services, however, were assessed in a different way, based on the total wealth of a household. Households were divided into five grades from very wealthy to destitute—with the majority of the population in the destitute grade. Wealthy households were required to take on duties, such as tax collection, that were difficult, time-consuming, and sometimes financially burdensome. If the household included a regular official, no one in it had to perform these services.[6]

To avoid these duties, Yüan Ts'ai reported, some families would falsify their actual division. A wealthy household about to divide in three could become three wealthy households, tripling its labor service obligations. By recording only nominal shares for two of the new households, there would be only one wealthy one and two poor ones, with little in the way of service obligations. The problem would occur in the next generation. According to Yüan Ts'ai, sometimes the sons of the man accorded the property "on paper" wanted to keep it all. Judges were then in a bind, for a decision in accord with the documents violated their sense of justice (3.57).

Yüan Ts'ai recommended sympathy for those who had to sell land, but he fully recognized that many of his contemporaries were unscrupulous. "Inhumane wealthy men," when they saw how desperately a seller needed money, would pretend to resist purchase to get a low price, then pay only ten percent, making the seller return again and again to be

---

[6] McKnight, *Village and Bureaucracy*, pp. 38–72, 109–121.

doled out a few strings of cash or be given commodities
(3.64). "Inhumane wealthy men" of this sort were also casti-
gated in legal decisions of the time.[7]

Because of all of these potential problems, Yüan Ts'ai
provided a long list of the steps to be taken whenever a piece
of land was bought. To understand Yüan Ts'ai's prudent,
business-like concern for anticipating complications, it is
useful to look closely at this list of steps. First, a broker was
needed to take the documents showing ownership (if inherited, the family division "lot-books") and compare them
with the government register. Second, the boundaries of the
plots had to be inspected and the tenants asked about the
accuracy of the owner's statements. Third, the owner's relatives had to be questioned to make sure none of them had a
claim to the property as a coparcener. Fourth, if the seller was
a widow selling her children's property, one had to check to
see that the government had verified her need to do so, for
widows were not supposed to dispose of their sons' inheritance for their own purposes. Fifth, if the proposed sale was
not a complete sale but a revocable one (a *tien mai*), the
original deed had to be seen to make sure there were no prior
revocable sales. Sixth, once the purchase contract was drawn
up, the "fine print" had to be checked carefully to see that the
price, date, and boundaries were filled in. Seventh, witnesses
had to be found, especially if a widow or minor marked the
contract rather than signing it. Finally, Yüan Ts'ai urged that
all transactions be done in cash, not in promissory notes or
commodities (3.60).

Yüan Ts'ai perceived deception and misrepresentation as
so common in land sales that wariness was definitely warranted. According to him (and confirmed in the *Judicial*

[7] See, for example, *CMC*, pp. 294–98, 355–59, 413–14.

Decisions),[8] some people did not quit the land they had sold, some buyers did not produce the money they had promised, and some people sold land that they had no legal right to sell (3.60). Relatives would try other ploys. Yüan Ts'ai described how a man, in dividing the family property, might plan in advance to make the division convenient for his eventual purchase of his brother's land (1.27). Because of all these sorts of trickery, Yüan Ts'ai urged never letting affection for the other party lead one to neglect recording all details in a contract (3.63). At the same time he recommended that the buyer offer a little more than the going price for land from a neighbor or relative, especially if it had special advantages. That is, never depend on your special rights: someone else might come along and make a higher bid, and then "regrets will be too late" (3.61).

To maintain good title to a piece of land, one had to pay the taxes, provide the labor service assessed on it, and see that any division among members of the family was accurately recorded. Yüan Ts'ai recommended that in preparing a budget, the money for taxes should be set aside first (3.69). He also noted that many people would hold off paying taxes till the last minute, when the government often offered discounts and accepted inferior commodities to get the collection completed. This he saw as pursuit of piddling profit at the expense of peace of mind (3.70).

Were Yüan Ts'ai's business-like attitudes common ones among *shih-ta-fu* of his time? Those fully committed to Ch'eng-Chu Neo-Confucianism would have had to abstain from most of the activities Yüan Ts'ai describes, even perhaps from worrying about the fine print on deeds of sale, and certainly from paying close attention to the operation of

---

[8] See, for example, *CMC*, pp. 253–56, 314–15, 328–31, 340–42.

businesses they owned. But none of the philosophers ever implied that most people were in fact immune to consider-ations of profit; to the contrary they described them as motivated by little else. Whereas the philosophers depicted anyone who pursued gain as morally inferior, Yüan Ts'ai distinguished between those who did it honestly, without harm to others, and those who used fraud and deception. One can probably assume that most shih-ta-fu who had property to manage looked on their business activities as Yüan Ts'ai did, not as Ch'eng I did.[9] Since the Sung was a period of great economic advance in agriculture, industry, and commerce, many men with talent and education must have been carefully planning how to invest their money, whether in land or in business.[10]

[9] In this I differ from Sung Hsi on the characterization of Sung shih-ta-fu's views on merchants (Sung-shih yen-chiu lun-ts'ung, pp. 1–17). He divides shih-ta-fu into three categories: ordinary, corrupt, and pure. The ordinary saw themselves as socially superior to merchants, the corrupt joined merchants in extracting profit from the people, and the pure strongly condemned such activities. This seems to me to ignore a very large gray area. Shih-ta-fu who may well have looked down on merchants as a group, and held themselves above corrupt or deceptive practices, still clearly bought and sold land and invested money in commercial and industrial ventures. Moreover, as Sung himself documents, they readily accepted educated sons of merchants into their midst. See also Shiba, Commerce and Society, pp. 212–13 and passim.

[10] On the land ownership and land management of shih-ta-fu in the Sung, see Chikusa Masaaki, "HokuSō shidaifu no shikyo to baiten," and Aoyama Sadao, "HokuSō o chūshin to suru shidaifu no kika to seikatsu ronri." Aoyama cites considerable evidence that shih-ta-fu of the eleventh and twelfth centuries assumed that an absolute minimum level of land-owning needed to support their style of life was about 200 mou, and those with 1000 mou would often still describe themselves as poor. (By way of comparison, J. P. McDermott, "Land Tenure and Rural Control," p. 133, estimated that a tenant needed about 15 mou to support himself from the land.) Aoyama also gives examples of involvement in lending money and trade and manufacture. See also Harriet T. Zurndorfer, "The Hsin-an ta-tsu chih and the Development of Chinese Gentry Society 800–1600," pp. 186–87 for evidence that families who produced many chin-shih also had

The Business of Managing a Family

Yüan Ts'ai, of course, did not think all *shih-ta-fu* were as prudent and as scrupulous as they should be; but in trying to convince them to change he argued that caution and fairness were sound business practices, useful in the long run. He assumed this argument would carry weight with them.

PRUDENT SPENDING

Yüan Ts'ai recognized that acquiring property and producing an income from it would not, in themselves, ensure the survival of the *chia*. It was also essential that everyday expenses be kept down and that money be set aside for taxes, weddings, funerals, and emergencies. In this conviction, Yüan Ts'ai echoed the statements of many other Sung *shih-ta-fu*.[11] His analysis, however, was more circumstantial and less moralistic than the usual sermons on frugality.

Everyday expenses Yüan Ts'ai referred to as the "hundred matters" of food, drink, clothing, houses, gardens, carriages, horses, servants, furnishings, and hobbies (2.55). These could be done on a low and scrimpy scale or on a lavish one (2.53). Yüan Ts'ai was not against luxury, but it had to be kept in accord with one's financial resources: spending becomes reckless then it is done without consideration of one's means (2.55).

From Yüan Ts'ai's experience, overspending most commonly resulted when a family tried to maintain a standard of living after major sources of income or perquisites had been

members who were active in commerce. A good example of an educated family who had members become salt merchants without giving up their scholarly traditions is found in *Fang-chou chi*, 15/15b–17a. Compare also *Lu Hsiang-shan ch'üan-chi*, 28, pp. 205–206 and *Lü Tung-lai wen-chi*, 7, pp. 177–78.

[11] See the discussions of the ideas of Ssu-ma Kuang and Lu Chiu-shao above in chap. 2, "The Family as a Corporate Unit." See also *CTTL*, passim.

cut off. A man who started poor and built up a fortune would retain many of his old habits and "every day his income exceeds his expenditure" (2.53). By contrast, the "son of a rich family easily falls into bankruptcy." When a wealthy family divided into two or three families, the expenditures would increase several fold. If, added to this, the division took place on the death of a high official, the effects were even worse. Not only had the high official brought in a large salary, but most of his family's needs had been met by the government. While in office his family had "many people at their beck and call," assigned to them by the local government. They also received frequent gifts, with the result that their clothing, food, and furnishings "may well [have been] splendid and costly, but the money for them [did] not come from the family assets" (2.53). Even when sons recognized the situation and planned to reduce their scale of living, their efforts were often unsuccessful. When they did not understand the need to economize, especially when they did not know exactly how much income the family had from its assets and the level of expenditure that these assets would support, there was no hope that they would escape bankruptcy.

The mechanism triggering bankruptcy, in Yüan Ts'ai's observation, was most often debt. Even reasonably frugal families could fall into debt if they encroached on the money set aside for taxes. Later, to pay the taxes, they would borrow at interest, or deal with a tax broker, who would charge an even higher rate. When the family had a stupid or "unworthy" son, debts could be contracted easily because these sons made such easy targets for "aggrandizers" (*chien-ping chih chia*), families on the rise who were busily buying up property. Yüan Ts'ai mentioned how such "aggrandizers" kept their eyes open for a property-owning family with a stupid or unworthy son. They would then offer to lend the young man money, encouraging him by great shows of friendliness. "For several years afterwards, they may not ask for repayment, waiting for the interest to mount up" (3.66). Once the interest equaled the principal, they would try to make him sell his land to pay the debt. "Although the law strictly forbids this, many get away with it" (3.66, cf. 1.52).[12] Another route to the bankruptcy of the *chia* was the piecemeal sale of its property to meet expenses such as weddings and funerals. Too many people, in Yüan Ts'ai's view, considered these situations emergencies for which they would sell land, hoping later to buy it back. Yüan Ts'ai disapproved of this, but he disapproved as much of failing in the obligations to daughters of dowries and to parents of tombs (2.56).

I should hardly need to explain how Yüan Ts'ai's perceptions of the economic behavior of those around him, his notions of fairness in business, and his strategies for avoiding bankruptcy related to the day-to-day behavior of *shih-ta-fu* of his time. Perhaps it is useful to highlight just three aspects: (a) He assumed that money-lending was a common concomitant of landownership, one shameful only if the interest charged was truly exorbitant. (b) He was fearful of taking on debt, which considering what he says of interest rates was probably a well-founded attitude. (c) He portrayed the finances of well-to-do households, especially ones with officials, as so complicated that bankruptcy could easily occur because no one actually had a good grasp on the size of assets and income and the extent of expenses.

---

[12] Yüan Ts'ai may be referring to either of two types of illegalities. According to Lien-sheng Yang (*Money and Credit*, p. 95), interest owed was not supposed to be counted as capital borrowed with interest charged on it. Moreover it was considered illegal to plot to take over another's family property. This, however, as Yüan Ts'ai implied, was a vague offense and difficult to punish. See *CMC*, pp. 227–30, 328–31.

MANAGING TENANTS AND BONDSERVANTS

Yüan Ts'ai's main audience, *shih-ta-fu*, did not plow or weed, make tools or tend shop. Rather, as he assumed, they employed tenants, bondservants, and hired workers to perform manual labor for them. Thus those with land needed to know how to select and manage tenants, and those with businesses needed the ability to recognize and motivate good managers and servants. Even families without businesses had numerous servants in their homes whose management required skill and attention.

In Yüan Ts'ai's opinion, most people did not recognize how important their tenants were to their welfare. He said, "The plowing and planting of a family are the product of the toil of the tenants. How can you then not value them?" (3.48). Common mistakes that landlords made were to let their managers or younger relatives harass tenants, to allow themselves to be manipulated by a tenant's enemies into raising the rent, to force a tenant to take a loan at high interest, or to try to take over land the tenants owned themselves. Much better, in Yüan Ts'ai's view, was to be considerate of tenants' needs, giving them gifts on the occasions of births, deaths, and marriages; lending grain at low interest over the growing season; and reducing rent in years of flood or drought. Indeed, the master was advised to love them as though they were kinsmen, for which they could be expected to repay him by providing for his food and clothing (3.48).[13]

Just as tenants were needed for rented-out farms, bondservants were needed for homes, businesses, and family-

[13] On tenantry in the Sung, see the article by Peter Golas, "Rural China in the Song," which reviews the extensive and complex Chinese and Japanese literature on this subject. See also Mark Elvin, *The Pattern of the Chinese Past*, pp. 69–83, and McDermott, "Land Tenure and Rural Control," pp. 206–236.

managed farms. Thirty of Yüan Ts'ai's 206 essays dealt with the selection, training, supervision, and treatment of servants, indicating how important this subject was to him. Yüan Ts'ai used several terms to refer to bondservants: *pi-ch'ieh* ("maids and concubines"), *pi-p'u* ("male and female servants"), *nu-p'u* ("male slaves and male servants," or "male bondservants"), *nu-pi* ("male and female slaves"), and *nu-li* ("slaves," or more specifically "male slaves"). The exact legal and social status of those he had in mind is not always clear. Yüan Ts'ai was, of course, addressing an audience who was familiar with current institutions of servitude, so he did not need to spell out all the details. In many passages he would seem to be using his terms in a very general sense, perhaps best understood to mean "menials," or menials of one sex. Behind these terms there could have been considerable variability in specific functions, obligations, age, legal status, and so on.[14] Yüan Ts'ai referred to maids who wove and menservants who tilled as well as ones who worked in shops and ones who did household chores. Although he spoke of them being "bought," he never mentioned how much a maid or manservant cost; on the other hand, he never treated price as a major concern, by contrast to maintenance.

From Yüan Ts'ai's remarks, maids seem to have been more conspicuous in domestic life than menservants, an impression also sustained in anecdotal writing.[15] Maids could be

[14] A great deal of scholarly effort has been expended trying to determine the exact legal status of various categories of employed people, especially ones who worked the land. (See McDermott's attempts to unravel these issues, "Land Tenure and Rural Control," pp. 140–236.) Yet all agree that those classified as *p'u* or *pi* were in the position of greatest subordination to their master and could not bring accusations against him or otherwise challenge his authority.

[15] Maids are ever-present in anecdotes of well-to-do houses, but they also appear where one would be less likely to expect them. For example, in *ICC chia*, 5, p. 41 a widow living with her widowed daughter-in-law has two maids of her own.

Part One

hired for limited periods of time (according to the law, for no more than ten years, after which they were to be returned);[16] or they could be bought on a revocable contract (*tien-mai*), allowing them to be redeemed after a stated period of time; or they could be bought outright, perhaps for legal purposes then called "concubines" rather than bondmaids.[17] Thus being a maid did not have to be a permanent condition, and most maids would have been young. Yüan Ts'ai reported, however, that unscrupulous men often made it difficult for a family to regain its daughter or wife by selling her to someone else or by simply failing to return her (3.41).[18] Likewise, wet nurses might be taken with the family when it moved, making it impossible for them ever to return to their own families (3.40).

Yüan Ts'ai assumed a plentiful supply of maids and advocated using a broker to arrange a contract for one (3.43).[19] In his time many of the young girls up for sale were brought in from elsewhere; these girls could well have been the daughters of poor peasants who sold them to traveling agents, but as Yüan Ts'ai noted, they might also have been kidnapped.[20] He wrote that if, on questioning, it turns out

[16] Only her parents could legally indenture or sell her. In the Sung or Yüan story, "Artisan Ts'ui and His Ghost Wife" (Y. W. Ma and Joseph S. M. Lau, eds., *Traditional Chinese Stories*, pp. 252–63), an artisan was asked whether he planned to marry off his daughter or "present" her to someone as a maid. He said he was too poor to pay for a dowry and so would have to "present" her. A contract was drawn up, the couple received the payment, and the new master promised that when her term of service was up, he would give her in marriage to a local worker.

[17] See Niida, *Tōsō hōritsu*, pp. 161–92, 371–90, 422–47. See also *Sung hui-yao chi-pen*, hsing-fa 2/155b.

[18] See *O-chou hsiao-chi*, 5, pp. 56–77.

[19] Brokers who dealt in bondservants are mentioned in *Tung-ching meng-hua lu*, 3, p. 119 and *Meng-liang lu*, 19, pp. 181–88.

[20] The magnitude of the kidnapping problem seems to have been great. One magistrate in an area where kidnapping was said to be endemic freed 2,600 people who had been forced into servile status. See *SS* 300, p. 9967.

that a maid was kidnapped, "report it immediately to the authorities; out of concern for her safety do not return her to those who offered her to you for sale" (3.44). If a girl was too young or too confused to prove that she could be legally bought by giving a reasonable explanation of her background, Yüan Ts'ai said to pay her a little in wages and return her at once should she ever be discovered by her relatives (3.45). In Hung Mai's anecdotes, stranded women often became maids; sometimes they later encountered their husbands or relatives.[21]

Yüan Ts'ai made no mention of the market for men-servants, perhaps because fewer were purchased. Nevertheless, men could also be bought on long-term or indefinite-term contracts, and brokers also handled them.[22] Men more often seem to have been engaged in productive work, for instance in businesses, in which adults would be more useful than teenagers. Yüan Ts'ai never discussed men's completing their terms of service, nor their parents' selling them. He portrayed them as voluntarily working for others because they lacked the wherewithal to support themselves (3.37). Nowhere did Yüan Ts'ai imply that bondservant status was hereditary, but he did refer to bondservants as a kind of person with certain cultural traits (3.30), which makes more sense if we imagine a largely hereditary group. This assumption is strengthened by Yüan Ts'ai's suggestion that one marry one's male and female bondservants, presumably to each other (3.42).

In the case of either men or women, temporary servitude was still servitude. Yüan Ts'ai's use of vocabulary associated with true slavery (i.e. *nu, pi, li,* classical terms for people who were born slaves with no release from bondage scheduled) seems to be entirely appropriate in the context of the day-to-

[21] *ICC chia* 3, p. 22; 13, pp. 115–16; *ping* 8, pp. 435–36.
[22] See note 17.

day behavior of the household. So long as their contracts
were in effect, maids and menservants were slaves to their
masters and mistresses who might beat them, order them to
do almost anything, and provide for them less than minimal
food and shelter. Yüan Ts'ai strongly disapproved of cruelty
to servants, but he saw it as commonplace in his social world.

Literary sources largely confirm Yüan Ts'ai's depiction of
the relations between masters and servants. Servants who
were beaten to death figure several times in Hung Mai's
anecdotes.[23] In the Sung or Yüan story, "Artisan Ts'ui and
his Ghost Wife," a runaway maid was beaten to death when
recaptured.[24] Yüan plays also often depict slaves and servants
being beaten.[25] Indeed, a disinclination to strike servants
seems to have warranted special notice. For instance, in his
Sung shih biography, Wei Hsien-mei was praised for his great
equanimity and generosity because when some slaveboys
knocked over a table, breaking the dishes in front of guests,
all Wei did was ask them to reset it.[26]

In Yüan Ts'ai's categories, a major distinction between
maids and menservants was that maids were grouped with
concubines, *ch'ieh*. Those not involved in some industrial
operation, such as weaving, were confined to the women's
quarters, making them much more members of the
household than menservants, who might well work and
sleep elsewhere. It is even possible that some young girls were
bought as *ch'ieh* so that there would be no time limit on their
term of service, their actual status in the household no higher
than that of maids. A sample contract included in a Yüan
dynasty encyclopedia shows how a single transaction could

[23] *ICC ting* 9, pp. 612–13; *chia* 15, p. 130, *ting* 2, p. 549.
[24] Ma and Lau, eds., *Traditional Chinese Stories*, pp. 252–63.
[25] See, for instance, the translation of "Rain on the Hsiao-hsiang," by J.
I. Crump, in *Chinese Theater*, pp. 247–309.
[26] *SS* 249, p. 8805.

be termed "hiring out" a girl who agreed to be a *ch'ieh*, the payment termed a "bridal present" and the broker a "go-between."[27]

Yüan Ts'ai did speak also of what we call concubines, that is, women whom the master treats as secondary wives. He called these women "maids or concubines" (*pi-ch'ieh*) a man "keeps" or "favors." Yüan Ts'ai, perhaps somewhat puritanical by temperament, tried to discourage "favoring" maids by pointing out the potential problems in establishing heirs (see Chapter 5), but he took it as normal: "*Pi-ch'ieh* come into close contact with their master, and some make use of this to form a sexual relationship" (3.21). Whether *pi* who were already married before being purchased were acceptable as quasi-concubines, Yüan Ts'ai never made clear, but from other sources it seems likely that they were.[28]

Yüan Ts'ai largely divided his social world into two kinds of people: superior men (*chün-tzu*) and inferior men (*hsiao-jen*). Bondservants by definition belonged to the category of inferior men (3.30). Other members of this category were peasants, artisans, and tradesmen (2.39). Occasionally an inferior person was endowed by Heaven with honesty and sincerity, but to Yüan Ts'ai that was the exception, not the rule (2.39). Most were endowed by Heaven with stupidity, stubbornness, forgetfulness, and bad tempers (3.30). Yüan

[27] *Hsin-pien shih-wen lei-yao ch'i-cha ch'ing ch'ien*, 11, p. 755.

[28] See Niida, *Tōsō hōritsu*, p. 379. How common it was to have sexual relations with maids can be seen in the great praise given Chang Yung (946–1015). He bought a maid, and four years later when he was transferred, her parents arranged a marriage for her. It turned out she was still a virgin. See *Hou te lu*, 4, pp. 2037–38. Further confirmation that *pi* (maids) were commonly looked on as suitable for bearing one's children is seen in an anecdote in the *Ch'i-tung yeh-yü*, 16, p. 206. Two friends had attained similar rank, but one had three sons and the other none. The one with three offered to help the other by giving him a *pi* who had already born a son for him. The woman then went back and forth between the two families, and the half-brothers became friends.

Ts'ai saw this as a fact of life and urged the family head to be lenient and patiently repeat his instructions, reminding himself that "the natural stupidity of inferior people is like this" (3.30).

Despite their moral and intellectual inadequacies, Yüan Ts'ai made it a point to note that servants were living beings. Even oxen, horses, pigs, sheep, cats, dogs, chickens, and ducks are provided shelter from the elements and bondservants deserve as much. "This thoughtfulness," he said, "characterizes the benevolent person who recognizes the underlying similarity between us and other beings" (3.38).

Yüan Ts'ai proposed several principles for the selection and management of bondservants. One major danger he saw in choosing menservants was corruption of the family's young men. Clever and attractive servants might entrance young men who would waste their time and money on them. Unpretentious and straightforward servants willing to work were the ones to choose (3.28).

In Yüan Ts'ai's opinion managing servants called for patience and sympathy but not weakness. To maintain consistent and firm control, he recommended delegating authority over the servants. He described some masters as trying to keep an eye on everything themselves, deciding how every little thing should be done and then constantly fretting about whether the servants had done it properly. Others went to the opposite extreme and supplied no direction; when dissatisfied with the result, they would curse and beat the servants. The best course, according to Yüan Ts'ai, was to appoint one person as a supervisor whose only task was to watch the others, for then "the success of the work will double" (3.31).

Disciplining servants, as Yüan Ts'ai saw it, required an understanding of their point of view and limitations. Servants entirely incapable of following direction should be replaced; trying to bring them into line by punishment was not a wise policy. "The master might go overboard in beating them and cause injury; their type, resenting this, might make trouble, some of which is unmentionable" (3.32).[29] Servants who were not beyond correction should be beaten when they did something wrong, but the master should not beat them himself because doing so would detract from his authority. In his anger he would fail to count the strokes he inflicted, thus seeming arbitrary and out of control. Instead the master should "reproach them calmly and order someone else to beat them, setting the number of strokes in accordance with the seriousness of the offense. Contradictory as it may seem, by not showing excessive anger [he] will gain authority" (3.33). Yüan Ts'ai also urged forbidding the women or young men in the family to beat their servants on their own (3.33).

Some of the more serious offenses servants could commit, in Yüan Ts'ai's view, were stealing, engaging in illicit sexual relations, and running away. If, from the nature of the case, severe penalties were warranted, the master would be well advised to turn the servant over to the government authorities, thereby avoiding the awkwardness of the servant's dying from a beating given at home (3.32).[30]

Bondservants were not entirely powerless; Yüan Ts'ai saw that they could cause their masters a lot of trouble, especially by dying. He worried that a servant's relatives might accuse the master's family of bringing about the servant's death directly or indirectly, that is, by beating, by neglecting an

[29] An example of the kind of trouble that could occur is found in *SS* 266, p. 9171. Ch'ien Jo-ch'ung beat his servant for making wine. The servant then took a knife and seriously injured him and his young son.

[30] In an anecdote in *ICC ting* 2, p. 549, an official brought a charge against his bondservant (*p'u*) for having sexual relations with his maid (*pi*). In this case, the judge sentenced him to penal servitude elsewhere, but the official, not satisfied, bribed a guard to have him killed.

illness, or by provoking a suicide. Thus Yüan Ts'ai said a
servant who became ill should be sent home to relatives who
could provide care and witness the cause of death. Consequently servants and slaves with local relatives were to be
preferred (3.42). If they had no relatives, they should be
sent to a neighbor's when ill so that the cause of their death
would be publicly known. "Also have the local mutual
security group record their statements and inform the government of it. Then if they die there will be no complications" (3.36). Another solution to the problem of no local
relatives was to choose mates for male and female servants
who then would be able to care for each other in illness and
old age (3.42).

Suicide by bondservants seems to have been a frequent
occurrence in Yüan Ts'ai's social milieu. He described detailed procedures for saving the servant's life when the
suicide attempt was discovered early and for reducing legal
complications in the case of death. He discussed hanging,
self-inflicted wounds, and jumping into wells and ponds. In
all cases, if there was no hope of resuscitation, he said to leave
everything as it was and immediately summon the local
police representatives (3.35).

Yüan Ts'ai paid little attention to the distinction between
hired workers and bondservants or that between a servant
who worked in the house and one who worked in a business
or on a farm. He quoted a "saying" of the *shih-ta-fu*, "Do not
be vexed that you keep too many maids (*pi*): Teach them to
spin and weave and they will be able to produce clothing for
the body. Do not be vexed that you keep too many menservants (*p'u*): Teach them to plow and plant and they will be
able to produce food to fill the stomach" (3.37). The failure
to distinguish between home and work was common in
premodern productive enterprises and therefore need not be

surprising.[31] The failure to make much of the distinction between bondservants and hired servants probably means there was not much difference from the master's point of view. Yüan Ts'ai assumed a plentiful supply of "lesser people" (*hsiao-min*) who lacked the resources to support themselves and therefore had to work for others. The only compensation Yüan Ts'ai mentioned was food and shelter. Indeed, he took great pains to try to convince masters that they should provide for these physical needs. "If they keep servants, then [rich families] should take care of their physical needs in return for the labor they perform. The virtue in this is great. And their sort will gladly perform strenuous toil for you so long as you keep them warm and fed" (3.37).

To anyone in the twentieth century, Yüan Ts'ai's descriptions of the behavior of servants and his advice about how to deal with them will seem suffused with social prejudices. But however much they disturb modern sensibilities, these attitudes were taken entirely for granted by Yüan Ts'ai's contemporaries. Indeed, in this regard I can find no difference between Yüan Ts'ai and the classicists or philosophers.[32] That upper class families needed servants, that the servants

[31] See Peter Laslett, *The World We Have Lost*, pp. 1–21.

[32] Note Ssu-ma Kuang's instructions for strict discipline of servants and Chu Hsi's praise for women who managed their servants properly, above in chap. 2, "The Family as a Corporate Unit." It is interesting to note in this regard that Wing-tsit Chan, in translating the *Chin-ssu lu*, used the phrase, "employing a wet nurse" for the Chinese *mai nai-pi*, literally "to buy a wet-nurse maid." In a note he took exception with Japanese commentators who took "buy" and "maid" seriously, saying "buy" merely meant to employ (*Reflections on Things at Hand*, p. 178, n. 25). Although buying or indenturing maids may have been in some sense the equivalent of hiring nurses today, there were nevertheless important differences, and Chinese of the time considered that they were indeed buying people for periods of time according to the terms of the contract. To suggest that this was simply "employment" is misleading.

had to be controlled through firm and consistent discipline, and that the servants and their masters were different sorts of people in talents and character were simply among the "facts of life" of Yüan Ts'ai's day.

PROVIDING SAFETY AND SECURITY

Minimizing the dangers of fire, accident, theft, and robbery was, to Yüan Ts'ai, a serious responsibility of family managers, and he provided detailed suggestions for precautions to be taken. Kitchen stoves he singled out as the major cause of fires. If embers were left in them and firewood was stacked nearby, it could catch fire (3.11). If clothes were left to dry over a covered smoldering fire all night, they could start a fire (3.12). Tenants' houses caught fire when silkworm frames were set over fires, or because ashes were carelessly disposed of near manure or thatched structures (3.13). Thatched houses were especially inflammable, as were places where oil or coal was stored (3.14).

To make it possible to put out fires quickly, Yüan Ts'ai advised making sure there was a nearby souce of water (such as a well). But the water itself would not be enough unless there were people to carry it. Therefore, Yüan Ts'ai insisted, it was essential to live in a populated area with neighbors (3.10). Anyone who wants to live in a quiet, isolated place in the mountains would be wise to build cottages for tenants in a circle around the house as a security measure (3.2).

Yüan Ts'ai gave some thought to other types of accidents, especially ones that prove fatal to children. Thus he urged that wells and ponds have railings around them and that barriers be erected to keep children away from anything dangerous—fast-flowing streams, sharp drops, and farm machinery. He argued that it was foolhardy to depend on the child's attendant to keep him or her away from dangers (3.17).

Guarding against theft was a perpetual problem, at least as much a worry to the family head as fire and accidents. Yüan Ts'ai saw no foolproof way to be free of this danger but argued that it could be mitigated.[33] He said that to avoid tempting thieves and robbers, one should not display valuables or store silk (3.6). In addition, one should keep the gates, walls to the compound, and the house walls in good repair (3.1). The next step to take was to arrange for patrols of one's property every night, which would have the added advantage of facilitating early detection of fires. Yüan Ts'ai advocated having someone patrol outside the property, making at least ten full circuits each night. Inside the walls of the compound, the younger men and bondservants would also take turns making patrols (3.4). If they heard anything at all suspicious, or if something made a dog bark, those on patrol would sound an alarm (3.3).

Because it was possible that all of these precautions could fail and armed robbers enter the compound, Yüan Ts'ai insisted that the family manager had to have defense and escape plans. "As a routine matter " he had to "have the young men in [the] family and the male servants maintain the weapons and know what steps to take to defend against attack" (3.7). As a precaution, the house should have a side exit by which the old people, the children, and the women could leave quickly, for Yüan Ts'ai stressed the need to prevent the robbers from capturing a family member and holding him or her hostage (3.7).

Obviously, from the measures he proposed, Yüan Ts'ai

[33] Concern about robbery was not new to the upper class. For a Later Han precedent, see Patricia Ebrey, "Estate and Family Management in the Later Han as Seen in the *Monthly Instructions for the Four Classes of People*."

did not see the local government as capable of suppressing robbery and banditry. Major uprisings were rare in the 1160s and 1170s, but sporadic and unorganized banditry seems to have been endemic.[34] Officials regularly wrote memorials complaining about the failure of the local government to stop it, a failure they attributed either to moral weakness or to inadequate institutional resources.[35] To Yüan Ts'ai, the causes of lawlessness did not matter so much as what one could do about it; family heads would be best advised to see to their own defense.

DEALING WITH THE OUTSIDE WORLD

Yüan Ts'ai perceived a highly interdependent social world; the head of a *shih-ta-fu* family had to deal on a regular basis with people outside his direct control, including poor kinsmen, neighbors, and shopkeepers. Cordial relations with them were important not only because one often needed to depend on them but also because conflict with them could lead to unpleasantness and costly lawsuits.

To Yüan Ts'ai, the way to avoid social conflict was, above all, to cultivate the socially necessary virtues described above in Chapter 3. That is, one should avoid envy, disdain, and eagerness to criticize others; one should be willing to forgive and forbear; and one should avoid giving offense. Yüan Ts'ai noted that facial expression and manner of speaking were as likely to offend as the words themselves, especially if one was in a bad mood (2.34). He also thought it was a good idea never to tell embarrassing secrets even to close friends and relatives. Sometime later they might get angry at you, and you would never forgive them if they then threw your guilty

---

[34] Some of the incidents of rioting and small uprisings in the Southern Sung are listed by Liang T'ai-chi in "Tu 'Yüan-shih shih fan,'" pp. 43–44.
[35] See McDermott, "Land Tenure and Rural Control," pp. 14–26.

secret back at you (2.33). Since relatives and old friends in the countryside were often poor, it was also advisable not to wear fancy clothes, drive elegant carriages, or ride superior horses. Your apparent importance would intimidate them, making you in turn feel uneasy (2.45).

In regard to relations with peers, Yüan Ts'ai made it clear that slowness to criticize was especially important; he said one should not advise people on court behavior, administrative methods, scholarship, ethics, managing property, or filial piety unless he had been fully successful in these endeavors himself (2.29). He also urged particular attention to the exchange of favors, for accepting a favor places a person in an inferior position. "Whenever you see the person who gave [you the favor], you will be deferential, and the person who extended the favor to you will look condescending" (2.61). These favors could include things so slight as a meal.[36]

Yüan Ts'ai did not think that all offenses could be forgiven nor all people won over through tolerance, submission, and inoffensiveness. Indeed he described a variety of bad types common in the countryside. There were villages with an old person of little integrity who, "claiming that he is immune from punishment, shamelessly curses and humiliates others on little or no grounds" (2.35).[37] There were also wealthy or high-ranking families who would use their influence to maltreat others. "Out of perversity they will surely prove a menace to any property adjoining theirs—houses, grave plots, hills, forests, fields, or gardens—stopping only when they possess them. They will seize whatever they take a fancy to, clothes, food, furnishings, small as such items may be" (2.38). There were also people who liked to stir up litigation

[36] This fear of obligations is at odds with the basic concept of *pao* described by Lien-sheng Yang, "The Concept of 'Pao' as a Basis for Social Relations in China."

[37] There were special legal privileges for people over 60. See 2.35 n. 38.

(2.38) and clerks and magistrates who took bribes (2.67). Some people formed gangs from among their numerous relatives to seize people's property, beating them up if they resisted (2.38). All of these "bad types" are also condemned in other Sung sources.[38]

Yüan Ts'ai's general advice in all these cases was to keep out of trouble (2.39). Avoid them: do not let their ways rub off on your family members (2.22). Just as important, do not try to reprove or control them. "Those who are impulsive in word and action and who may purposely do something they know is wrong—these people will certainly violently brush aside those who try to reprove them. Men who are well-adjusted to living in their community not only avoid reproving someone like this, they also know enough not to get caught in the middle of an argument between him and someone else" (2.26). The same applied to other people's unworthy sons; Yüan Ts'ai said he had "never heard of anyone reforming such young men by advice and scolding" (2.28).[39] In the cases of bullies who would bribe the government so that complaints to it would be useless, he advised taking no direct action, waiting instead for Heaven to punish them (2.38).

Yüan Ts'ai had relatively little to say concerning contact with kinsmen. Marriages with maternal and affinal relatives were fine but had to be handled delicately to avoid the

---

[38] See *CHTK* 2, pp. 11–17; *Sung hui-yao chi-pen*, hsing-fa, 2/133b.

[39] Some of Hung Mai's anecdotes seem designed to lead one to the same conclusion. Perhaps the best one is in *ICC ting* 5, pp. 585–86. When the income from selling a huge tree on a family grave plot was divided among the twelve families who jointly owned it, 40 cash remained. The man who hosted the meeting took it, saying it would repay his expenses. A nephew objected, started a fight, and ended up with a broken leg. This frightened the buyer, who then wanted his money back. When a few of the families refused, there was another fight and an eventual lawsuit. All twelve of the families were ruined, and many had to move away.

appearance of slights (1.58). Yüan Ts'ai advocated being generous to relatives (patrilineal and through marriage) and argued that outright gifts were much better than loans because unpaid debts invariably lead to grudges, and most loans between relatives never get repaid (1.37, 1.38). He also advocated taking in destitute and homeless relatives, including widows and children, but warned that one should first put the financial aspects of such charitable relationships on paper or at least make them public (1.48, 1.61). He argued against setting up charitable estates for lineage members on the grounds that the income from them, given in equal shares to all, does little good.[40] As the lineage grows the shares become small, and those who have plenty are encouraged to be even more dissolute and never give their shares to the truly needy. Yüan Ts'ai thought endowing a school for the common use of lineage members would make better use of the money (1.65).[41]

It is difficult to assess how common these attitudes toward kinsmen were. Certainly many Sung writers were quick to praise the moral and social excellence of lineages and charitable estates (see Chapter 2). Even though only a very small proportion of the *shih-ta-fu* in the Sung acted on these values, I have found no evidence of anyone scoffing at them. Yüan Ts'ai's fear of property disputes with affinal relatives may have been more common; at any rate in the light of cases in the *Judicial Decisions* this fear was not unfounded.[42]

---

[40] On lineages, see above, chap. 2, "Ancestors and Lineages."

[41] An inscription for a charitable school established along the lines Yüan Ts'ai proposed is found in Chu Hsi's collected works, *CWKCC* 80/2a–3b.

[42] For instance, one case concerned a woman née Chang who had married into the Wu family. After her husband and son had both died, she supported herself by cultivating land she had brought with her from her own family. When she became ill, no one in the Wu family would take her in, so she returned to the Chang family. A distant relative of her husband then brought a suit against her two nephews (who presumably were the

On the whole, Yüan Ts'ai seems to have considered neighbors a more crucial element of a *shih-ta-fu*'s social world than kinsmen. To avoid disputes with them, a man had to make sure that his livestock did not wander into neighbors' yards. The best solution was to have everything fenced. "By keeping people from going to and fro across your property, you will avoid the need to make accusations against them" (3.54). Yüan Ts'ai saw *shih-ta-fu* who maltreated their neighbors as extremely shortsighted:

> One day an enemy may come and attack their family or burn their house, but the neighbors will warn each other, "'If we put out the fire, afterwards not only will we receive no reward, but that man will bring charges against us, saying we stole his family's goods. Who knows how long the case will be at court? If we do not go to his aid to put out the fire, all we'll receive is one hundred blows." The neighbors would willingly take the beating to enjoy watching the mansion burn to the ground, with none of the furnishings passed down to the surviving generations. (3.10)

Yüan Ts'ai's class consciousness in the non-Marxist sense is most clearly revealed in his discussions of how to deal with those termed inferior people. Throughout his book Yüan Ts'ai used the terms superior man (*chün-tzu*) and inferior person (*hsiao-jen*) in two senses, moral and social. For instance, he apparently was making a moral distinction when he said, "Superior men are considerate, cordial, dignified, and cautious in their speech.... Inferior people are sharp,

---

ones caring for her) for illegally using property that belonged to the Wu family. This suit was dismissed, but the next year, after the widow had died, this Wu again tried to get her property by having his grandson made heir to her dead son, without even letting the Chang family be reimbursed for the funeral expenses. *CMC*, pp. 45–58.

unkind, exaggerated, and specious in their talk" (2.22). In other places, however, he used "inferior person" as a label for those of low social and economic status, especially those who had to work for others. The ambiguity of the terms he pointed out himself when he asserted that not every superior man in the social sense was a superior man in the moral sense. The opposite he said was also true: "Among the class of peasants, artisans, merchants, and bondservants there are some whom Heaven endowed with honesty and sincerity and who can be entrusted with business and assets. They are called 'the superior men among the inferior people'" (2.39).[43]

Since, Yüan Ts'ai implied, most socially inferior people were also morally inferior, a superior man had to take this into account in his dealings with them. Whenever passing through markets or stopping at teahouses and wineshops—places frequented by inferior people—he had to be sure to be dignified in speech and deportment to avoid being insulted (2.43). When doing business with inferior people, he had to recognize that they were seldom faithful or trustworthy. That is, shopkeepers would dress up inferior goods by adding substances like water or glue and then try to sell them through flowery sales pitches (2.41). Craftsmen, in order to secure business, would promise to have something done by a certain date, then time and again make excuses and new promises. To Yüan Ts'ai such behavior was part and parcel of their occupations: "Inferior people act these ways day in and day out without the slightest compunction" (2.41). Never-

---

[43] An example of a servant entrusted with property is found in the Sung or Yüan story, "Artisan Ts'ui and His Ghost Wife," Ma and Lau, eds. *Traditional Chinese Stories*, pp. 252–63. Another early story, "The Honest Clerk" (Hsien-yi Yang and Gladys Yang, trans., *The Courtesan's Jewel Box*, pp. 27–41), provides a portrait of a store clerk loyal to his master against all temptation.

theless many "superior men" would get angry: "Wanting to show them a lesson on the spot, they will sometimes go so far as to beat them or sue them." If only they could "have pity on the inferior person's ignorance and the pressures which lead him to self-serving expediency, then [they] could calm down a little when these annoyances occur" (2.41). Yüan Ts'ai's views of artisans and tradesmen thus differed little from his views of servants.

As Yüan Ts'ai saw it, inferior people were often laughing at superior ones and trying to find ways to take advantage of them. A good way was flattery, which easily fools the high-ranking; another was pandering to their weaknesses (2.31). Immature sons, without experience in social interaction, Yüan Ts'ai saw as especially easy victims for these sorts of inferior men (2.50).

The government and its representatives were, of course, another important element in Yüan Ts'ai's world. As mentioned earlier, Yüan Ts'ai strongly urged obeying the letter of the law in everything concerned with property and taxes as a matter of both duty and prudence. He urged getting taxes in early if at all possible and never falsifying deeds or documents of division in the hope of avoiding labor service or taxes. Moreover, he recommended preventive measures aimed at avoiding lawsuits, such as the variety of steps to be taken when a bondservant was ill or property was purchased.

Yüan Ts'ai's advocacy of dutiful behavior on the part of subjects was not matched by a conviction that the government would respond to them fairly or competently. One of the major reasons for avoiding lawsuits was that their outcome was so much in doubt. In Yüan Ts'ai's opinion, many judges were not astute enough to see through the complexities of land disputes (2.65), others would accept bribes to decide cases unfairly (2.67), and others were easily manipulated by bullies (2.38). In fiscal matters, some officials would add unauthorized imposts, and others would require the local service workers to perform unreasonable services (2.67, 2.68).

When an individual was confronted with oppressive or corrupt officials or clerks, Yüan Ts'ai saw little recourse other than keeping out of their way. He said that it was seldom of any use to bring charges against them. "The accused official will get letters from the high and mighty pleading for protection; the accused clerks will use government funds to pay bribes, will destroy records, and will alter the legal dossiers" (2.66). Officials, for their part, favored subjects who "dare not utter a word, swallowing their sounds and sucking in their breath, when they suffer from corrupt officials" (2.67), and they tried to slander as "unruly" any populace that made lists of the official's wrongs and brought charges against them.

Lack of confidence in the judicial process was certainly common in Yüan Ts'ai's time. Literary examples of false suits, unperceptive judges, and corrupt clerks abound in Yüan drama.[44] The *Chou-hsien t'i-kang*, a guide for magistrates and prefects written by a contemporary of Yüan Ts'ai, often referred to "unperceptive judges" and the ill effects of the rich and the powerful bribing the clerks.[45]

As mentioned in Chapter 3, a negative and often fearful tone pervades much of Yüan Ts'ai's discussion of social relations outside the family. In that sphere it was not the good one could do through local leadership, nor even the good one could gain from appropriate connections, that Yüan Ts'ai emphasized. Rather it was the dangers that one would be wise to avoid. He saw much satisfaction in orderly manage-

---

[44] See, for instance, "The Mo-ho-lo Doll" in Crump, *Chinese Theater*, pp. 311–92, and "Snow in Midsummer" and "The Wife Snatcher" in Yang and Yang, trans., *Selected Plays of Guan Hanqing*," pp. 13–66.

[45] *CHTK* 2, pp. 11–17.

ment of a large and prosperous family, but he did not propose taking the next step in the classical scheme to local leadership. To the contrary, he warned against the dangers of trying to resolve other people's disputes and of standing up to bullies and oppressive officials. In part this was a fear of lawsuits, which would waste one's patrimony. But in many cases the only dangers Yüan Ts'ai mentioned were humiliation and embarrassment.

Yüan Ts'ai's conception of his social world may have been no more fearful and negative than that of many of his contemporaries, but it certainly conflicted with what classicists and philosophers believed the attitude of local gentlemen should be. This is perhaps best seen by comparing Yüan Ts'ai's advice with that of Chu Hsi in his "Supplemented" version of the village compact first devised by Lü Ta-fang and his brothers. As a means of improving local behavior, this compact called for monthly meetings of village men who would agree to encourage each other in virtue and work, to reprimand each other on their failings, to observe polite forms in all their social interaction, and to aid each other in distress. Charts were to be kept to keep track of everyone's moral progress under the supervision of a chosen elder. The compact gave a list of virtues (such as serving parents, teaching children, controlling servants, and being honest) and vices (such as quarrelsomeness, insubordination, and selfishness). It also gave detailed rules for seniority to be used in determining orders of deference. Chu Hsi added a full description of a ceremony the men should perform before a portrait of the former sages.[46] Yüan Ts'ai would have agreed that the specified virtues were needed and the specified vices deplorable but would have seen monthly

---

[46] *CWKCC* 74/25a–32a.

meetings and charts as utopian solutions. If the town had anyone really in need of reform, having everyone else reprimand him would be more likely to result in violence than harmony, at least as Yüan Ts'ai saw things.

CHAPTER 7

Conclusions

Yüan Ts'ai assumptions, perceptions, opinions, and strategies have been analyzed in the four chapters above. Sometimes it may have seemed as though his thoughts were analyzed too closely, considering that he was not an especially profound thinker. But that was on purpose. My goal has been to look at the preoccupations of a relatively normal upper class man with the attention to conceptual distinctions usually reserved for the treatises of major thinkers or the statements of illiterate informants. In this last chapter I will try to probe further what Yüan Ts'ai's ways of thinking had to do with the culture of the upper class in his age.

Yüan Ts'ai's "ways of thinking" do not directly correspond to the culture of his society or class. Like everyone else, he made a selection, part consciously, part unconsciously, part through accidents of personal history, from the stock of ideas potentially available to all his peers. Yüan Ts'ai was a critic of the behavior of some members of his society and a critic of other critics as well (especially the more unbending classicists). Moreover, he discussed some subjects that others seem to have avoided in writing, and he recognized certain patterns underlying interpersonal relations that many of them seem not to have noticed.

Intellectual and political historians have already shown many divisions among Sung thinkers and statesmen: James Liu has studied the factionalism of the eleventh century; Winston Lo and Hoyt Tillman have shown the divergence between the utilitarians and the Ch'eng-Chu school; Robert Hartwell has shown how scholars differed in their use of historical example, from moral didacticism to historical analogism; Conrad Schirokauer has analyzed the opposition to Chu Hsi and his students; George Hatch has analyzed the divergent strands in the thought of Su Hsün and Su Shih.[1] But almost all of this work has focused on differences in political theories or metaphysics. It seems to have been largely assumed that all educated men agreed on the Five Cardinal Relations and the ethics of family life.

Indeed, that would have been my conclusion also if I had tried to generalize about the thinking of the Sung educated class through a comparison of Chu Hsi and Ssu-ma Kuang. Their shared convictions, especially their belief that ritual rules were the key to regulating the relations among relatives and their condemnation of individually owned property, would have been taken as the underlying presuppositions of family life. Where they diverged, especially Chu Hsi's shift of emphasis from the complex family to the descent line, would have been taken as indicating the points of tension or ambiguity in an otherwise coherent system of thought.[2]

The principal differences between Yüan Ts'ai and Sung classicists and philosophers have already been noted. Yüan Ts'ai based his arguments on "common sense" analysis of consequences and not on the teaching of the sages. Moreover, he was more concerned with the outcome of actions than with the motivations behind them. He was tolerant of

---

[1] James T. C. Liu, *Reform in Sung China*; Winston Wan Lo, *The Life and Thought of Yeh Shih*; Hoyt Tillman, *Utilitarian Confucianism*; Robert M. Hartwell, "Historical Analogism, Public Policy, and Social Science in Eleventh- and Twelfth-Century China"; Conrad Schirokauer, "Neo-Confucians Under Attack"; George Hatch, "The Thought of Su Hsün" and "Su Shih."

[2] Indeed, Makino Tatsumi wrote an article much to this effect. See *Kinsei Chūgoku sōzoku kenkyū*, pp. 11–27.

differences in personality and reluctant to place blame when people did not get along. He had no disdain for calculative thought aimed at bringing prosperity and harmony to one's family, and toward that end he encouraged tolerance and compromise rather than insistence on principle or duty. Finally, he had very little interest in form or ritual for its own sake.

The differences between Yüan Ts'ai and the philosophers on family matters could be viewed as a further indication of the plurality of Sung thought. But that would be a mistake. The ideas of Yüan Ts'ai and Chu Hsi on these topics were not parallel, with people free to choose one or the other. Rather, I argue, they represent quite distinct cultural phenomena. Yüan Ts'ai's general ideas had deep roots in the culture of the *shih-ta-fu* of his age, that is, the pattern of ideas and discriminations that underlay their behavior, whereas those of Chu Hsi and even Ssu-ma Kuang were only tangentially related to the behavior of the class.

Many of the differences between Yüan Ts'ai and the classicists can be traced to the very high value that Yüan Ts'ai placed on preserving the family. Indeed, the reason why Yüan Ts'ai discouraged fathers from berating their sons or treating them unfairly was not any belief in the rights of sons but a fear of the consequences of these actions. As Yüan Ts'ai noted in a different context, once disaster occurred, it did not matter who was to blame. If berating your son led to his becoming defiant and unworthy, your moral rectitude would not save your family from decline. The desire to preserve the family was certainly a sentiment Yüan Ts'ai shared with many members of his social class, though he went further than anyone else in articulating all of its ramifications and implications. As discussed above, Ssu-ma Kuang, Yeh Meng-te, and Lu Chiu-shao also wrote as though this desire were natural and reasonable, even if it sometimes led to counterproductive activities.

In many ways concern with preserving the *chia* can be viewed as a fear of loss of social status. No one thought that those whose ancestors were poor and humble had to preserve exactly the status they had inherited. Rather, it was those whose ancestors had built up their family's assets and reputation who were warned about the ease with which it all could be lost. Probably in any society with substantial social mobility there will be anxiety about slipping, but in China there was extra pressure because of the conception of the *chia*.[3] The *chia* was the family as a ministate: intrinsic to it were social position, reputation, and material resources. Because the *chia* was seen as a trust from one's ancestors, losing one's patrimony was not merely a sign of personal incompetence but also a failure in one of the highest responsibilities a man had.

Many characteristics of Yüan Ts'ai's world view have already been shown to have been common among his contemporaries. A few others still deserve attention. One of the clearest contrasts between Yüan Ts'ai and the philosophers is his mode of argument. Even so-called utilitarian thinkers such as Ch'en Liang and Yeh Shih regularly supported their arguments by citation of classical authorities. Yüan Ts'ai, by contrast, almost always offered benefits to be attained: an action would reduce interpersonal friction, save trouble, or preserve the family. This was exactly the sort of reasoning used in guides for magistrates and prefects, our best source for the everyday thinking of local officials. In these books, of which the *Admonitions for Magistrates* (*Tso-i tzu-chen*) and *Guidelines for Local Administrators* (*Chou-hsien t'i-kang*) are the

[3] Ping-ti Ho discusses the fear of downward mobility in the Ming and Ch'ing dynasties in *The Ladder of Success*, pp. 141–47.

best surviving examples, the emphasis was on how to achieve recognized political objectives. The important points were to know one's true goals, make do with the subordinates one finds, get along with local notables, and know when to accept less than complete success. Consider the two passages below from the *Guidelines*:

Guard Against Buying and Selling by Relatives

When gentlemen-officials (*shih-ta-fu*) are at home out of office, they have their relatives around them and are on close, affectionate terms with them. After they take up office, their relatives often engage in private commerce, falsifying names and concealing tax obligations. They may travel long distances to the official's residence, seeking to sell goods there. The official cannot refuse them because it would be against human feelings. Some put them up in the official compound; others send them to a monastery. They distribute their wares to the people or clerks, or entrust them to a broker. The relatives want a profit of several-fold. Sometimes the official even gives them a trading pass to help get them on their way. Once this has given rise to lawsuits, you know who will be blamed! You should take preventive action before it gets this far.

As for poor relatives who come to visit, you must treat them politely and give them gifts from your salary, then quickly send them on their way. Do not let them tarry!

In Blaming the Clerks, Reflect on Yourself

Today officials all say, "The clerks are avaricious and must be disciplined. The clerks are stubborn and must be regulated." Now, the greediness and stubbornness of clerks should certainly be disciplined and regulated. But you must first reflect on your own leadership of the clerks. After all, rich people do not become clerks; those who become clerks are all poor. In their desire for the resources they need to live, to care for their elders and children, and to pay for funerals and marriages, they are just the same as us. But in seeking their support from the public, they have to depend on bribes.

The great officer receives his appointment from the ruler and consumes the salary given by the ruler. Still some are dissatisfied; they steal from the public and take from the people. They force the clerks to provide everything they need for their own family. Then they turn around and call the clerks covetous and stubborn! What should we think of that? Therefore I once said, "Only if you are as pure as jade and have never had a single blemish on your record should you sternly rebuke the clerks."[4]

Not only did the *Guidelines for Local Administrators* employ a rhetorical style very similar to that used in the *Precepts*, but much of its advice seems to have been based on similar perceptions of social life and human proclivities. The passages quoted here show ideas about commerce, kinsmen, and social inferiors similar to Yüan Ts'ai's, and like the *Precepts* they urge precaution, self-reflection, and sympathy. Other passages echo Yüan Ts'ai in noting that very few things ever turn out as one wants them to, in suggesting that one avoid dealing with others while angry, and in worrying about how to handle incorrigible and deceptive people.[5]

Another indication that Yüan Ts'ai's ideas and assumptions were basic ones in the culture of his time is that they help explain the customary law of the period. Whereas Ssu-ma Kuang and Chu Hsi condemned individual property,

[4] *CHTK* 1, p. 5.
[5] See *CHTK* 1, pp. 8–9; 2, pp. 15–16.

remarriage of widows, premortem division, and adoptions that were not oriented specifically to ancestral succession, Yüan Ts'ai accepted the same standards as the law—all much less stringent. Indeed, it is probably more accurate to assume that the relationship was the other way around, that the courts enforced the type of standards educated men like Yüan Ts'ai considered right and reasonable.[6]

Finally it should be noted that Yüan Ts'ai's ideas are coherent and consistent and could quite plausibly have been practiced by ordinary, decent people. The coherence of Yüan Ts'ai's views can be understood by recalling his "ultimate values" discussed in Chapter 3. Almost all of his advice falls into place once one understands his belief in human variability and Heavenly response and the values he placed on social harmony and especially on the preservation of the family.

By this point I think it can be granted that Yüan Ts'ai's ideas

---

[6] Yüan Ts'ai's ideas correspond in rough ways to what has been described as Chinese peasant culture, at least with regard to concern with family survival, fear of humiliation, and avoidance of overt social or political conflict. One difference should, however, also be noted: Yüan Ts'ai revealed no sign of any deep need for a social superior to provide authority, a trait that some scholars have posited as a central feature of Chinese political culture (Richard Soloman, *Mao's Revolution and the Chinese Political Culture*, pp. 105–122). Yüan Ts'ai portrayed family heads as ultimately dependent on their own wits and the moral response of Heaven. The reason for disciplining their sons or economizing on expenses was not that the sages or the emperor or the magistrate had told them to but because, after thinking it over carefully, it was the sensible thing to do. Indeed, family heads had constantly to assess the situations they were in and decide on the appropriate course; they were fully responsible themselves if they made faulty decisions and, for instance, had to accept the blame if their children's marriages did not succeed. This sense of autonomy and personal responsibility may well derive from the education that *shih-ta-fu* received and their belief that they were the heirs to a long tradition of social and political leadership. But in Yüan Ts'ai's case it can hardly have come from Ch'eng-Chu Neo-Confucianism, as Thomas Metzger concluded (*Escape from Predicament*, pp. 49–190).

and assumptions did not all derive from the Classics or the writings of great teachers, that their divergences were often paralleled in other contemporary sources, and that the cultural principles reflected in the *Precepts* and related sources were ones of great importance in shaping the day-to-day behavior of the *shih-ta-fu*. Granting all this, we can turn to the question of the relationship between this broad cultural complex and the teachings of the philosophers. These teachings were, after all, an element in the culture of many educated men. The ways in which the general culture of the upper class and the doctrines of its teachers reinforced, contradicted, and provoked each other is an extremely complex question, worthy of detailed study in its own right; but some broad outlines can be suggested here.

Yüan Ts'ai was what we would call a decent man. He wanted all people to take care of their own responsibilities but not at the expense of hurting others. He insisted on the importance of honesty and good faith in all of a person's dealings. He sought an end to quarreling and ill will but was sympathetic to the variety of unfortunate circumstances in which people could find themselves.

He was also a sensible or pragmatic man. Although he had a clear idea of what the ideal state of affairs would be, he was willing to set lower goals when the ideal seemed unattainable. Thus he laid down very few absolute rules and never urged self-sacrifice as the only honorable course.

The difference between decency and virtue lies largely in its attainability. Decency can be demanded of everyone; or to put it the other way, achieving what a culture asks of everyone is considered decent. Virtue is an extreme or absolute, full mastery of which very few ever achieve or are expected to achieve. Philosophical discourse in China, as elsewhere, concerned itself much more with what constituted virtue than with what constituted decency.

The difference between pragmatism and principles lies largely in the willingness to compromise. Pragmatism was not so neglected in Chinese philosophy as decency was. In discussions of government, some thinkers regularly fell to the side of being pragmatic or utilitarian. They usually advocated study of the evolution of institutions and the details of current situations. Others opposed such thinking, insisting that one concentrate on timeless principles and the purity of intentions, such as concern for the welfare of the people and loyalty to the ruler.

The connection between what most upper class men considered decent and reasonable and the philosophy of their teachers was neither simple nor direct. It occurred within a context involving the material order, the socio-political order, the culture of the upper class, the teachings of the classical scholars, and the classical texts themselves. The material order (level of technology, availability of resources) and the classical texts acted as the "givens" of the system, influencing others more than they were influenced by them. The commercial and agricultural revolutions of the Sung have been shown to have affected social organization and political institutions in a great variety of ways.[7] Social and political institutions were in turn systematically related to culture. That is, how men responded to new economic opportunities or political institutions depended on notions in their heads, but these notions could also change as they came to deal with new situations. As early as the Han, the introduction of free sale of landed property and the abolition of

---

[7] See Laurence J. C. Ma, *Commercial Development and Urban Change in Sung China*, Ping-ti Ho, "Early-Ripening Rice in Chinese History"; Yoshinobu Shiba, "Urbanization and the Development of Markets in the Lower Yangtze Valley"; and Robert M. Hartwell, "Financial Expertise, Examinations and the Formulation of Economic Policy in Northern Sung China" and "Transformations of China."

hereditary stipends had led men to develop new arrangements of family life. Later developments had similar effects. I would think that some of Yüan Ts'ai's calculative thought could be traced to the great growth of commerce in the Sung and the interpenetration of the scholarly and mercantile worlds. Of course, they also owed much to the statecraft tradition, especially that developed for management of smaller units like counties. Perhaps equally important, increased social mobility made the rise and decline of families a matter of common knowledge and a very real concern of those who took seriously the role of family head.

In a similar fashion, teachers and philosophers had a complex relationship with the culture of their social peers. From childhood the teachers interacted with those around them and learned to take for granted the principles, beliefs, and attitudes of members of their society. At an early age they began to study the Classics, perhaps with a parent but usually soon with a teacher. These Classics were written over a thousand years earlier and by and large call for outlooks and values especially suited to a "feudal" age. Yet among the doctrines they were taught was the universal validity of the values expressed in the Classics. Thus a continuing intellectual problem for classically trained scholars, and a stimulus for much of their philosophical writings, was the conflict between the culture they grew up in and what they thought this culture should be from their reading of the Classics.

From my comparison of the *Precepts for Social Life* and the writings of Ssu-ma Kuang and Chu Hsi, I suspect that a key to the interaction of the culture of the educated and the doctrines of their teachers was use of the same terms or ideas for different purposes. In many particulars Yüan Ts'ai, Ssu-ma Kuang, and Chu Hsi all concurred in their observations and their injunctions. For instance, they all thought that most of their contemporaries spoiled their children and were inclined to indulge themselves. Moreover, their cures were largely alike, strictness in the early years and frugality achieved by reducing desires in adulthood. But this similarity hides a fundamental difference, at least between Yüan Ts'ai and Chu Hsi. For Yüan Ts'ai indulgence was not inherently evil; the problem was its effects on the survival of the family as a property-owning unit. Spoiled three-year-olds became "unworthy sons" who spent recklessly and got into trouble, ruining their families in the process. To Chu Hsi, indulgence was a clear case of the pursuit of "human desires" and wrong no matter what the consequences. Yüan Ts'ai defined frugality as living within one's means and did not condemn comfort that one could afford. Chu Hsi, of course, would have considered it as bad for a rich man to indulge his desires as a poor one.

Sometimes even when Yüan Ts'ai and Chu Hsi used the same words, they could mean different things by them. For instance, both agreed that to be *kung* (public or impartial) was better than to be *ssu* (private, partial, or selfish). But their range of reference differed. Yüan Ts'ai used these terms largely in the context of the complex family. To be concerned with the common interest of all the brothers and impartial in distribution of resources was to have a *kung* attitude. To be concerned only with one's wife or children to the detriment of brothers or their children was to be selfish or partial (*ssu*). Yüan Ts'ai did not see concern for them per se as selfish; he would call it selfish only when it led to harming others in the family. To Chu Hsi, to be *kung* was to be motivated by righteous principles (*i*), to be *ssu* was to be motivated by interest. Chu Hsi quoted a statement by Ch'eng I that the love between father and son begins as *kung* but becomes *ssu* when personal concern is attached to it.[8] To

[8] *CSL* 7, p. 214; 6, p. 191 (Chan, trans., p. 195, 175).

give another example, Yüan Ts'ai wished people to be honest and respectful of their seniors, using terms like *hsin* and *ching*, also often used by philosophers. But to him to be *ching* was to "behave with deference and speak with humility," and he saw it as a quality most of his contemporaries possessed (2.13). It was not the serious, attentive, composed approach to life that Neo-Confucian philosophers described as *ching* and saw as a major element in self-cultivation.[9]

Another way that the same words could be used to different purposes was through metaphor. All three writers, continuing a tradition of great antiquity, likened the family to the state. To Yüan Ts'ai this was a two-way metaphor: one should govern the people as one manages a family and manage the family as one handles an office. He wrote, "When gentlemen and officials (*shih-ta-fu*) live at home, if they could reflect on the time they spent in office, then they would not intercede with requests, seize power, and upset current practices. When they are in office, if they could reflect on their time at home, they would not provoke resentment through harshness and cruelty" (2.40). For Chu Hsi the metaphor was usually one way: a man was as kindly and dutiful in his capacity as an official as he was in his roles as a father or a son. For instance, in a funerary inscription, Chu Hsi praised a man because he loved the commoners as he loved his children, supervised the clerks as he supervised his household servants, dealt with his colleagues as he dealt with his friends, was as sparing of government revenue as he was of his private assets, and managed public affairs as he managed household affairs.[10]

The very great but often misleading verbal similarity in the statements of men like Yüan Ts'ai and those of classicists and philosophers could mask considerable differences and

[9] See A. C. Graham, *Two Chinese Philosophers*, pp. 68–69.
[10] *CWKCC* 94/6a.

deflect conflict. This masking would allow men to think they had chosen to adhere to philosophically approved values while, at a less conscious level, they were acting on other, long-established principles of prudent family management, which they had learned from sources other than their teachers.

This process of accommodation and obfuscation can perhaps be more clearly seen if we consider what happened after the Sung. In the early and mid-Ming when Chu Hsi's writings, especially his commentaries on the *Four Books*, became required reading for anyone aspiring to an official career, it seems as if certain ideas could not be directly expressed in expository writing; among these were Yüan Ts'ai's pleas for tolerance, compromise, and calculative concern for the prosperity of descendants. But authors could take up concerns of Yüan Ts'ai's on which there was seeming agreement with classicists. For instance, thrift, strictness, filial piety, and wifely submission were fully acceptable to philosophers but also (and for other reasons) essential to the survival of the family as an economic unit. Probably for this reason they are repeated ad nauseum in the hundreds of "family instructions" of Ming and Ch'ing times.[11] Whatever advice Yüan Ts'ai offered that was objectionable to the Ch'eng-Chu orthodoxy, such as compromising principles for the sake of harmony or prudentially planning to avoid impoverishment, could be left unstated, to be conveyed in less direct ways. One such avenue of expression seems to have been vernacular fiction. Patrick Hanan described the "highest value" in the "folly and consequence" stories of the mid-Ming as the "preservation and stability of the family, includ-

[11] See Hui-chen Wang Liu, "An Analysis of Chinese Clan Rules." See also the "instructions" from genealogies collected by Taga Akigoro, *Sōfu no kenkyū*, pp. 581–675.

Conclusions

ing its economic basis." Sexual misadventure and the idleness of a spoiled son were portrayed as major threats to this stability.[12]

At the same time, adjustments were not strictly verbal; changes in family customs were also made. Practices that appealed to the philosophers could be adopted with no sense of hypocrisy by people otherwise little concerned with the pursuit of moral purity, so long as they in no sense undermined their own goal of the preservation of the *chia*. Good examples are forbidding remarriage of widows and endowing charitable estates for lineages. Even punctilious performance of ancestral and other family rituals could be copied, so long as they were relegated to special occasions and not allowed to set the tone for all of the interaction of family members (which was exactly what Ssu-ma Kuang and Chu Hsi had wanted them to do).

The circulation of Yüan Ts'ai's *Precepts* was clearly affected by these changes in intellectual orthodoxy. (See Appendix A.) During the fourteenth century, before the full acceptance of Ch'eng-Chu orthodoxy, large parts of the *Precepts* were copied into two encyclopedias for popular reference. Of proportionately greatest interest to the editors of these reference books was anything to do with property or servants, subjects on which Yüan Ts'ai had little agreement with the Ch'eng-Chu philosophers. During the early and mid-Ming when Ch'eng-Chu orthodoxy was at its height, the *Precepts* was little known. By the late Ming, however, the strength of the Ch'eng-Chu tradition declined, and there was a shift in emphasis within Neo-Confucian philosophy toward thinkers like Wang Yang-ming (1472–1529) who stressed moral values that were easy for all to practice. In this period the

[12] Patrick Hanan, *The Chinese Vernacular Story*, p. 60.

(169)

Precepts for Social Life, not surprisingly, was reprinted in several collectanea. Moreover, a condensed version was prepared for the *T'ang-Sung ts'ung-shu*, which gave special weight to the items on moral values in the middle chapter. In the Ch'ing dynasty there was a revival of statecraft, an often utilitarian turn of thought comparable to Yüan Ts'ai's, even if usually directed toward government rather than family. Probably as a consequence, in this period it was again acceptable to discuss family matters from the point of view of harmony and prosperity rather than ethics and ritual, and the *Precepts* was reprinted and excerpted several times. The enormous (10,000 *chüan*) imperial encyclopedia, the *Ku-chin t'u-shu chi-ch'eng*, finished in 1725, included almost everything in the *Precepts* except the items on moral values, quoting many of the items on property and family harmony several times. By the mid-eighteenth century even Confucian scholars could quote from the *Precepts*, as long as some selectivity was used. The excerpts made by the scholars Ch'en Hung-mou in 1742 and Wang Tzu-ts'ai in 1841 show similarities. Each one quoted extensively from Yüan Ts'ai's comments on how to achieve harmony in complex families but was nearly silent on planning, wills, or adoption, subjects that could be considered more "calculative" and therefore morally objectionable.[13]

The ready acceptance the *Precepts* found in the eighteenth and nineteenth centuries is perhaps best comprehended by thinking of the social values and "facts of life" presented in the great eighteenth-century novel, *Hung-lou meng* (*Dream of*

---

[13] It is also interesting to note that in this period the *Precepts* was reclassified. Until the eighteenth century, in bibliographies it had been placed under "miscellaneous doctrines" rather than under "Confucians" (*ju-chia*). The massive catalogue prepared on orders of the Ch'ien-lung emperor, the *Ssu-k'u ch'üan-shu tsung-mu t'i-yao*, 18, p. 1900, reclassified it as a "Confucian" text, noting that it would indeed improve customs.

Red Mansions).[14] Not only do many particulars of the two works match in such areas as the recruiting, disciplining, and motivating of servants and agents, but one of the major themes of the novel seems straight out of the *Precepts*: the decline of a family because it produced too many unworthy sons and its senior members failed to show prudence in budgeting and investment. Although Yüan Ts'ai showed no particular sympathy for romantic personalities of Chia Pao-yü's type, I cannot help but think he would have had much advice and chiding to offer Pao-yü's father, Chia Cheng.

I do not of course mean to imply that Yüan Ts'ai's book had any great influence on *shih-ta-fu* of the Ch'ing. The point is that Yüan Ts'ai articulated views that were not shaped by any one or two books but that were deeply embedded in the culture that underlay the family system, the business practices, and the social habits of *shih-ta-fu*. This cultural complex was much greater than any one thinker or book and had its own logic of development. Even so influential a thinker as Chu Hsi—if his ideas were directly counter to it, as they were in many aspects of family life—could only hinder direct expression of these values and assumptions; he could not suppress or redirect the entire cultural tradition.

[14] See the not yet finished translation by David Hawkes (*The Story of the Stone*) or the complete one by Gladys and Hsien-yi Yang (*The Dream of Red Mansions*).

PART TWO

Precepts for Social Life

By Yüan Ts'ai

Abbreviations Used to Indicate Sources Quoting the Precepts

(1) *Chü-chia pi-yung shih-lei* (14th century)
(2) *Shih-lin kuang-chi* (14th century)
(3) *T'ang-Sung ts'ung-shu* and the "Expanded" *Shuo fu* (early 17th century)
(4) *Ku-chin t'u-shu chi-ch'eng* (1725) (Parts of the *Precepts* are quoted under twenty-four categories. When more than one "4" is given, it is because the passage is quoted more than once.)
(5) *Wu chung i-kuei* (1742)
(6) *Sung-Yüan hsüeh-an pu-i* (1841)

On the inclusion of parts of the *Precepts* in these books, see Appendix A. The numbers in parentheses appear flush right on the line below each item.

PREFACE

Thinking about how to be good and how to bring others to become good are what the superior man concentrates on.

Mr. Yüan Chün-tsai of San-ch'ü[1] is a person of integrity whose conduct is refined. He is widely learned and has written extensively. With the talent of a thoughtful official, he has promoted morality and love in his service as magistrate. The music and singing in Wu-ch'eng[2] did not go beyond this.

One day, Mr. Yüan brought by the three-chapter book that resulted from his efforts. As he showed it to me, he said, "This book can promote cordiality in interpersonal relations and bring improvement to habits and customs. I am going to print it and circulate it in this town." He asked me to criticize it and write a preface for it.

During the course of several months I read it over many times and became quite familiar with its style. The first part is called "Getting Along with Relatives," the second, "Improving Personal Conduct," and the third, "Managing Family Affairs." Each has several dozen entries. The wording is to the point and comprehensive. The ideas are earnest and generous ones, yet they are expressed with subtlety. Anyone who puts them into practice can indeed become filial, brotherly, faithful, forgiving, and good, and thus behave like

[1] San-ch'ü was the popular name for Ch'ü prefecture as well as the name of a mountain in the prefecture.

[2] An allusion to *Analects* 17 : 4 (Waley, trans., pp. 209–210). Wu-ch'eng was the city where Confucius' disciple Tzu-yu held office. Although it was a small, unimportant place, he was able to transform the people through education.

a scholarly superior man. But how can this book be enjoyed only by the people of Le-ch'ing?³ It ought to reach all areas! How can it be practiced in only one age? Later generations deserve to have it!

Mr. Yüan wished to offer to one city what he had originally written for himself. In the future it will reach the emperor and benefit the people. Thus we can see his desire to bring goodness to all those in the empire.

I was a fellow student with Mr. Yüan at the National University, and now I also benefit from his residence in my native place. I have learned much of value from him. Thus I have the presumption to introduce his book with this convoluted essay. However, I want to rename the book, *Precepts for Social Life*. Isn't this title more appropriate! Yüan Chüntsai's formal name is Yüan Ts'ai.

I, Liu Chen, Dignitary of Deliberations, Co-Administrator of Lung-hsing prefecture, write this preface on the 15th day of the first month of the *wu-hsü* year of the Ch'un-hsi reign [1178].⁴   (1)

---

³ Le-ch'ing was the name of the county where Yüan Ts'ai was magistrate when he wrote this book. It is located on the seacoast of Chekiang province.

⁴ Liu Chen was from an educated family in Le-ch'ing and received his *chin-shih* in 1158, five years before Yüan Ts'ai did.

In recent generations, old teachers and experienced scholars have often collected their sayings into "Recorded Quotations," to be passed on to their students.[1] Their goal has been to share with the world what wisdom they have acquired. But their points are involved and abstruse, beyond the reach of students, who do not become enlightened even if they diligently recite and ponder the text. Imagine how difficult these must be for ordinary or inferior people! Popular works such as short tales or anecdotes about poets, however valuable they may be in themselves, are of no use in moral instruction on social relations. There are also "Family Instructions" written to admonish sons and grandsons, but these are usually sketchy in coverage and limited in circulation.[2]

I, Ts'ai, am a simple rustic who enjoys commenting on social customs and affairs. By nature I am forgetful; sometimes other people can repeat what I have previously said while I myself have no recollection of it. Consequently, I

---

[1] Yüan Ts'ai is probably referring to the "Recorded Quotations" of Sung Neo-Confucians, such as Chang Tsai (1020–1077), Ch'eng I (1033–1107), and Hsieh Liang-tso (1050–1103).

[2] The most famous "Family Instructions," the *Yen-shih chia-hsün* (*YSCH*), was written in the sixth century. (See *Family Instructions for the Yen Clan*, trans. by Teng Ssu-yü.) This book is the exception to Yüan Ts'ai's generalization, being both broad in coverage and wide in circulation. But most "Family Instructions" whose names have been recorded seem to have been brief, and only a few from the T'ang and Sung dynasties have survived until today. A large selection from them was, however, published by a contemporary of Yüan Ts'ai, Liu Ch'ing-chih (1130–1195), in the *Chieh-tzu t'ung-lu* (*CTTL*).

have taken to writing down my comments, and these in time have become a book. Many people have borrowed it to make copies, but as I could not meet all of the demands, I have had wood blocks carved in order to publish it.

In antiquity when Tzu-ssu discoursed on the Way of *Centrality and Commonality*[3] he said that men and women of little intelligence could understand the elementary points, and ones of inferior character could practice them. But even the sages were not fully able to understand or practice the most elevated points in order to investigate Heaven and Earth.[4] Now, the investigations of Heaven and Earth found in our predecessors' "Recorded Quotations" go on for page after page. So I have instead strung together some essays on points that ordinary men and women can understand from their own observation. I have addressed them to the general public, making my points clear enough even for farmers, old villagers, and women who live in seclusion. People will differ on the parts they like best, considering one point right and the next wrong, but there will certainly be one or two items that will evoke a response in them so that they engage in fewer disputes and avoid legal trouble. Thus the popular ethos will return to a pure and cordial state. Should the Sage reappear, what I have done will not be rejected.[5]

At first I gave this book the title "Instructions for Improving the Popular Ethos." My colleague, Governor Liu, renamed it "Precepts for Social Life," which seems an

---

[3] Tzu-ssu was the grandson of Confucius and the reputed author of *Centrality and Commonality* (*Chung-yung*), one of the thirteen classics as established by Sung Neo-Confucians.

[4] *Chung-yung*, 12 (Legge, trans., *Classics* I, pp. 391–92). Yüan Ts'ai has condensed the passage somewhat.

[5] Yüan Ts'ai is echoing a passage in *Mencius*, 3B:9, in which, in reference to his defense of Confucius' teachings, Mencius says, "When the sages rise up again, they will not change my words." (Lau, trans., p. 115.)

exaggeration. Three times I asked him to change it, but he would not consent, leaving me no choice but to accept what he said.

> Written on the fifteenth day of the *ssu-hai* year of the Ch'un-hsi period [1179], by Yüan Ts'ai of Wu-p'o in San-ch'ü, at the Le-ch'ing county courtroom.
> [Later Edition] Written on the day of the summer solstice of the first year of the Shao-hsi period [1190], by Yüan Ts'ai of Wu-p'o in San-ch'ü, at the courtroom of Hui-chou's Wu-yüan county.[6]

My classmate Mr. Cheng Ching-yüan[7] sent me a letter that said:

> Formerly Wen-kuo Kung had some ideas on the same subject you address, but he modestly called his book *Precepts for Family Life*; he did not use the term "social life."[8] If you wish rules for society in general, then there is the book of the Viscount of Chi.[9] Now I fear people might accuse the person who suggested the title of flattery and think you were presumptuous to accept it. It would be best for you to retain your old title.

Mr. Cheng's was an accurate analysis that cut me to my heart. Although I did not dare follow it, I inscribed it here to

[6] On the two editions, see Appendix A.

[7] Cheng Po-ying (styled Ching-yüan) and his brother Cheng Po-hsiung were among the leading scholars of Le-ch'ing.

[8] Wen-kuo Kung is Ssu-ma Kuang. The ideas in his *Chia fan* are discussed in Part One, chap. 2

[9] The Viscount of Chi was one of the leading officials of the last ruler of the Shang dynasty (ca. 1100 B.C.). He was traditionally believed to be the author of the "Great Plan" (*Hung-fan*) in the *Shang shu* (*Book of Documents*). This text bears little resemblance to Yüan Ts'ai's work, consisting in advice to the ruler on overall cosmology, moral cultivation, and political policies. See Legge, trans., *Classics* 3, pp. 320–44.

let the reader know that if it had not been for Prefect Liu's death I would have privately changed the title.

    Respectfully, Ts'ai[10]   (4)

---

[10] The order of the prefatory material given here is that of *YCL*. *CPTC* and *SK* have the author's preface at the end of the book as a postface; the author's note follows Liu's preface. *PCMS* has only Yüan Ts'ai's preface; *PYT* only has this preface as a postface; and *KCTS* has none of the prefaces.

CHAPTER I

Getting Along with Relatives

I.I PERSONALITY DIFFERENCES[1]

The personal relations between fathers and sons and between older and younger brothers are the closest there are, and yet sometimes they are not harmonious. With fathers and sons, discord often is due to the father's high demands.[2] With brothers it is often the result of disputes over property. In cases where neither of these is involved, outsiders who observe the disharmony may be able to see who is right and who is wrong on particular issues but still be puzzled about why the parties are at odds.

I think such inexplicable disagreements are the result of personality differences. Some people are relaxed, others tense; some are tough, others timid; some are serious, others lighthearted; some are disciplined, others indulgent; some

---

[1] In the *CPTC* edition (but not the 1179 editions), each item is preceded by a title. The titles are generally brief sentences that convey the overall message in the item. It is probable that the 1179 edition did not have titles but that Yüan Ts'ai added them when reprinting the book in 1190. Here, mostly for the sake of English style, titles have been retained but reduced to noun phrases giving the topic rather than sentences giving the message.

[2] Mencius also spoke of the problems caused by fathers' putting too high demands on their sons. See *Mencius* 4A:15 (Lau, trans., p. 125): "Between fathers and sons there should not be demands for goodness (*tse-shan*). If there are, alienation will result, and of inauspicious circumstances, none is worse than alienation." See also *Mencius* 4B:30 (Lau, trans., p. 135).

like calm, others prefer excitement; some have narrow vision; others are farsighted. Given such differences in personality, fathers may try to insist that their sons' personalities conform to their own, but this cannot always be. Older brothers may insist that their younger brothers' personalities accord with theirs, but likewise this is not always possible. If their personalities cannot be made to conform, neither can their speech and conduct. This reality is the fundamental cause of disharmony between fathers and sons or between brothers.

The worst cases are when some action needs to be taken, for all the personality differences then come into play. One will consider right what the other considers wrong; one will say to do first what the other says to do last; one will think speed essential while the other says to take time. Given such differences, if everyone expects to get his own way, disputes will certainly result. If the disputes are not settled, they will be repeated two or three, even ten or more times. Feelings of discord start in this way, and sometimes people end up disliking each other for the rest of their lives.

If people could awaken to the way this works, and older family members could understand the feelings of their juniors and not demand that they be the same as them, and juniors could look up to their seniors but not expect them to accept all their advice, then whenever action needs to be taken everyone would cooperate and obstinate disputes could be avoided. Confucius said, "In serving his father and mother, a son offers advice. If he sees that his opinion is not followed, he is even more respectful and does not oppose them. He may feel discouraged but not resentful." [3] Such was the main method for achieving familial harmony taught by the Sage. It is worth pondering carefully.   (3, 4, 5, 6)

[3] *Analects* 4:18 (Waley, trans., p. 105).

I.2   THE VALUE OF REFLECTION

When a father or a son, rather than concentrate on fulfilling his own duties, prefers to criticize the other, discord is especially likely to arise gradually between them. If each were capable of reflection, such a situation could be avoided.

A father should say, "Today I am someone's father, but in the past I was someone's son. If the way I served my parents was perfect in all respects, then my sons would have seen it and heard it and would imitate my ways without waiting to be told. If the way I served my parents had some flaws, how can I, with a clear conscience, blame my son for the same sorts of things?"

A son should say, "Now I am someone's son, but one day I will probably be someone's father. The way my father now rears and supports me deserves to be called generous. If I treat my son exactly the way my father treats me, then I will be able to hold up my head without shame. If I don't meet his standards, not only will I be failing my son, but how will I be able to face my father?"

Those in our society who are good at being sons generally prove to be good fathers, and those who were not able to be filial to their parents tend to be cruel to their sons. There is no reason for this other than that the wise are capable of reflection, and so avoid doing wrong in all situations, while the unwise, being incapable of reflection, often are resentful as sons and violent as fathers.[4] It seems then that this discussion of reflection will be understood only by the wise.   (4)

I.3   PARENTAL KINDNESS AND FILIAL OBEDIENCE

Kindly fathers often have sons who ruin the family. Filial sons are sometimes given little attention by their fathers. The

---

[4] Reflection (*tzu-fan*) is also advocated by *Mencius* 4B:28 as a way of finding the fault in oneself instead of in others (Lau, trans., p. 133–34).

reason is that the average person will tend to retreat when he runs into strength but become reckless when he encounters weakness. If the father is stern the son is intimidated and does not dare to do wrong; if the father is lenient, then the son indulges himself and is impulsive in his conduct. The father often forgives the son who is unworthy but berates continually the one who is simple and honest.[5] Only wise and worthy men are free from this failing.

The principle that when one party is strong the other will be weak also accounts for the cases where the elder brother is friendly but the younger one is disrespectful; or where the younger brother is respectful but the older one is unfriendly; or where the husband is proper in his behavior but his wife is disagreeable; or where the wife is acquiescent but her husband does not treat her properly.

If fathers would compare their own sons to the unworthy sons other people have, and if sons would compare their own fathers to the foolish fathers other people have, they would be able to appreciate their own. Sons then would respond to kindly fathers by being even more filial and fathers would respond to filial sons by being even more kindly, and there would be no fear of either party overwhelming the other.

Similarly, if brothers put each other's shortcomings in comparative perspective and husbands and wives did so also, their relations would never be marred by lack of friendliness and deference between brothers or proper and agreeable behavior between husbands and wives.[6]   (4, 4)

[5] On the meaning of the term "unworthy sons," see Part One, chap. 4, "Father–Son Tensions."
[6] This passage and the two preceding ones can be viewed as a response to *YSCH* 5, "Family Management," which says, "When a father is kind but the son is refractory, when an elder brother is friendly but the younger brother is arrogant, when a husband is just but a wife is cruel, then indeed they are the bad people of the world; they must be controlled by punishments; teaching and guidance will not change them. If ferule and wrath are

Getting Along with Relatives

1.4 TOLERANCE

It has always been the case that the good and the bad come mixed in human relations. Some fathers and sons are not both good; some older and younger brothers are not both superior people; sometimes a husband is dissolute or a wife violent. Rare is the family free from this problem. Even the sages and great men of the past had little they could do in such cases.[7]

This problem can be compared with an ulcer or a tumor. Despite all its evil it cannot be excised from the body; the most you can do is take it easy and live with it. By comprehending how this works, you achieve peace of mind. This is what the men of antiquity meant when they said that it is so difficult to comment on the relations between parents and children, siblings, or husbands and wives.[8]   (5, 6)

1.5 SUBMISSION

The relationship of a son to his father or a younger brother to his elder brother is like that of a soldier to his officer, a clerk to the official above him, or a bondservant to his master: that is, they may not consider themselves peers who may dispute points whenever they please. If a senior's words or actions are unmistakably remiss, all that the junior may do is voice some suggestions in a tactful way. If the senior compounds his mistakes by offering twisted excuses, the junior should listen even more submissively and not argue with him. Elders ought to reflect on this matter.   (3)

---

not used in family discipline, the evil practices of mean-spirited sons will immediately appear" (from Teng Ssu-yü, trans., *Family Instructions for the Yen Clan*, p. 16).

[7] The ancient "sage rulers" Yao and Shun had "unworthy sons" and so did not leave the empire to them. Shun had parents who were nearly impossible to please. *Mencius* 5A:2, 6 (Lau, trans., pp. 129–40, 144–45).

[8] An allusion to *Han shu* 66, p. 2884.

Part Two

1.6 FORBEARANCE

People say that lasting harmony in families begins with the ability to forbear.[9] But knowing how to forbear without knowing how to live with forbearing can lead to a great many errors. Some seem to think that forbearance means to repress anger; that is, when someone offends you, you repress your feelings and do not reveal them. If this happens only once or twice it would be all right. But if it happens repeatedly the anger will come bursting forth like an irrepressible flood.

A better method is to dissipate anger as the occasion arises instead of hiding it in your chest. Do this by saying to yourself, "He wasn't thinking," "He doesn't know any better," "He made a mistake," "He is narrow in his outlook," "How much harm can this really do?" If you keep the anger from entering your heart, then even if someone offends you ten times a day, neither your speech nor your behavior will be affected. You will then see the magnitude of the benefits of forbearance. Those referred to as excelling at forbearance act this way.   (4, 5, 6)

1.7 DISLIKE AMONG RELATIVES

Dislike among blood relatives may start from a very minor incident but end up ingrained. It is just that once two people take a dislike to each other they become irascible, and neither is willing to be the first to cool off. When they are in each other's company day in and day out, they cannot help but irritate each other. If, having reached this state, one of them would be willing to take the initiative in cooling off and would talk to the other, then the other would reciprocate,

---

[9] See the anecdote about Chang Kung-i cited in Part One, chap. 3, "Social Ethics."

and the situation would return to normal. This point is
worth deep consideration.   (4, 6)

1.8   SERVING THE HEAD OF THE HOUSEHOLD

In a family that is flourishing, all the members, young and
old, cooperate harmoniously, probably because there is
nothing to fight over when everyone can have what he or she
wants. But in a family in economic straits, the family head
often berates and reviles his wife and children, whether or
not they have done anything wrong. Unable to provide food
and clothing and beset with worries, the man has no place to
vent his accumulated frustrations except on his wife and
children. If they would just recognize this fact, they would
see that he needs to be served with particular attention.

                                                             (3, 4)

1.9   OLD PEOPLE'S FANCIES

People advanced in years sometimes resemble children in
their behavior. They like to make small monetary profits;
they take delight in little gifts of drinks or fruit; they enjoy
playing games with children. If their sons could understand
this and indulge them, then they would be perfectly happy.

                                                          (3, 4, 5)

1.10   SINCERITY IN FILIAL CONDUCT

True filial conduct is rooted in sincerity. Even if little details
are omitted and nothing elaborate is ever done, such filial
conduct is enough to move Heaven and Earth and evoke a
response from the ghosts and gods.

I have seen contemporaries who did not make any sincere
efforts to serve their parents yet tried to feign respect through

use of their voice, smile, and manner. These people should consider themselves lucky if they avoid being condemned to death by Heaven and Earth and the spirits. They have no hope that their posterity will be sincerely filial or that their house will flourish.[10]

Once you become aware of this truth, then in relations with people you will be sincere. Any superior man of discernment who compares the long term results of sincerity and insincerity will find ample proof for my point.   (4, 4)

1.11   FILIAL SENTIMENTS

Babies are closely attached to their parents, and parents are extremely generous with their love for their babies, doing everything possible to care for them. The reason would seem to be that not long has passed since they were one flesh and blood, and besides, a baby's sounds, smiles, and gestures are such that they bring out the love in people. Furthermore, the Creator has made such attachment a principle of nature, to ensure that the succession of births will continue uninterrupted.[11] Even the most insignificant insect, bird, or animal behaves this way. When the young first emerges from the womb or shell, these creatures suckle it or feed it pre-chewed food, going to all lengths to care for it. If something threatens their young, they protect it, heedless of their own safety.

[10] On the concept of retribution implied here, see also 2.15 and 2.19.

[11] The Creator (*tsao-wu-che*) is a term for a supervising deity that was used by Chuang Tzu and taken up again by Sung literati. See also 2.6, 2.7, and 2.52. Concerning Su Shih's use of the term, Burton Watson has written: "[He] repeatedly refers to a supernatural force which he calls 'The Creator' . . . and which he often describes in terms of a child. It is a force which moves throughout the natural world, childlike in its lack of thought or plan, yet capable of influencing the destinies of all beings in the universe. And when man learns to be equally free of willfulness and to join in the Creator's game, then everything in the natural world will become his toy" (*Su Tung-p'o*, p. 22).

When human beings are full grown, distinctions in status become stricter and distance becomes established; parents then are expected to express fully their kindness and children to express fully their filial duty. By contrast, when insects, birds, and animals mature a little, they no longer recognize their mothers nor their mothers them. This difference separates human beings from other creatures.

It is impossible to recount fully how parents care for their children in their earliest years. Thus the children will never be able to repay them for the care they received, even if they are solicitous of their parents their whole lives, entirely fulfilling their filial duties. How much more true is this for those whose filial conduct has been imperfect!

I would ask those who are not able to fulfill their filial duties to observe how people care for infants, how much they love them. This ought to bring them to their senses. The life-giving and life-nurturing principles of Heaven and Earth reach their fullest manifestation in man. But how do men repay Heaven and Earth? Some burn incense and kneel in prayer before the "void" (*hsü-k'ung*). Some summon Taoist priests to offer sacrifices to God (*Shang-ti*). In this way they think they are repaying Heaven and Earth.[12] In fact, they are only repaying one part in ten thousand of what they owe! And this is even more true of those who resent and blame Heaven and Earth! Such errors come from not reflecting.

(4)

I.12   PARENTAL BLINDNESS

Very often parents, during their son's infancy and childhood, love him so much they forget his faults; they give in to his every demand and tolerate his every action. If he cries for no

[12] For popular religious practices in this period, see Jacques Gernet, *Daily Life in China on the Eve of the Mongol Invasion*, pp. 197–215.

reason, they do not have the sense to make him stop, but blame his nanny. If he bullies his playmates, his parents do not have the sense to correct him, but instead blame the other children. If someone tries to tell them that their child was the one in the wrong, they reply that he is too young to be blamed. As the days and months go by, they nurture his depravity. All this is the fault of the parents' misguided love.[13]

As the boy grows older, the parents' love gradually lessens. They get angry at the slightest misdeed, treating it as a major crime. When they meet relatives and old friends, they relate every incident of misbehavior with great embellishments, guaranteeing that the boy gets labeled very unfilial, a label he does not deserve. All this is the fault of the parents' irrational disapproval.

The mother is usually the source of such unreasonable likes and dislikes. When the father fails to recognize this and listens to what she says, the situation can become irretrievable. Fathers must examine this situation with care. They must be strict with their sons when they are young and must not let their love grow thin as the sons reach maturity.   (4, 4)

I.13   OCCUPATIONS FOR SONS AND YOUNGER BROTHERS

People who have sons must see to it that they get occupations. An occupation will keep those in modest circumstances from destitution and those with wealth and official rank from getting into trouble.[14]

As a general rule, the younger members of rich and honored families indulge in wine and women and are addicted

[13] Much the same idea was expressed in *YSCH* 1, pp. 3–4 (Teng trans., p. 3) and *SMSSI* 4, p. 45.
[14] Cf. 2.58 on the trouble that young men from high-ranking families get into.

to gambling, fancy clothes, and splendid carriages. Spending their time with lackeys, they ruin their families. It is not that at heart they are unworthy, but that the urge to do mischief arises when they have no occupation to fill up their days. Riffraff encourage them in their wrongdoing whenever they see a chance to gain some food or drink or money for themselves.[15] It is acutely necessary for young people to give thought to this. (1, 3, 4)

1.14 EDUCATING YOUNG FAMILY MEMBERS

When rich and high-ranking families teach their boys to read, they certainly hope that they will pass the civil service examinations and also absorb the essence of the words and actions of the sages.[16] But you cannot demand that your children all succeed, since people differ in their destinies and their intellectual capacities. Above all, you should not make them give up their education because they are not succeeding in the goal of entering civil service.[17]

When young people are well-read, they gain what is called the "usefulness of the useless."[18] Histories record stories. Literary collections contain elegant poems and essays. Even books on Yin-Yang, divination, magic, and fiction contain delightful tales. But there are so many books that no one can exhaust them in a few years. If young people spend their mornings and evenings amid such books they will certainly profit from them, and they will not have time for other affairs. Moreover, they will make friends with professional

[15] Cf. 1.39 on dealings with riffraff.

[16] On education in the Sung, see Thomas H. C. Lee, "Life in the Schools of Sung China."

[17] Notice how much more mild Yüan Ts'ai was in chiding a career orientation in education than were the Ch'eng brothers and Chu Hsi. See Part One, chap. 2, pp. 45–46.

[18] Allusion to *Chuang Tzu* 26 (Watson, trans., p. 299).

scholars and carry on discussions with them when they visit one another. Then how could they spend whole days like those who get enough to eat but apply their minds to nothing and get into trouble with riffraff? (4)

1.15 STARTING EDUCATION EARLY

When people have several sons, the care they give them in food, drink, and clothing must be equal. At the same time they must teach them to be scrupulous in observing distinctions based on age and rank and must teach them to distinguish wisdom from folly and truth from falsehood. If sons are shown equality when young, when grown they will not get into disputes about property.[19] If they are taught the niceties, when grown they will not cause trouble through willful and arrogant behavior. If they are taught to make value judgments, when grown they will not do wrong.

Nowadays, people treat their sons in the contrary fashion. They are generous to those they like and stingy with those they dislike. But if in the beginning sons are not treated equally, how can the parents prevent them from later getting into disputes? Parents also let their sons insult their seniors and bully their juniors. But if such behavior is not corrected by reproof and punishment at the start, how can the parents prevent them from later becoming defiant? Parents also sometimes hate their good sons and love their unworthy ones. But if treatment starts unfairly, how can the parents prevent them from one day becoming bad? (4)

1.16 EQUAL TREATMENT FOR EACH SON

Discord between brothers, so great that it ends in ruining the family, often is caused by parental partiality. In clothing,

[19] On such disputes, see 1.22, 1.27, and 1.62.

food and drink, in word and action, the parents favor the one they love and slight the one they don't. The beloved one becomes more outlandish in his desires and behavior day-by-day, and the neglected one is resentful. With time these feelings build up into deep hostility between the sons. This is what is meant by the phrase, "To love him is precisely to hurt him."[20]

If parents love their boys equally, the boys will naturally get along, and both will do well. Wouldn't this be best?

(4, 4)

1.17 PARENTS' WORRIES

When parents see that one of their sons is in financial need, they worry about him.[21] Out of sympathy they favor him in distributing food and clothing. The well-off sons occasionally send things to the parents, which they pass on to the poor sons. The reason for this state of affairs is the parents' feeling that sons should be equal. But sometimes a well-off son resents his parents' actions. Apparently he has not considered that if he were the one in need, his parents would be doing the same for him. (3, 4, 4, 5, 6)

1.18 CHERISHING SONS AND GRANDSONS

Even if your sons and grandsons act against your wishes, you should not take a deep dislike to them. In all probability, the son or grandson you love best will turn out to be unfilial or die young. The one you dislike may easily be the one to care

---

[20] Lu Chiu-shao used almost the same expression in his discussion of parents' failure to bring up their sons properly (*SYHA* 57, p. 117).

[21] The difference in the sons' situations could be due to their private assets (discussed in 1.24, 1.26, and 3.56). It could also be a consequence of division before the death of the parents (on which see 1.62).

for you in old age and provide for your burial and sacrifices. This generalization also applies to other blood relatives. I suggest you take heed from other people's experience.

(3, 4)

1.19 SPOILING THE YOUNGEST CHILD

Among boys of the same mother, the oldest is often despised by his parents while the youngest is doted on. I once gave this perplexing phenomenon careful thought and now think I know the explanation. In the first and second year of life, a baby's every action, smile, and word makes us love him. Even strangers love little babies, so need I speak of their parents! From his third and fourth to his fifth and sixth years, the child becomes willful, screams and yells, and is generally contrary. He breaks things and is foolhardy. Everything he says or does elicits disapproval. Moreover, he is often obstinate and intractable. Therefore even his parents detest him.

Just when the older boy is at the most insufferable stage, his younger brother will be at the most adorable. The parents then transfer their love from the older to the younger boy, whom they love all the more. From then on the parents' affections follow separate courses. When the youngest son reaches the detestable stage, there is no one who is lovable,[22] so the parents have no one to transfer their love to and continue to dote on him. This is how the development seems to proceed.

Sons should recognize where their parents' love lies. Older ones ought to yield a little and younger ones ought to practice self-restraint. In addition parents must wake up to what they are doing and try to compensate a little. They should not do whatever they like or they will make the older

[22] This follows the reading in the 1179 editions. The *CPTC* edition has "when the last son passes the adorable stage he is still not without faults."

ones resentful and the younger ones spoiled, leading to the ruin of the patrimony. (4)

1.20   SPOILING THE FIRST GRANDSON

Whereas parents often dislike their oldest son, the grandparents often dote on him excessively. This situation is also perplexing. Could it be that the grandparents transfer their love for their youngest son to him? (4)

1.21   OBEYING PARENTS AND PARENTS-IN-LAW

Even though sons are basically similar in character, a father who remarries will find dissatisfaction primarily with the sons of his first wife.[23] Even if the father has not remarried, if he favors a serving girl it will have the same effect.[24] The father's bias is certainly the result of his intimate relations. For his part, the son ought to obey his father singlemindedly; in time the workings of Heaven will reestablish harmony.

Even though sons' wives are largely alike in nature, parents particularly dislike them when their own unmarried daughters also live at home. This is undoubtedly caused by the parents' favoritism. For her part, a wife should obey her husband's parents singlemindedly; after her respect has been manifested for a long time, her husband's parents will come to realize their mistake.

What if the son's father or the bride's in-laws to the end do

[23] Children with stepmothers are of course nearly universally pitied. The *CMC* cites the case of a man who tried to disinherit the sons of his first wife and leave his property to his second wife's son by her former husband. The stepmother hated the former wife's children and always slandered them (*CMC*, pp. 211–18). Ssu-ma Kuang relates the case of a stepmother who sold her husband's seven-*sui* daughter as a bondmaid, claiming she had lost her (*SMCC*, 72, p. 883).

[24] On treating female bondservants as concubines, see 3.21–3.26.

not see the truth? Then there is nothing a son or a wife can do except be more respectful; they simply must put up with it.

(4, 4, 4)

I.22   COMPLEX FAMILIES

Discord among brothers, sons, and nephews who live together need not start with major disagreements. The cause could be one person among them who does not set his mind on the common interest. He takes a little extra for himself; no matter how little it is, still it is taking from the others. Or, when there is something to divide among everyone, he tries to get the largest share; the others become resentful of this and so quarrels start, bringing financial ruin to the family estate. Thus a desire for small gains brings about a major disaster.

When people recognize this truth they all keep the common interest at heart. When individual funds are to be used, all use their individual funds; when common funds are to be used, all use the common funds.[25] When there is something to be distributed to everyone, it is divided evenly, even if it is fruit or candy, worth only a few dozen coins. Then what cause is there for quarrels?   (4, 4)

I.23   HARMONY BETWEEN SENIORS AND JUNIORS

When brothers, sons, and nephews live together, the elders sometimes use their seniority to maltreat the young. They arrogate control of the assets, using them for their private purposes to keep themselves warm and well fed. They do not allow the younger ones any knowledge of the receipts for

[25] On the distinction between common and individual funds, see Part One, chap. 5, "Family Property."

income and outlay. Sometimes the younger ones reach the point where they cannot avoid hunger and cold, which inevitably gives rise to disputes.[26]

On the other hand, sometimes the seniors manage the affairs with utmost fairness, but the younger ones do not accept their leadership. They steal from the family's assets to finance their own unworthy activities and are especially hard to get along with.

If only the elders could take charge of the major policy decisions and let the younger ones share in management of the details, then the elders would certainly consult with the younger ones and the younger ones certainly would do as their elders tell them. Each would devote himself to the common good, and lack of contention would result naturally. (1, 4, 4, 5, 6)

1.24 UNEQUAL WEALTH AMONG BROTHERS

Wealth and liberality will not be uniform among brothers, sons, and nephews.[27] The rich ones, only pursuing what's good for them, easily become proud. The poor ones, failing to strive for self-improvement, easily become envious. Discord then arises.

If the richer ones from time to time would make gifts of their surplus without worrying about gratitude, and if the poorer ones could recognize that their position is a matter of fate and not expect charity, then there would be nothing for them to quarrel about.[28] (3, 4, 4, 5)

---

[26] Yüan Ts'ai is referring to the conflicts between collateral relatives living together (elder and younger brothers or uncles and fatherless nephews), not lineal ones (father and son or grandfather and grandson).

[27] The phrase "brothers, sons, and nephews" is usually used here in the context of the complex family. If that is the case here the differences in their wealth would be due to individual funds. See 1.26.

[28] On Yüan Ts'ai's conception of fate, see 2.2, 2.4, 2.6, and 2.7.

1.25   EQUITY IN FAMILY DIVISION

The laws established by the government relating to division of family property are nothing if not complicated in regard to circumstances and exhaustive in detail. Nevertheless, some people in fact embezzle common family property to operate a private business; they may claim on the bill of sale or mortgage that the property was bought with their wives' assets or register it under a false name.[29] The courts find it difficult to get to the bottom of such cases.

Some people actually start from poverty and are able to establish themselves and set up prosperous businesses without making use of any inherited family resources. Others, although there was a common family estate,[30] did not make use of it, separately acquiring their individual wealth from their own efforts.[31] In either case, their patrilineal kinsmen will certainly try to get shares of what they have acquired. Lawsuits taken to the county and prefectural courts may drag on for decades until terminated by the bankruptcy of all parties concerned.

Richer relatives capable of reflection should think: "If I used common property to set up my private business and do

[29] On the complexities of land ownership, see Part One, chap. 6, "Wealth and Income." The term "mortgage" is used here for *tien*, partial or redeemable sale. Note here that Yüan Ts'ai is implying that "wife's assets" are not merged with family property.

[30] "Common family estate" (*tsu-chung ts'ai-ch'an*) means property to which several relatives (brothers, uncles, and nephews) have equal claim. It is family property that will eventually be divided. This concept is referred to as "common property" (*chung*) below.

[31] Yüan Ts'ai implies here that a man who had not yet divided his property from that of his brothers or nephews could claim exclusive rights to the earnings from businesses he established without use of capital from the common estate. This may have been a common sentiment (see below 3.56) but does not seem to have been recognized by statutory or case law. See Part One, chap. 5, "Family Property."

not share the proceeds with my poor relatives, how can I avoid a guilty conscience? Even if I built the business on my own, it would be an act of benevolence to share openly with my poor relatives and a deed of unobtrusive virtue to do it anonymously. Wouldn't this be better than lawsuits that drag on for years, distracting me from family duties and incurring wasteful travel expenses, gifts to court clerks to bid for their help, and bribes to officials?"[32]

The poorer relatives also ought to think to themselves: "Even if he really embezzled common property, he prospered because of his own hard work and management. How can all his profits be distributed? And what if it really was his own property? For me to try to get it then certainly would be shameful."

If only people would recognize these truths, then even if the shares they receive are slight, at least they wouldn't waste anything on lawsuits.   (1, 2, 4, 4, 5, 6,)

1.26   INDIVIDUAL ASSETS IN COMPLEX FAMILIES

When brothers, sons, and nephews live together, it sometimes happens that one of them has his own personal fortune. Worried about problems arising when the family divides the common property, he may convert his fortune to gold and silver and conceal it. This is perfectly foolish. For instance, if he had 100,000 strings worth of gold and silver and used this money to buy productive property, in a year he would gain 10,000 strings; after ten years or so, he would have regained the 100,000 strings and what would be divided among the family would be interest. Moreover, the 100,000 strings could continue to earn interest. If it were invested in a

---

[32] *PYT* adds "expensive witnesses" after "wasteful travel expenses."

pawnbroking business, in three years the interest would equal the capital. He would still have the 100,000 strings and the rest, being interest, could be divided. Moreover, it could be doubled again in another three years, ad infinitum.[33] What reason could there be to store it in boxes rather than use it to earn interest for the profit of the whole family? I have seen contemporaries who lend their individual funds to their relatives to use in family businesses and later take back only the capital lent.[34] These families become wealthy on an equal basis, and the brothers, sons, and nephews stay together generation after generation. Such is the reward gained for having thought through how to get along well with others.

Sometimes a person embezzles common funds and deposits them with his wife's family or other families related through marriage. The money ends up being used by those people, and the embezzler does not dare ask for it back. Even if he does, he is not likely to get it. Another person will buy land in the name of his wife's family or other families related through marriage and all too often end up losing it. Yet another will place land in his wife's name. Frequently what happens then is that, after he dies, his wife remarries and takes the property with her.[35] Superior men should give careful thought to these problems and keep them in mind.

(2, 4, 4, 5)

---

[33] In 3.47 and 3.65 Yüan Ts'ai discusses in more detail the ways of investing money and gives further information on the rates of return from various businesses. There, however, his tone is more cautious. He argues against charging excessive interest on loans, warns against the possible problems that could arise in entrusting money to others to manage, and so on.

[34] "Whole family" and "relatives" both are referred to as *chung*, the group who share a common estate.

[35] On widows remarrying, see also 1.48, 1.50, and 1.51.

I.27 DIVIDING ESTATES

When brothers live together and A is rich, he always worries about being bothered by B. But within a decade or two, A may go bankrupt and B may grow rich and honored. Or A may die, leaving sons unable to stand on their own. Occasionally it happens that B ends up being bothered by A.

When brothers divide property, their ploys often turn against them. The first example is of the person who expects his coparcener[36] to mortgage his land and has hopes of redeeming it. He divides every plot and section of the fields evenly, perhaps giving his coparcener each side and keeping the middle for himself. But often he has to sell his own fields before his coparcener needs to sell anything. In fact, there are many cases where the coparcener turns the tables on him and uses his rights as a neighbor to redeem his land.[37] The second example concerns cousins whose fathers have died. When they divide their common property, if they do it "equally," only those with no brothers will be well-to-do and those who have several brothers will gradually decline after the division; thus those with many brothers don't want the division to be on an "equal" basis.[38] But it may turn out that the ones with brothers prosper more than the one with a full share. The third example concerns the man who insists on a division of property because his brothers all have many more dependents than he does. Yet after the division, he gradually declines and doesn't do as well as his more encumbered

[36] Coparcener (*ying-fen-jen*) is a technical legal term for the men who stood to gain shares of the common property (or group-share property, *chung-fen ch'an*) during the next division.

[37] On the rights of neighbors and relatives to have first option on buying land, see Part One, chap. 6, n. 3.

[38] By "equal" Yüan Ts'ai means *per stirpes*. See Part One, chap. 5, "Division of Property Among Heirs."

brothers, who prosper as before. The fourth example is the person who goes to court to seek a second division of the property because he thinks the first was unfair. Yet after this division, he goes bankrupt and in the end is not as well-off as those he took to court, who prosper as before.

If only people today would recognize that clever strategies cannot overcome the workings of Heaven, the impulse to go to court would be checked.[39]   (4, 4)

1.28   MUTUAL AFFECTION AMONG BROTHERS

One of the most beautiful things in the world is adult brothers living together after their father's death.[40] But if one of them dies young, his brothers will have less affection for his sons than they had for him and neither the orphans nor their uncles can be counted on to be fairminded. There are uncles who cheat their nephews and nephews who are rude to their uncles. I have seen ones who fight with each other with more bitterness than strangers ever could. What in days past had been beautiful becomes very ugly.

Therefore when brothers ought to divide, get it settled quickly. If they love each other, separate funds will not do damage to their filial piety or morality. Their performance of filial and moral obligations will suffer much more if they start quarreling.   (4, 4, 5, 6)

1.29   SHARED COURTYARDS

When brothers, sons, and nephews share a compound but have separate households, each one should give full attention

[39] The philosophy expressed here, that good and bad circumstances will tend to balance themselves out over a lifetime, is stated more directly in 2.6 and 2.7.

[40] Literally: living together out of righteousness, which means beyond their father's deaths and after all of them are full grown.

to common concerns. Each must prevent his youngsters and servants from bothering the others. Even very minor things, when repeated, can cause irritations. When one person is diligent in seeing to the sweeping and cleaning of the common courtyards and halls but another pays no attention to it at all, the diligent one will be resentful. It is even worse when the noncontributing one lets his small children and servants regularly mess the place up and won't let anyone else stop them. Angry rebukes and ill will easily develop this way.

(4, 4, 5, 6)

1.30   REMAINING UNRUFFLED

A household may include a scoundrel who maliciously makes trouble for everyone else. You should try to reason with him if his misbehavior only happens occasionally. When he doesn't even do one thing right in one hundred, and you have to confront him day in and day out, it can be extremely provoking. Similar situations can exist with neighbors and co-workers.[41] In such cases, you should try to be philosophical and deal with the scoundrel as a fact of life beyond your control.

(4, 4)

1.31   AFFECTION FOR YOUNGER BROTHERS AND NEPHEWS

The older and younger brothers of your father are called "senior father" and "junior father." Their wives are called "senior mother" and "junior mother." Mourning obligations to them are one degree less than for mothers and fathers.[42] The meaning behind these customs is that the care

---

[41] Cf. 2.26–2.28 on dealing with unworthy people.

[42] Ssu-ma Kuang gives mourning for father as grade 1, mother as grade 2a, and paternal uncle and paternal uncle's wife as 2c (*SMSSI*, 6, pp. 69–70). *Yüan tien chang* 30 is closer to what Yüan Ts'ai says, giving

and guidance they provide nephews are essentially parental, not far from that of true parents. Likewise, brothers' sons are called "equivalent sons," which means that their obedience and service are filial, not far from that of true sons. Therefore, orphans never end up without means of support if they have paternal uncles and aunts, and old people without heirs never end up with no place to go if they have fraternal nephews. This is the basic idea behind the rituals set by the sages and the laws established by the rulers.

People today sometimes act contrary to these principles. They love their own sons and neglect their brothers' sons. They take advantage of the fact that their nephews have no parents to seize their assets, thinking up ploy after ploy to do them harm. Such people can then hardly expect filial obedience from their nephews, and the nephews naturally look on them as enemies.   (4)

1.32   SETTING A GOOD EXAMPLE

A man with several sons may love each and every one of them yet treat his own brothers like enemies. Frequently the sons, adopting their father's attitudes, are rude to their paternal uncles. Such men fail to recognize that their brothers are their father's sons and their sons will someday be a group of grown brothers. If you do not get along with your brothers, then your sons will observe and imitate you, assuring that they become perverse and wicked. Sons who are impolite to their uncles will gradually come to be unfilial to their fathers.

Consequently, if you wish your sons to get along, you must set an example for them by your behavior toward your

---

both father and mother as grade 1. These grades not only served the practical purpose of specifying the length and severity of mourning for each relative but also, since early times, had come to be used as a shorthand code to indicate comparative closeness in kinship relations.

brothers. If you wish your sons to be filial, you must first teach them to serve their uncles properly.   (4, 4, 5, 6)

1.33   TATTLETALES

In most families there are younger members or women who are fond of passing gossip. Even a household composed of sages could not avoid disputes in such circumstances. After all, no one can be perfect in everything he does, nor can his every action meet general approval. If backbiting is something you would rather avoid, do not pass on stories; the others then will know nothing of them. If starting arguments is what you prefer, all you need to do is tell others the stories you've heard; before long resentment and hatred will be built up. And if in passing gossip between two parties you embellish the stories in the process, the ill will between the two parties can reach a point beyond hope of reconciliation.

Only people of great perception are able to close their ears to gossip, rendering the tattletales powerless to create friction between them and their relatives.   (2, 4, 4, 5, 6)

1.34   OVERHEARING CRITICISMS

When living in a complex family, you should let the others know when you are coming or going by calling or by shuffling your sandals. Arriving silently is unacceptable because, should the others be discussing you, all concerned will be embarrassed and at a loss for what to do. It is even worse when there is an unenlightened person in the family who loves to hide in dark places and eavesdrop on people. His reports start incidents and cause quarrels, making it impossible to live with such a person for long.

Do not assume that homes are secluded and vacant. If you are quick to find fault with others, you must always worry about whether they can hear you. There is a popular saying, "The walls have ears." It is also said, "By day speak not of men, by night speak not of ghosts." (1, 2, 4, 5, 6)

1.35 WOMEN'S OPINIONS

Many cases of family discord begin because a woman, by what she says, incites animosity between her husband and other family members of his generation. The reason for this is that a woman has limited experience and lacks a sense of the common interest or of fairness. Moreover, when she addresses members of the household as "father-in-law," "mother-in-law," "elder brother," "younger brother," "elder brother's wife," "younger brother's wife," she is using arbitrarily fixed terms, not ones derived from natural relations. Therefore she can lightly forget favors and easily nurture resentment. Her husband, unless he is farsighted, will be unintentionally affected by her, with the result that unpleasant incidents will occur in the family.[43]

I cannot relate all the kinds of situations that occur. Some brothers, sons, and nephew will have nothing to do with each other the rest of their lives even though they live in adjoining rooms. Some brothers will refuse to adopt a nephew as an heir when they have no sons of their own. Others who have several sons will not give one to a brother to adopt as an heir. There are brothers who will insist that all of them share equally in supporting their parents, even though one is poor, preferring to see the parents neglected than do anything extra.[44] Some brothers would rather see

[43] Compare the comments of Liu K'ai quoted in Part One, chap. 4, pp. 85-86.
[44] Yüan Ts'ai seems to be referring here to cases where full division of the property took place before the death of the parents. On such division see 1.62.

their parents left unburied than make an exception to the principle of all contributing equally, out of sympathy for one brother's poverty.[45]

I once knew a farsighted man who understood that women cannot be changed by lecturing to them. So outside the home he maintained his love and affection for his brothers. He privately aided them when they were in distress and supplied them when they were in need, never letting the women know anything of his acts. His poorer brothers loathed his women but loved him all the more. When it was time to divide the estate, they did not use their financial need as an excuse to covet his property. I think the reason is that men of this high-minded and farsighted sort, by ignoring their women and being generous to their brothers in advance, secure their affection. (1, 2, 4, 4, 4, 5, 6)

1.36   SERVANTS' TALK

The ease with which women gossip is often made worse by contention among the maids.[46] Maids are ignorant and lowly and almost totally without insight. They think that reporting other people's faults displays loyalty to their mistress. A perceptive woman will listen to absolutely nothing they say so that they will not dare bring slander to her anymore. If she listens to them and believes them, and

---

[45] A case of this sort is found in *ICC chia* 7, p. 58. A man blamed his failure to bury his parents on his brothers' unwillingness to cooperate fully.

[46] The term translated here as women means literally "wives and daughters" (*fu-nü*), that is, the women who are full family members, not the lower ranking household members. The term translated here as maids means literally "maids and concubines" (*pi-ch'ieh*), a term Yüan Ts'ai uses regularly for female household members of menial social status. Since in this context he is commenting on their subservience to the mistress, not the master, the term maids conveys his meaning accurately enough. Maids are discussed in much more detail in 3.19–3.45.

thereby grows fond of them, the maids will certainly tell stories time and again. Soon their mistress has made enemies with the other people, and the maids have fully attained their objectives.

Maids are not the only ones who act this way; male bondservants are often as bad. If the master believes what they tell him, collateral relatives, relatives through marriage, and old friends will develop ill will for each other, and the good servants and tenants will be unfairly punished.[47]

(1, 2, 4, 4, 4, 5, 6)

1.37   LOANS TO RELATIVES

The poorest among your agnatic relatives, relatives through marriage, and neighbors are likely to ask to borrow something as soon as they are short.[48] Even loans of rice, salt, wine, or vinegar of little monetary value become an annoyance when repeated day in and day out.

When borrowed clothes or tools are damaged or pawned, you as lender remember every detail and day after day wait to be compensated. Sometimes the borrower not only fails to make restitution, but he acts as though nothing ever happened; indeed he tells people, "I've never borrowed a speck from him." When such talk gets back to you, how can it help but arouse your indignation?   (2, 4, 4)

1.38   AIDING RELATIVES AND FRIENDS

Making loans to relatives and friends is not as good as providing outright gifts to the best of your ability. You will

---

[47] *PYT* adds one more sentence, "Men of discernment ought to think of further examples themselves and come to their senses."

[48] On making loans see also 3.67 and 3.68.

expect repayment of anything termed a loan and have no choice but to ask for it. When the requests are repeated, the debtor becomes indignant. In his anger he will say, "I want to repay, but he is wrong to keep demanding it, so I'll postpone it awhile." On the other hand, if you do not demand repayment, the borrower will say, "He doesn't humbly request the money, so why should I put myself to the trouble of repaying it?" Therefore, the loan will remain unpaid whether you demand payment or not, and the outcome will be hostility either way.

Most of the time when poor people borrow they never intend to repay.[49] Even if they have good intentions, what can they repay it with? In other cases people borrow to operate a business; but they often fail in their business because they are short of luck or business sense. When they take the loan, they are deferential and agreeable to you; they would willingly swear an oath on the sun attesting to their sincere gratitude. But when it comes time to repay, they resent not being able to take a knife to you.

Many are the friends and relatives who hold grudges over money. The popular saying is, "The unfilial resent their parents; the indebted resent those who made them loans."[50] It is so much better to show consideration for financial distress and give aid outright according to the extent of your resources. Then you will not worry about being repaid, and no one will resent you.   (1, 2, 4, 4)

1.39   KEEPING TRACK OF SONS AND GRANDSONS

Fathers and grandfathers, especially if they are high officials, are likely to be ignorant of their sons' and grandsons' faults.

[49] Cf. 3.67 and 3.68 on lending and borrowing.
[50] A rhyming, parallel couplet, typical of proverbs.

The reason is that the young men's misbehavior is easily concealed from the older men's eyes and ears. Outsiders know what is going on, but they do no more than laugh to themselves; they do not bring these matters to the attention of the father or grandfather.

When the high official is from a rural area, the local people who come to see him are effusive in praising his virtues and would not dream of mentioning the misdeeds of the official's heir. It is even worse when the official thinks his heir is virtuous and that other people must be slandering him. Therefore, the young man may fill the universe with his bad deeds without his father or grandfather knowing anything of it. In addition, sometimes there are families with reasonably strict family discipline in which the mothers may still cover up their sons' evils and keep the men from knowing of them.

When a young man in a rich family is unworthy, he will indulge in wine, women, and gambling, and hang around with riffraff, thus ruining the family but that's about all. It is much worse with the sons and grandsons of high officials. When such young men live in the countryside they do all sorts of mischief. They extort wine and food from people. They demand to borrow money, valuables, or goods, which they do not return. They force people to sell them things but do not pay up. They keep the company of riffraff, who they let make use of their connections to abuse others. They encroach on the property of honest people and then make false accusations against them, using high-flown language. When local villagers do something wrong to break the law, they take the blame, saying, "I am responsible." When a villager is involved in a court case, they fake notes from their father or grandfather to go and beg favorable treatment from the county and prefecture, trying to make wrong seem right. They order around workers and use the boats; they get tax exemptions and pardons for people. All these things they do to gain money to amuse themselves with wine and women.

When these young men accompany their seniors, they privately order merchants and government clerks to buy them goods and commission the government monopoly agents to make them purchases but in no cases pay the full value. When the clerks fill a post, are excused of a crime, or make a good profit, they always demand their cut. They set low prices when buying maids and concubines and make the agent pay the difference.[51] Sometimes they hang around with the servants in government offices. They interfere with the government monopoly affairs and get tax exemptions for others, as well as make other unreasonable demands.

These young men lack any consideration for their fathers and grandfathers when they are brought before the law and punished. Therefore, their elders ought to be aware of these doings and be on a constant watch for them. If the elders can keep making inquiries about their sons and grandsons, they may manage to avoid the worst. (1, 4)

1.40 JUNIOR FAMILY MEMBERS OF BAD CHARACTER

You should not let intellectually deficient or financially corrupt sons or younger brothers serve as officials. The ancients said that your descendants will prosper if you do many deeds of unostentatious merit while trying law cases.[52] This means that if you benefit people without their knowledge, you will enjoy blessings. Now, the intellectually deficient will cer-

---

[51] That is, they demand that their agent buy them a maid or concubine at a price so low that the agent has no choice but to add money himself in order to get one.

[52] An allusion to *Han shu*, 74, pp. 3142–50 (Watson, trans., pp. 186–90).

tainly entrust all of the lawcases to the clerks who will alter the facts to cover up for the wrong and trip up the right. This is exactly the opposite of acts of unostentatious merit.

The ancients also said, "What the Taoists avoid is conspiring."[53] This means that if you harm people without their knowledge, you will in time suffer disaster. Now, the financially corrupt will certainly conspire with underlings in the sale of official decisions. Thus wrong is made to seem right; people suffer injustice but have nowhere to bring their complaints. How can this be called anything but conspiracy?

Gentlemen and officials (*shih-ta-fu*) should try to count the number of their hometown's official families of thirty years ago who still survive today. They will find only a handful. The decline of the others was brought about precisely in the ways related above. The farsighted will certainly see the truth in what I say here.   (4)

1.41   FAMILY PROSPERITY

Fathers, brothers, and sons who live together will be a mixture of good and bad. If the ones who are quarrelsome, stingy, or wasteful of the family's estate die first, then the family's fortune will be difficult enough to determine. If the kindly, generous, diligent, and careful ones die first, then the family will be beyond salvage. This idea is also expressed in the proverb, "No one should say the family has not yet achieved eminence; the son to achieve it is not yet born. No one should say a family is not yet ruined; the son to ruin it is not yet grown."[54]   (4, 4)

---

[53] Slightly altered from *Shih chi*, 56, p. 2062. The point of this passage was that a military advisor, who had laid a lot of plots to harm people, would not have a good fate (Watson, trans., 1, p. 167).

[54] Each sentence is a rhymed couplet, typical of proverbs. The basic idea in this item is elaborated in 2.51–2.59.

1.42   AGES TO ADOPT SONS

Poor people who adopt should do it when the boys are young. The reason is that poor people have no land or houses to provide for their declining years and so must depend on their children for sustenance. They have no choice but to clothe, feed, and care for adopted sons from their infancy to create an emotional attachment between them.

Rich people who adopt should do it when the boys are grown. Present day rich people often conceal the fact of an adoption. Consequently they want to adopt the boy young, before he knows anything.[55] Sometimes they adopt the children of extremely lowly people, who when grown turn out to be unworthy. If out of fear that they will ruin the family, the parents then consider expelling them, it will give rise to lawsuits.

When adoption takes place after the adoptee has grown up, his qualities can be roughly judged. Those who are genial, honest, and possess self-control will surely be able to serve their adoptive parents as they served their natural ones. Moreover, they will neither bring about the ruin of the family nor be the cause of lawsuits.   (2, 4, 4)

1.43   GIVING UP SONS FOR ADOPTION

Having too many sons is certainly something to worry about. But you cannot on that account lightly give them to others. You must wait until they have matured a little so that you can see whether they are genial, honest, and self-controlled before you give them away. When you do so both families will be blessed by the adoption.

---

[55] Consequently men sometimes did not discover they were adopted until they were adults. See, for instance, the case of Shen Chi-chung in *SS* 456, p. 13407.

If you give a boy away while he is still in diapers and by chance he turns out to be unworthy, not only will he ruin the other family but that family will try to return him to yours, which often leads to lawsuits and the ruin of your family also. In such cases, both families suffer the consequences.

(2, 4, 4)

1.44 ADOPTING SONS OF OTHER SURNAMES

Adopting a boy with a surname different from yours[56] presents problems not only because the spirits of your ancestors will be dissatisfied with the offerings made to them[57] but also because after several generations a marriage surely will occur with someone of the boy's original surname. Since the legal prohibitions against such marriages are very strict,[58] people often hide the facts, thereby laying the groundwork for disputes and lawsuits. Even if no one reports the marriage and the courts take no action on it, how can you forget the moral principle involved?

When boys are adopted in Chiang-hsi,[59] they do not give up the surname they were born with; they just put the name of their adoptive family in front of it so that it looks like a double-character surname. Even though this practice is not recognized by law or mentioned in the Classics, people do it because they have such a strong dislike for the failure to distinguish surnames.

(4)

[56] Legal only when the boy was three *sui* or younger. See *SHT* 12/8b and *CMC* pp. 14–16.

[57] One of the very few references to ancestor worship in this text. See also 2.54.

[58] *SHT* 14/1b says, "All those of the same surname who marry will be sentenced to two years penal servitude. Those who are mourning relatives will be dealt with according to the statute on incest."

[59] Name of a circuit, largely overlapping with the modern province of that name (Kiangsi).

1.45 SELECTING HEIRS

A person of the same surname whose generational sequence is not correct should not be made an heir.[60] Even flying geese and the smallest creatures keep their ranks. But human beings will violate this order. When it reaches the point where an uncle bows to a nephew, can anyone be comfortable so far as principle is concerned? What's more, such actions can cause disputes.

If there is no choice but to adopt a younger brother or a brother's grandson to carry on your sacrifices, you should care for the boy as a son and have him inherit your property.[61] Then the one who receives the care will serve the one who cares for him as though he were his father. This is like the ancient system of wearing mourning clothes for your elder brother's wife[62] or the present day idea of double succession to father and grandfather. So long as the generational sequence is not disturbed, there is no great harm.

(4)

1.46 THE STATUS OF SONS OF CONCUBINES AND POSTHUMOUS SONS

Adopt, raise, and educate from the earliest possible time any child born to women set up in separate houses or born after

[60] That is, only someone in the generation younger than yours should be an heir (i.e. someone the same generation as a natural son).

[61] Both of these would be violations of generational sequence. Liu K'o-chuang in a judgment said popular custom allowed the adoption of a (classificatory) younger brother (*HTHSTCC* 193/10a–17b). In the Sung it became legally permissible to adopt someone as a grandson when there was no close agnatic relative of the right age to be adopted as a son. See Niida, *Tōsō hōritsu*, pp. 515–16.

[62] Normally one avoided one's older brother's wife and did not wear mourning for her. Exceptions were allowed in the T'ang because it was recognized that this violated natural feelings when the brothers were very different in age and the younger brother as a child was cared for by his sister-in-law (*T'ung tien*, 92, p. 500c).

the death of the father.[63] This will avoid lawsuits after your death. If the boy is left with his mother and by imitating those around him becomes a lowly, uneducated sort of person and then later wants to join your family, the situation will be very troublesome. Daughters can be as much trouble.

If you have illicit relations with a promiscuous person, or if you have a maid who is expelled for some reason, you must establish while you are still alive whether or not you fathered any children by the woman. Otherwise after your death there may be children who seek to join the descent line, and the facts of the case will be murky. Your sons and grandsons will be the ones to suffer. (4)

1.47   LENDING ANCESTRY

There are people in our society who raise orphans and abandoned children and then have them become Buddhist or Taoist monks when they are grown. These boys take the family's surname and use their ancestors[64] for the records. And when a kinsman leaves to become a monk, he might borrow the ancestry of a privileged person.[65] Although this generally causes no great harm, later on some may return to lay status and rejoin the descent line; then the officials will have the documents as evidence and will not be able to discern the falsity of them. Be on guard against this from the beginning.

[63] Yüan Ts'ai is referring not only to children of concubines but also to children of one's deceased brothers who might otherwise have followed their mothers when they remarried.
[64] Literally, their three generations, that is, their father, grandfather, and great-grandfather.
[65] A privileged person was a high official who was entitled to nominate relatives for office under the "protection" (*yin*) privilege.

1.48   FOSTER CHILDREN

When a virtuous man sees that the child of a patrilineal relative or relative through marriage is poor, he often takes the boy into his house and clothes, feeds, educates, and cares for him just as though he were his own son. But because popular customs are as degenerate as they are, the boy may covet his benefactor's property. When he dies the boy will try by all means to succeed him, saying that he appointed him an heir. Therefore it is hard to do great acts of charity.

There is only one course to take. Before anything has happened, have the foster child live separately and be sure he is called by a name appropriate to his station.[66] If your succession is not yet settled and this outsider's boy is older than your own sons, it is especially important to clear up any confusions in advance.

In order to avoid trouble later on, men who marry a woman who has sons by her previous husband and women who take in a husband[67] who has sons by his previous wife must decide at the start whether or not the sons are to be reared. Whether the boys will be brought into the house and whether they will share in the household economy[68] must be declared publicly and reported to the authorities, thereby preventing disputes before they begin.

Foster sons who perform services for the family ought to be rewarded as soon as possible. Likewise, foster brothers

[66] That is, do not number him among the sons, let him call the sons "elder brother," "younger brother," and so forth.

[67] Widows with orphans could "take in" husbands to help support their ex-husband's sons using the ex-husband's property. See, for instance, *CMC*, p. 147.

[68] Literally, whether they would "live together," implying that they had pooled their resources and would get a share when the family property was eventually divided.

who perform services or do favors ought to be given part of the family property. Do not hold to the letter of the law to the total disregard of gratitude and morality. (2, 4)

I.49   THE PROPERTY OF ORPHANED GIRLS

When orphaned daughters have shares in the family property, marry them with as generous dowries as possible.[69] When it is fitting that they get land, they should certainly be given it in accordance with the law. If you think only of the present and begrudge it, you will certainly be sued after the marriage. (2, 4)

I.50   MARRIAGE NEGOTIATIONS FOR ORPHANED GIRLS

Widows who remarry sometimes have daughters not yet of marriageable age. If there is a person with a strong sense of integrity among her affinal or maternal relatives, you should negotiate a marriage into his family and have the girl raised by the parents of her future husband, with the marriage to take place after she has grown up.[70] If the girl accompanies

[69] On the property rights of orphaned girls, see Part One, chap. 5, "Women and Property."

[70] Nishida Taiichiro, in his translation of the *Precepts*, p. 56, following the annotation of Katayama Shin, interprets the phrase *chiu-ku*, "mother and father in-law," not to mean the girl's future in-laws but the widow's previous in-laws, that is, the girl's paternal grandparents. I find this less plausible, first because in a majority of the cases when a man dies, his parents would already be dead, and second, when they were alive, that solution would be simple and obvious. It seems more likely that Yüan Ts'ai was addressing the more troublesome case when there was no one from the deceased husband's family to leave the girl with. Having a girl reared by her future in-laws is not improbable for the period, since the Yüan encyclopedia *Shih-lin kuang-chi* included a passage condemning it. See n. 80 below. On Nishida's and Katayama's editions of the *Precepts*, see Appendix A.

her mother to her stepfather's house, doubts and suspicions
will arise that cannot be cleared up.[71]   (2, 4, 4, 5, 6)

1.51   SECOND WIVES

One of life's great misfortunes is to reach middle age and then
lose your wife. Your little boys and girls have no one to care
for them; there is no one to manage the cooking, sewing, and
other work of the women's quarters. Thus you have little
choice but to remarry.

Men who take a girl directly from her parents' home find
that a middle-aged man cannot cope with the feelings of a
young woman. Men who marry a widow may find that she
has affairs with other men. Moreover, she will not be easy to
control. She also will find it hard to forget the sons she had by
her former husband, and, if she bears a son for you, she will
not be able to avoid dividing her affections.[72] Therefore, it is
extremely difficult to remarry at middle age.[73]

Women who are consistently wise, refined, chaste, and
friendly do in fact exist; it is just unusually difficult to locate
them.[74]   (4)

[71] In her stepfather's house she would be living among men not related
to her and therefore not under a strong incest taboo that would keep them
from having sexual relations with her. Yüan Ts'ai makes clear that this is a
very awkward situation.

[72] The sons by her former husband would often have been left with his
family.

[73] In *YSCH* 1, pp. 57–58 (Teng, trans., pp. 12–15), Yen Chih-t'ui also
worried about remarriage, but more because of the legal complications
and disputes caused by having half-brothers. He went so far as to advise—
as an alternative to remarriage—the assignment of wifely duties to a
concubine of low status whose sons would not be full half-brothers. Sons
of women of low status seem to have had more rights in Yüan Ts'ai's
society, which he discusses in 1.46 and 3.20–3.25.

[74] *PTY* adds one more sentence: "Those who remarry ought to select
carefully."

1.52   WOMEN AND BUSINESS

The saying that women do not take part in outside affairs[75] is based on the fact that worthy husbands and sons take care of everything for them, whereas unworthy ones can always find ways to hide their deeds, whatever they are, from the women.

Many men today indulge in pleasure and gambling; some end up selling their lands, even their houses, without their wives' knowledge. Therefore, when husbands are scoundrels, even if wives try to handle business matters, it is of no use. Sons must have their mothers' signatures to sell family property, but there are sons who falsify papers and forge signatures.[76] Some also borrow money at high interest from people who are trying to annex property and who would not hesitate to bring their claim to court.[77] Other sons sell contraband tea and salt to get money, which the authorities, if they discover it, will make them pay for.[78] Mothers have no control in such matters. Therefore, when sons are scoundrels, it is useless for mothers to try to handle business matters.

For women, these are grave misfortunes, but what can they do about them? But wouldn't it be great if husbands and sons could only remember that their wives and mothers are helpless and suddenly repent!   (4, 4, 4)

[75] Compare the statement in the "Patterns for Domestic Life," "Men do not speak of what is inside, nor women of what is outside." *Li chi*, "Nei ts'e" (Legge, trans., I, p. 454).

[76] This principle is repeatedly reiterated in Sung law. For examples of sons who violated it, see *CMC*, pp. 118–22, *Mien-chai chi*, 33/20a–24b.

[77] To foreclose on the property for payment of the debt. See below 3.66 for schemes of "people trying to annex property" (*chien-ping chih jen*).

[78] Tea and salt were government monopolies. The penalties for dealing in these goods illicitly could be much heavier than mere monetary compensation.

Getting Along with Relatives

1.53   THE FINANCIAL AFFAIRS OF WIDOWS

Some wives with dull-witted husbands are able to manage
the household affairs, calculating the outlays and income of
money and grain, without letting anyone cheat them. Some
with unworthy husbands are able to manage the finances
with the help of their sons without it ending in the ruin of the
family and its property. Occasionally there are even widows
whose sons are young who are able to raise and educate their
sons, keep the affection of all their relatives, manage the
family finances, and even prosper. All of these are wise and
worthy women. But the most remarkable are the women
who manage the family's support after their husbands have
died leaving them with young children.[79] Such women
could entrust their finances to their husband's kinsmen or
their own kinsmen, but not all relatives are honorable, and
the honorable ones are not necessarily willing to look after
other people's business.

When wives themselves can read and do arithmetic, and
those they entrust with their affairs have enough to live on
themselves and some sense of fairness and duty, then affairs
will usually work out all right. When these conditions do not
prevail, the usual result is the ruin of the family.

(4, 4, 4, 5)

1.54   CHILDHOOD ENGAGEMENTS

Do not negotiate marriages for your sons and daughters
while they are little. In general, for a woman, what you seek

[79] Chu Hsi, in his funerary inscriptions, gives several examples of such
competent women. See Part One, chap. 2, p. 50. For a counter example of
a widow with a young child who had the family assets stolen by a
bondservant before she even had several recently deceased family members buried, see *ICC ting* 10, p. 625.

(221)

is someone she can trust to take care of her, and for a man what you seek is a mate; if you make plans with only the present situation before you, you will certainly have regrets later on. For wealth and honor come and go in no fixed pattern, and the character of boys and girls can only be discerned after they are grown.

It is fine when nothing changes after an early engagement is contracted. But often yesterday's rich are today's poor and yesterday's honored come to be despised. Also sometimes the prospective son-in-law turns out to be dissolute and unworthy or the prospective bride recalcitrant and unruly. If you honor the agreement, preserving your family will be difficult. But to renounce it is unethical and may lead to lawsuits.

Be warned![80]   (2, 4)

1.55   MATCHING PERSONALITIES

In arranging marriages do not be greedy for eminence or wealth. If the boy's and girl's characters do not match, they will be unhappy their whole lives. Moreover, with discord between them, troublesome incidents will occur.   (2, 4)

1.56   MATES THAT MATCH

You may wish to choose a bride for your son or a son-in-law for your daughter, but first you must evaluate your own child. If your foolish and vulgar son marries a beautiful woman, they will get along very poorly and there will be troublesome incidents. If your ugly, clumsy, and spiteful daughter marries a superior man, it could even end in divorce

---

[80] The Yüan encyclopedia *Shih-lin kuang-chi* adds at this point a paragraph against the practice of taking in a future daughter-in-law as a child. Most likely this paragraph was added by an anonymous copyist.

should they disagree. The parents' failure to choose judiciously is to blame when marriages between unsuitable people lead to discord.

(2, 4, 5, 6)

1.57   MATCHMAKERS' STATEMENTS

The ancients said that the people of the Chou period hated matchmakers because they contradict themselves: they fool the girl's family by saying the boy is rich; they fool the boy's family by saying the girl is beautiful.[81]

This has gotten worse of late. Matchmakers deceive the girl's family by saying the boy does not seek a full complement of dowry presents and in fact will help in outfitting the bride. They deceive the boy's family by promising generous transfer of goods, and they make up a figure without any basis in fact. If the parties simply believe what the matchmaker says and go through with the marriage, each side will accuse the other of dishonesty and the husband and wife will quarrel. There are even cases where the final result is divorce.

Matchmakers may be indispensable in marrying one's children, but do not give such full credence to what they say. What you ought to do is check out everything carefully from the start.   (1, 2, 4, 5)

1.58   ARRANGING MARRIAGES BETWEEN RELATIVES

When people plan marriages they often want to "use a marriage connection to make a marriage connection" in

---

[81] Paraphrase of *Chan Kuo ts'e* Yen 1: "Su Tai said, 'The Chou despised matchmakers because they make two reports. They go to the boy's family and say the girl was beautiful. They go to the girl's family and say the boy is rich.'" (Crump, trans., p. 532.)

order to show that the ties between the families are not forgotten. This is a fine element in popular customs. But there are women of narrow vision who will use their close ties to the other family as an excuse to be lax; they offend the other party, then quarreling starts, and soon no one is getting along. Marriages suddenly arranged between complete strangers are better than this. Therefore, when arranging a marriage with relatives, it is essential not to omit courtesies on account of familiarity. In addition you should not severely criticize each other's preparations, forgetting that the original reason for the marriage was to strengthen your ties. When both families are careful and complete in their etiquette, there need be no other worries.

There are girls who marry into their father's sister's house and are singularly despised by their father's sister; the same is true if they marry into their mother's brother's house or their mother's sister's house. These resentments arise because at the beginning the marriage was not taken seriously and the courtesies were slighted. Again this is the fault of not examining the situation beforehand. (2, 4)

1.59   WOMEN'S SYMPATHIES

Without going overboard, people should marry their daughters with dowries appropriate to their family's wealth. Families with ample property should not consider their daughters outsiders but should give them a share of the property. Nowadays people sometimes have incapable sons and so have to entrust their affairs to their daughter's families; even after their deaths, their burials and sacrifices are performed by their daughters. So how can people say that daughters are not as good as sons?[82]

[82] This may be something of a proverbial phrase, as it appears fairly often in epitaphs for women.

Generally speaking, a woman's heart is very sympathetic. If her mother's family is wealthy and her husband's family is poor, she wants to take assets from her mother's family to give to her husband's family. If her husband's family is wealthy but her mother's family is poor, then she wants to take from her husband's family assets to give to her mother's family. Her parents and husband should be sympathetic toward her feelings and accommodate some of her wishes.[83] When her own sons and daughters are grown and married, if either her son's family or her daughter's family is wealthy while the other is poor, she wishes to take from the wealthy one to give to the poor one. Her sons and daughters should understand her feelings and be somewhat accommodating. But taking from the poor to make the rich richer is unacceptable, and no one should ever go along with it.[84]

(2, 4, 5, 6)

1.60   OLD AGE FOR WOMEN

People say that, though a life span may be a hundred years, only a few reach seventy, for time goes by in a flash. But for those destined to be poor, old age is the hardest to endure. For them, as a general rule, until about the age of fifty, the passage of twenty years seems like only ten; but after that age, ten years can feel as long as twenty.

For women who live a long life, old age is especially hard

[83] By contrast, Ssu-ma Kuang says women should not make any gifts themselves, even of things given to them. See Part One, chapt. 5, "Family Property."

[84] See *Analects* 6:3: "The superior man helps those in distress but does not add to the wealth of the rich." (Waley, trans., p. 116.) It is interesting to note here that the woman looks on her parents' home as her "mother's family." This accords with Margery Wolf's concept of the ties among women in the uterine family. See *Women and the Family in Rural Taiwan*, pp. 32–41.

to bear because most women must rely on others for their existence. Of her relatives from before she was married, a good father is even more valuable than a good grandfather; a good brother is of even more value than a good father; a good nephew is even more valuable than a good brother. Of the relatives she acquires through marriage, a good husband is even more valuable than a good father-in-law; a good son is even more valuable than a good husband; and a good grandson is even more valuable than a good son. Women often enjoy wealth and honor in their youth but find their old age difficult to endure because of this principle.[85] It would be well for their relatives to be sympathetic.   (4)

1.61   TAKING IN RELATIVES

You cannot avoid taking in old paternal and maternal aunts, sisters, and wives of relatives through marriage whose children and grandchildren are unworthy and do not support them.[86] Precautions, however, must be taken. There is the danger that after a woman dies, her unworthy sons or grandsons might make absurd accusations to the authorities, claiming that the woman died because she was left hungry or cold,

[85] Yüan Ts'ai seems to be saying that a woman needs strong ties to people of the younger generation (sons, nephews, grandsons) to care for her in her old age, but unfortunately she is less likely to have strong ties to younger relatives than to ones of her own or earlier generations (father, brother, husband).

[86] Yüan Ts'ai's assumption here is that any respectable man would accept responsibility for women who had married close agnatic relatives, such as his father's brother's wife, his brother's wife, and so on. He is asking that they go beyond the call of duty to take care of other female relatives who were supposed to be other people's responsibility, such as his father's sister or his own sister, his mother's sister, and the wives of such relatives as his mother's brother, wife's brother, and so on. For an example of a man who took care of his father's sister and helped his own sister, see *Nan-chien chia-i kao*, 21, pp. 432–44.

or that she left trunks of goods. When the authorities receive such complaints, they have to investigate and trouble is unavoidable. Thus in order to avoid future problems, while the woman is alive make it clear to the public and to the government that she is bringing nothing with her but herself. Generally, in performing charitable acts, it is best to make certain that they will entail no future problems.

(1, 2, 5)

1.62 EQUALITY IN PROPERTY DIVISION

When the family head is old and tired of management, he often distributes the property to his heirs equally.[87] If the father or grandfather is impartial and fair-minded, and his heirs are able to assist each other and do not fritter the money away, then after the distribution, there will be no disputes; indeed, prosperity will ensue.

Sometimes a family head is generous with clothes, food, money, and goods to some of his heirs but stingy to others. This may be because one son was adopted from a collateral branch, or because one is by a first wife and another by a second wife, or because one of his sons died and he does not love the surviving grandsons, or even simply because he prefers certain ones even though they are all of the same status. If in such a case his behavior causes his heirs themselves to ask for an equal distribution, and he still secretly favors some over others, he will surely be laying the groundwork for future disputes.[88]

[87] Yüan Ts'ai could be referring to full division, legally possible when the parents order it. But since he uses *chi* ("give, supply") instead of the standard legal term *fen* ("give in division"), he probably means distributing for management and use, pending a legal division after the father's death.

[88] Note that the disputes over property are in the future. Sons could not sue about division of property while their fathers were alive.

Sometimes there is an unworthy person among the heirs, and the family head has no choice but to give him a share in order to save his other sons from trouble. In such a case periodically give the unworthy heir shares of the income in money and grain but not of the land.[89] If you give him land, he will consider it his personally owned share and will pester the family elders to give him the deeds so he can mortgage it.[90] Once it is mortgaged, he will set his greedy eyes on the other heirs' property.[91] Lawsuits will be the inevitable outcome, disturbing and doing harm to your worthy sons and grandsons, just as much as bankruptcy does. You must give this thought.

As a general rule, among ten or more well-behaved sons and grandsons, there will be one who is unworthy. There are cases where the dozen good ones all suffer because of the single bad one, even to the point where the family is ruined. The hundreds of stipulations in our laws can do nothing to prevent this; neither can the hundreds of plans laid by fathers and grandfathers. Those who wish to preserve and continue their family line should observe what has happened to other families to take stock of what may happen to their own. Do not fail to cultivate virtue and ponder carefully in order to lay plans for the long run. (1, 2, 4, 4)

1.63   POTENTIAL PROBLEMS WITH WILLS

Wills are written by wise men who want to plan for what will happen after their deaths. But the provisions in them

[89] The idea here seems to be that he would receive a regular allowance and no longer pool his expenses with his brothers.

[90] That is, even though the father had not meant this to be a permanent, legal division, the son would try to treat it as such and sell or *tien* the land allotted to him to gain money for other expenses. He would ask family elders (such as uncles) to serve as witnesses to the deed to reassure the buyer that he had the right to sell.

[91] Cf. 1.27 on seeking a second division.

must be fair if they are to preserve the family. Misconceived actions will be countless if you name an heir foolishly or cast aside a son capriciously because you give in to a bossy wife or a crafty concubine or take into account the way a second wife favors her own beloved sons and is niggardly to the others. Any of these courses will provoke lawsuits and bring your family to ruin.[92]

(4, 4, 4, 5)

1.64 THE TIME TO WRITE WILLS

Fathers or grandfathers who worry about disputes and law-suits between their heirs often intend to prepare wills but procrastinate, not recognizing that life is snuffed out as easily as a candle in the wind. Thus there are many cases where men die exasperated; gravely ill, they can neither utter words nor move their hands to write, though their minds are still lucid. Worse are those who become mentally confused.

(1, 4, 4, 4)

1.65 CHARITABLE SCHOOLS[93]

The purpose of establishing charitable estates is to aid poor kinsmen.[94] If your lineage is an old one, its members are sure

---

[92] Wills were enforced unless the plaintiff could convince the judge that the family head had been patently unfair. See *CMC*, pp. 137–39.

[93] This item is omitted in the *CPTC* edition; possibly Yüan Ts'ai deleted it when he issued his 1190 edition. Or, since the last page of a volume (*ts'e*) is the most easily torn off, this item could merely have been lost in transmission (relatively plausible since the 1190 edition is known through a single surviving copy). The text followed here is the *YCL* edition.

[94] Charitable estates were founded by many Sung gentlemen to provide subsidies for their kinsmen and support for lineage activities such as ancestral rites. The first and most famous charitable estate was set up by Fan Chung-yen (989–1052). See Denis Twitchett, "The Fan Clan's Charitable Estate, 1050–1760" and "Documents of Clan Administration, 1." For the account of an estate established in imitation of Fan's model by a contemporary of Yüan Ts'ai, see *Lu Fang-weng ch'üan-chi*, 21, p. 124.

to be numerous. Not only will each person's share become less and less, but the unworthy young men will not use their shares to aid the cold and hungry.

Furthermore, some will go so far as to mortgage their shares in the joint estate because of a bout of drinking or a toss of the dice. They will then get less than half; what is the use then? Also, if members' income is generous, they will be well fed to the end of their days with nothing to focus their minds on except disturbing their communities and causing trouble for the authorities.

Thus it is better to use the land to endow a charitable school. If it is attached to a temple, you can endow "monk land." Someone qualified as a classicist can be selected to teach. [From the endowment] the meals for the students can be supplied, and help can be given when they are in need.

Consider making monks out of those of inferior talents without land to take care of or a profession to follow. Then neither will they end up unable to care for their dependents, nor will they bring shame on the virtue of their ancestors; neither will they disturb people nor will they cause trouble for the authorities.[95]   (4)

---

[95] Yüan Ts'ai's point seems to be that it is better to make them monks than subsidize them from a charitable estate.

CHAPTER 2

Improving Personal Conduct

2.1   VARIATIONS IN INTELLIGENCE

Human intelligence certainly varies; indeed there is a great gap between the highest and the lowest in mental capacity. A person with high intelligence sees everything when he looks on someone with lower intelligence, just as one who climbs a high spot can see far into the distance. But when those with inferior intelligence gaze at those with high, they might as well be standing outside a wall trying to get a peek inside.

Two people with only a minor difference in intelligence can still talk with each other; when the difference is extremely large, interaction is not advisable, since conversation will only provide useless exercise for the tongue and jaw. Chess offers an analogy. If two players differ in their scores by only three or five moves, they are still acceptable opponents. But imagine what happens when a national champion plays with someone who has never seen the tallies or board before![1]   (3)

2.2   ARROGANCE

Since wealth and honor are assigned by fate and chance, you should not be arrogant to the residents of your community

---

[1] Cf. *Analects* 6:19: "One can discuss higher things with those of superior ability, but one cannot discuss higher things with those below average." (Waley, trans., p. 119.)

on such grounds. If you started out poor and attained wealth
yourself, or if you started out in a humble family and
achieved prominence yourself, other people may praise you
for your achievements, but you should not use them to
put yourself above your townsmen. If you enjoy luxury
because of the resources bequeathed to you by your ancestors, or if you gradually attained prominence because of the
patronage and sponsorship you received from your father or
grandfather,[2] then what makes you any different from the
ordinary person?[3] Those who try to use these advantages to
lord it over their fellow residents ought to be ashamed. They
are also pitiable.   (2, 4)

2.3   POLITENESS AND RANK

In society there are some benighted people who are unable to
treat all their fellow residents with equal politeness. Instead
they differentiate according to the person's wealth and status.
Their manners are deferential and their attitude respectful
whenever they meet a wealthy person or official. The more
the wealth and the higher the rank, the greater their deference and respect. But when they cast their eyes on poor
and humble people, their manners are rude and their attitude
contemptuous; moreover, they never display the slightest
sympathy. They totally fail to recognize that another
person's wealth and rank bring them no glory, nor does his
humble station humiliate them in any way. What use is
there in making these sorts of status distinctions? No cordial,
discerning gentleman would act this way.   (2)

---

[2] Yüan Ts'ai refers in part to attaining office through privilege based on
the ranks of the office held by a close relative. Cf. 1.47 n. 65.

[3] The idea that the wealth or rank a man achieved on his own was more
worthy of respect than that inherited had no classical precedence, nor does
it seem to have been a common idea in the Sung.

2.4 SUCCESS AND FAILURE

Personal conduct and changes in social standing are two separate matters; there is no basis for thinking that proper conduct will lead naturally to glory and honor and improper conduct to misery and frustration. If such were the case, Confucius and Yen Yüan would have been prime ministers, and throughout history there never would have been an inferior man occupying a top post.[4]

Careful conduct is a personal obligation, but you cannot expect it to have an effect on external events. If you hold such hopes and they are unfulfilled, your conduct will become remiss, your standards may change, and soon you may turn into one of those inferior people.

In the world today, often the stupid enjoy great wealth while the intelligent dwell in poverty and obscurity. The reason is that their lot is fixed. There is no point in trying to understand why it is so. If you could recognize this truth you would be contented with your situation and save yourself considerable trouble.   (2)

2.5 CHANGES IN CIRCUMSTANCES

Worldly affairs constantly change: this is the principle of Heaven. In the present world many people see a small degree of success[5] right in front of them and assume that they have nothing to worry about in life; in no time they end up ruined.

The general rule is that the astrological order changes every decade with the new *chia* year, and there is then a shift

---

[4] Confucius never held an important post, and his disciple Yen Yüan, known for never making the same mistake twice and being content in meager circumstances, died young.

[5] Following the reading of the 1179 editions.

in worldly affairs.[6] There is no need to look far for proof of this; just compare your community of ten or twenty years ago with the same community today. Some families have risen, others have declined, without any definite trends.

Unperceptive contemporaries are envious of the successful who have things go their way; they also laugh at the failures who are frustrated in all their endeavors. This envy and disdain are especially serious problems among relatives living together and among nearby neighbors. If people could recognize the vagaries of circumstances,[7] they would have more than enough to do taking care of their own affairs; they would hardly have the leisure to envy or ridicule others.

(I, 2)

2.6   THE ALTERNATION OF HARD WORK AND LEISURE

People who will enjoy wealth and honor in their late years have to suffer all sorts of hardships and difficulties in their youth and early adulthood. Those who enjoy wealth and rank from a young age never continue a life of leisure into old age.

The Creator calculates in several ways. People who pass the examinations early and those who receive assignments early get embroiled in conflicts in middle age and do not achieve their aspirations, or do not achieve eminence until they are old. When someone serves in office without conflict it must be because he was hard-pressed financially and had to worry about the need for food, shelter, and marriage.[8] In addition, early death often awaits the seemingly blessed, such

[6] In the sixty-year cycle used for designating years, every tenth year begins with the "stem" *chia* combined with one of six "branches."

[7] *PYT* adds a phrase here: "It's like the boards used to build a wall; sometimes the top ones may be put on the bottom, sometimes the bottom ones may be put on the top."

[8] *PYT* adds here "and experienced hardship and grief, but ..."

as those who gain office at an early age without having experienced hardship, those who enjoy the comforts of life by grace of the affluence of their fathers and grandfathers, and those who have never been frustrated in their desires.

Occasionally there are exceptions, people who from first to last enjoy wealth and official rank. They are highly blessed people but not the rule; there is only one like them in ten million. At present, people will scheme and plot to avoid any suffering and to enjoy their wealth and rank to the end of their lives. These people fail to understand how Heaven works. Even more deluded are those who resist these principles by making plans to ensure that their descendants will enjoy wealth and rank from childhood. In the end their human efforts will not be able to defeat Heaven.[9]   (1, 2)

2.7   YOUR ALLOTTED SHARE OF RICHES

Wealth and rank have their naturally allotted share. The Creator has already set for you a definite share; he has also set in place an unpredictable mechanism of chance that makes everyone in the world work hard, rushing around day and night, and that to the day they die they do not recognize. Without this mechanism, the people born on earth would have nothing to do, and this transforming process of the universe would stop.[10]

No more than one or two people get what they seek in their rushing around while millions fail to get anything.

[9] *PYT* adds a sentence at the end: "All they will accomplish is being laughed at by the Azure One." The phrase "Azure One" for Heaven is not found elsewhere in the *Precepts*.

[10] Cf. *Chuang Tzu* 18 (Watson, trans., pp. 190–91), "People who are rich wear themselves out rushing around on business, piling up more wealth than they could ever use.... The inaction of Heaven is its purity, the inaction of earth is its peace. So the two inactions combine and all things are transformed and brought to birth." Yüan Ts'ai is, of course, not fully adopting Chuang Tzu's stance in favor of inaction.

Part Two

Most people notice the one or two who succeed and so till the day they die they work hard and expend their resources, all to no avail. They are not aware that the ones who succeeded after rushing around were fated to do so.

Anything that is a part of your allotted share you will attain in the end, even if you do not rush around but merely while away the months and years. Therefore, perceptive and farsighted men transcend this mechanism of transformation and accept what comes and what goes. In their breasts they are tranquil, feeling neither grief nor joy, neither resentment nor blame. Such matters as rushing around and subverting each other are never anyone's aims, so why struggle toward such ends?

One of my senior friends said, "Death and life, poverty and wealth, are set from birth; the superior person wins his lot by being a superior person; the inferior person acting vainly makes himself an inferior person." This saying is highly apt. It is just that people do not comprehend it.

(2, 5)

2.8   ATTAINING TRANQUILLITY

Human beings, from the moment they begin to understand the world around them, have worries and frustrations. Babies cry and shriek when their wishes are not met. From childhood to youth to adulthood to old age, few things turn out as you wanted them to. Even the very rich and high-ranking, whom everyone else envies and looks up to as divine, have all had their disappointments, just like poor and humble people, though what they worry about is different. Thus we call this an imperfect world. Those who are dissatisfied with this world could gain a little peace of mind by comprehending this truth and accepting it without complaint.   (1)

(236)

2.9   SUCCEEDING THROUGH PLANNING

Let me comment on the plans people lay for even the most minor everyday affairs. Some plans succeed only after struggle, others approach success and then fail but succeed the next time. Success achieved in these ways brings long-lasting tranquillity and an end to worry. If something is achieved easily or by accident, later events will not turn out as hoped. The mechanisms of creation are this subtle and unpredictable. If you give it calm thought, you will recognize this principle and can free yourself from cares.   (1, 3, 5, 6)

2.10   PERSONALITY DEFECTS

People's Heaven-endowed qualities bias them in certain ways. The superior man knows in what ways he is inclined and so through cultivation compensates for his deficiencies, becoming a perfected person. Ordinary people, not recognizing their proclivities, act directly on their passions and so often make mistakes.

The *Book of Documents* speaks of nine qualities: affability, mildness, honesty, aptness for government, docility, straightforwardness, simplicity, toughness, and strength. These are part of one's Heaven-endowed make-up. The so-called accompaniments are dignity, firmness, courtesy, respectfulness, resolution, congeniality, uncorruptibility, sincerity, and integrity: these are what one attains by cultivation. They are the means by which the sages became sages.[11]

[11] The passage in the *Shang-shu*, "Kao-yao mu" (Legge, trans., *Classics* 3, p. 71) can be translated as follows: "affability combined with dignity, mildness combined with firmness, honesty combined with courtesy, aptness for government combined with respectfulness, docility combined with resolution, straightforwardness combined with congeniality, simplicity combined with uncorruptibility, toughness combined with sincerity, strength combined with a sense of duty."

The custom in later generations of wearing a belt of leather when one is hasty by nature and a belt made of bowstrings when one is slow is similar to this in principle.[12]

Inclinations are difficult for a person to recognize himself. You must ask other people about yours to learn of them.

2.11   PEOPLE'S STRONG AND WEAK POINTS

A person may have shortcomings in disposition and be-havior, but invariably he also has strong points. If you keep noticing what he lacks without seeing what he has to offer, then you will never be able to tolerate his company for any length of time. But if you keep in mind his strong points and do not dwell on his weak ones, you can maintain social contact with him all your life.   (1, 3, 4)

2.12   CONTEMPT, DECEIT, ENVY, AND SUSPICION

Those who regularly harbor feelings of contempt, deceit, envy, or suspicion in their dealings with others invite humili-ation. Gentlemen of character never act this way.

The contemptuous person is no better than others but enjoys slighting them. When someone not his equal asks him for something, he is rude to his face and ridicules him behind his back. If he could observe himself, he would break out in sweat from mortification.

The deceitful person speaks in a devious way. He acts as though he is extremely cordial but in his heart he is just the opposite. For a time people admire him. Yet after he has repeated his behavior two or three times the truth becomes evident and he is spit on by people.

The envious person always wants to be ranked the highest.

---

[12] *Han Fei tzu*, 24 (Liao, trans., I, p. 259).

Therefore, if he hears someone praised for his qualities, he becomes upset and resentful and discredits the report. He is overjoyed at reports that someone has shortcomings. How does this detract from other people? Precisely by adding to enmity.

The suspicious person twists whatever people say to find innuendos in it. He thinks, "He must be criticizing me for such-and-such," or "He must be making fun of me for such-and-such." The building of enmity between people often starts this way. The wise pay no attention when they hear people make fun of them, thereby saving themselves a lot of trouble.   (2, 5)

2.13   GOOD FAITH, TRUSTWORTHINESS, SINCERITY, AND RESPECTFULNESS

To show good faith and trustworthiness in speech and sincerity and respect in conduct are the arts the sage taught for gaining local esteem.[13] To secure your own advantage without harming anyone else when dealing with business matters and in crises to take care of yourself without hindering others is good faith. To fulfill promises to the last iota and to keep appointments to the dot is trustworthiness. To be cordial in your dealings and honest in your heart is sincerity. To behave with deference and to speak with humility is respectfulness. If you can put these virtues into practice, not only will you be esteemed by your community, but you will also attain whatever you seek.[14]

Concerning respectfulness, showing it costs nothing, so

[13] *Analects* 15:5 (Waley, trans., p. 194).

[14] By contrast, Chu Hsi says that merely showing good faith and trustworthiness in speech and sincerity and respectfulness in conduct is not enough. If it were, there would have been numerous sages over the centuries and the Way would have been transmitted, which to him was untrue (Ch'ien Mu, *Chu Tzu hsin hsüeh-an*, I, p. 383).

most of your contemporaries practice it.[15] But to make a show of respect when in your heart you feel contempt is to have mastered respectfulness but not sincerity. Superior men label this sycophancy, and no one has ever gained the esteem of his community through it. (2, 4)

2.14 CRITICIZING YOURSELF

Good faith, trustworthiness, sincerity, and respectfulness should be sought in other people only after you possess them yourself. If you find fault with others for lacking these qualities while you are not perfect in them yourself, people will find fault with you the same way. There are very few people at present who are able to reflect on their own good faith, trustworthiness, sincerity, and respect; but they all can find fault with others in these regards.

Even if you are perfect in these traits, you still should not go too far in criticizing others for lacking them. Today there are some people who fully develop these qualities in themselves—which is unquestionably good. But then they demand that others resemble them and go overboard in condemnation whenever someone acts contrary to their views. Those who are not magnanimous will merely provoke resentment in others.[16] (5)

2.15 THE SENSE OF SHAME

Nowadays when someone does a bad deed, if by luck no one else discovers it, he remains relaxed and complacent, afraid of

[15] Cf. 2.3.

[16] The idea that demanding (*tse*) too much of others and too little of oneself provokes resentment is also expressed in *Analects* 15:14: "He who is heavy in his expectations of himself and light in his demands on others will avoid resentment." (Waley, trans., p. 196.) See also 2.29.

nothing. Such people do not realize that an act can be hidden from the eyes and ears of men but never from the knowledge of the gods.

When you do something that in your heart you know is right, other people may know nothing of it, but the gods know it. When you do something that in your heart you know is wrong, whether or not other people know anything of it, the gods are aware of it. Your conscience is the gods, and the gods are blessings and misfortunes. Just as you cannot deceive your own conscience, so you cannot deceive the gods.

The *Book of Songs* says, "The visits of the gods cannot be foretold, but you cannot slight them." [17] The commentators explain this to mean that even when a person in his heart thinks the gods are present, still he cannot discern them. And it is much worse when he doesn't believe that the gods are right beside him and regards them with disdain, for he would stop at nothing then.

2.16 PRAYER

When people pray to the gods asking for their secret assistance in some yet unaccomplished good deed, even if their prayers have no effect, they will not be ashamed to speak of them. But when people pray to the gods, seeking their assistance for some bad deed, aren't they trying to deceive the gods? For instance, if you are plotting a robbery and pray to the gods, or you are engaged in unreasonable litigation and pray to the gods, should the gods in fact act on your words, this will enrage them, and you will have provoked disaster.

(2)

[17] From the *Shih ching*, Mao text 256 (Waley, trans., p. 302).

2.17 SELF–SATISFACTION

People who are fair and straightforward in their behavior should make use of these virtues to serve the gods; they should not be disrespectful toward the gods, thinking they can depend on their virtues. They should use their virtues to serve mankind; they should not be arrogant toward people, thinking they can depend on their virtues. Even Confucius made the statements, "Be respectful of the ghosts and gods," "Serve the officials," and "Hold great men in awe." [18] How much more true this is for people inferior to Confucius!

People whose conduct is reprehensible may become conscience-stricken and learn trepidation—thus they may be able to avoid calamity and preserve their lives. When superior men on occasion suffer calamity, often they have brought it on themselves through over-self-confidence.   (1, 5, 6)

2.18 REMORSE

Some people are able regularly to regret their errors in past actions, the mistakes they made in earlier conversations, and their lack of wisdom in prior years. As the saying goes, "Without being aware of it, they are making daily progress toward wisdom and virtue." [19] The ancients said, "Reaching sixty, one knows the errors of fifty-nine." [20] Can this fail to be an encouragement?   (3)

[18] *Analects* 6:20, 15:9, 16:8 (Waley, trans., pp. 120, 195, 206).

[19] An allusion to a statement by Tung Chung-shu in *Han shu*, 56, p. 2517.

[20] An allusion to *Chuang Tzu* 27 in which Chuang Tzu accused Confucius of never deciding what is right but continually revising his previous assessments. Hui Tzu defended Confucius, saying he was working to increase his knowledge (Watson, trans., p. 305).

2.19   EVIL DEEDS

People who fail in their efforts to do a bad deed must on no account resent Heaven or be angry at men.[21] Heaven is showing them love; in the future they will face no problems. If you see other people succeed in their bad deeds, do not be jealous. Heaven is rejecting these people. Once their evils have piled up, Heaven will destroy them, wreaking punishment either on them or on their descendants. If you wait for a while, this process will become obvious.   (3, 4)

2.20   THE REWARDS AND PUNISHMENTS METED OUT FOR GOOD AND EVIL DEEDS

People are often perplexed by cases in which a person does something bad and is punished but his descendants flourish; it seems to them as though Heaven has made a mistake. These people do not realize that the family of the person in question must have accumulated many more good deeds than bad ones. Since the good ones outnumbered the bad, the person who did wrong suffers punishment himself but does not prevent blessings from reaching his descendants. If a person commits many evil deeds and enjoys a long life, riches, and tranquillity, surely the accumulated merit of his ancestors will be depleted. Because Heaven has no affection for him, it has let him recklessly pursue evil, which will bring about his utter destruction.   (3, 4)

2.21   THE ABILITY TO FORBEAR

The ability to forbear can easily become a habit, so much so that when someone does something reprehensible or in-

---

[21] A proverbial expression going back to the *Analects* 14:37 (Waley, trans., p. 189) and *Centrality and Commonality* 14 (Legge, trans., *Classics* 1, p. 396).

tolerable, you can still remain as calm as before.[22] The inability to forbear also easily becomes a habit, so much so that you take offense at an angry look. Matters too trivial to argue about then lead to curses and litigation. Unwilling to let up short of victory, you do not recognize how much you lose from this kind of behavior.

When you can have a stable outlook unaffected by other people's manners, then you can attain great tranquillity of body and mind.

2.22   INFERIOR PEOPLE

In ordinary life, people should try to stay close to superior men and at a distance from inferior men. Superior men are considerate, cordial, dignified, and cautious in their speech. If you hear their speech from childhood and it enters your heart you will naturally be like them in your actions. Inferior people are sharp, unkind, exaggerated, and specious in their talk. If this type of talk is what enters your heart in youth, as you do things you will naturally talk the same way.

Likewise, if all day long you listen to the talk of people who are arrogant and love to insult others, without being aware of the process, you will come to act as they do. And if all day long you listen to people who are dissolute and undisciplined, without being aware of it you will come to act the same way.[23] There are a wide variety of cases like this.

[22] Cf. 1.4 and 1.6.
[23] Cf. *Hsün Tzu* 23 (Watson, trans., pp. 170–71): "If a man studies with a worthy teacher what he will hear will be the ways of Yao, Shun, Yü, and T'ang. If he associates with worthy friends, what he will observe will be loyal, trustworthy, respectful, and deferential behavior. Without his awareness each day he will advance toward benevolence and duty. His environment makes him do this. Now if he lives with bad men what he will hear will be deception and lies, what he will see will be wanton, depraved, and greedy behavior. Without his awareness, he will get closer to suffering punishment, such is the force of his environment."

Unless you have great power to retain your stability, you cannot avoid the problem of having your companion's habits rub off on you. (4, 5)

2.23   EXPERIENCE

What older people say may seem unpracticable, but they have a lot of experience. Even if a younger person is endowed with high intelligence, his knowledge cannot compare with theirs. But younger people habitually consider the old to be outdated and wide of the mark.[24]

In general, the old want to teach the young the truths they have personally learned to be valid from their own experience. Many young people get tired of listening to this and belittle the old ones. But as the years go by and they gain experience, the young ones will finally recognize the truth of their elders' advice and will acknowledge it with respect. But by this time they will have already tasted all sorts of danger and distress themselves. (6)

2.24   THE FAULTS OF SUPERIOR MEN

No one can escape making mistakes—not even sages and worthy men, and certainly not those of lesser abilities. How can a person's every action be perfect?[25] When you err, would anyone but your father or elder brother be willing to reproach you? Would anyone but your closest friends be willing to admonish you? Casual acquaintances will do no more than talk about you behind your back.

The superior man worries only about whether he has faults. He makes confidential inquiries to find out what other

[24] Yüan Ts'ai's observations here of how people act provide an interesting contrast to the generalizations about Chinese veneration of the aged.
[25] Cf. 2.30.

people say about him so that he can offer apologies and try to improve. When an inferior person hears that someone has been talking about him, he defends himself through forced arguments; he will even go so far as to sever all contact or sue the other one. (5, 6)

2.25 CONCISE SPEECH

If you speak simply and concisely, you will reduce the embarrassment you cause yourself and be less likely to provoke resentment in others. (6)

2.26 INFERIOR PEOPLE'S MISBEHAVIOR

Anyone who in speech or action thinks carefully, follows the rules, and reflects but still unfortunately makes a mistake is within the reach of reason and admonishment. But those who are impulsive in word and action and who may purposely do something they know is wrong—these people will certainly violently brush aside those who try to reprove them. Men who are well adjusted to living in their community not only avoid reproving someone like this, they also know enough not to get caught in the middle of an argument between him and someone else. This is how they avoid getting insulted.[26]

I once witnessed the case of a man who could not bear to see a good friend fall into error, so he privately and sincerely spoke to him of it. Contrary to his hopes, the friend got angry and said, "You and I were very cordial, yet even you slander me!" As Mencius said, "How can one talk with those who are not good-hearted." [27]

[26] Cf. 1.30 and 2.28. "Insulted" follows the reading of the 1179 editions.
[27] *Mencius* 4A:8 (Lau, trans., p. 121). The passage continues, "They feel safe amidst peril, find benefit in calamities, and take pleasure in the means of their own destruction. If it were possible to talk with these unbenevo-

2.27 SCOUNDRELS

Although people all detest the scoundrel, he also serves a purpose. Generally speaking, observing a bad person makes you more circumspect and less likely to do bad things yourself. Never observing a bad person leads to carelessness, perhaps even to the point where you do wrong unintentionally. Therefore families without scoundrels also lack conspicuous examples of filial and friendly behavior; villages without scoundrels also lack prominent examples of sincerity and cordiality.

Take whetstones as a comparison: The stone is worn down as the knife or ax is sharpened on it. Lao Tzu was making precisely this point when he said that the bad man is a resource for the good man.[28]

On the other hand, if you see a scoundrel and join in his evil activities, perhaps even competing with him to take the lead, then his presence is only harmful. What advantage could it have for anyone? (2)

2.28 UNWORTHY SONS

In rural communities there are unworthy young men who indulge in wine and women, gamble and roam about, keep the company of riffraff, and raise horses for hunting. These young men easily bankrupt their family's property and even sometimes become beggars or thieves.[29] When such is the unhappy fate of the family, the bad deeds of the young man's father or grandfather may have been the cause.[30]

---

lent people, how would there be such destruction of states and ruin of families?"

[28] Lao Tzu, *Tao te ching* 27 (Waley, trans., p. 177).

[29] Cf. 1.39 and 2.58.

[30] That is, because the ancestors had done bad deeds the family is now suffering, the agent of their suffering being their unworthy sons. Cf. 2.19 and 2.20.

I have never heard of anyone reforming such young men by advice and scolding. Even their closest relatives ought to deal with them as phenomena beyond their control. Arguing with them is pointless and can only increase the bitterness felt. (4)

2.29 CORRECTING OTHERS

Encouraging people to be good and dissuading them from being bad are certainly admirable activities; yet personal reflection is needed before undertaking them. If you offer advice before you have established yourself as a person of integrity, not only will people pay no attention to what you say, they also will look down on you for saying it.

Don't advise others on how to act at court unless your behavior at court has been praiseworthy. Don't advise others on administrative methods unless your administrative service has been effective. Wait until your talent and scholarship command respect before advising others on the essentials of advancing in learning. Wait until your personality and conduct are valued by others before advising them on the details of personal behavior. Wait until you have been able to attain wealth and comfort yourself before advising others on the ways to manage family affairs. Wait until you are able to live side-by-side with your parents in harmony and without disagreements before advising others about truly filial conduct.

If you do not meet these standards, won't you be laughed at when you offer advice?[31] (2)

2.30 LIGHTLY SPOKEN WORDS

A person may say the perfect thing and yet have others criticize him. He may take the most appropriate action and

[31] Does Yüan Ts'ai imply he is perfect in all these, since he offers advice on them all?

still have people say he was wrong. The reason is that people are only rarely of one mind, and their judgments are seldom uniform. When a superior man considers his speech and conduct in the light of his conscience, judges them by the ancient teachings, asks worthy people about them, and finds nothing in violation of principle in them, then he will not take any notice of such assorted comments, nor will he try to refute them.[32] None of the sages and worthy men of antiquity, or the chief ministers of this dynasty, or the current governors and magistrates have escaped gossip. So how can someone living in the countryside along with the registered commoners? Above all, how can you be surprised when people of the sort that hold no one in awe casually criticize you?

Generally, those who call good bad are jealous or hold bitter grudges. Such people are not the ones who set right-thinking public opinion. Disregard them and do not bother to refute them.   (2, 3)

2.31   PANDERING

There are people who will praise your best features and deliberately let you hear of it so that you will be pleased without realizing that they are trying to ingratiate themselves. This flattery is one of the most devilish ruses inferior people have. Such types flatter you to your face, which pleases you. When they go away and talk to other people, they may not refrain from making fun of you for having been fooled by them.

There are also people good at guessing your weak tendencies, who may take the initiative in that direction and lead

---

[32] Cf. *Analects* 12:4: "The superior man has neither fear nor anxiety.... When, after examining himself he finds nothing wrong, what does he have to worry about, what does he have to fear?" (Waley, trans., p. 163.)

you up to what you like. They please you because what they say happens to agree with what you have in mind. This pandering is another of the devilishly clever ruses used by inferior people. If they accurately judge your weaknesses and in fact you join them, when they go away and talk with other people, they may not refrain from making fun of you for being easily sized up. In such cases even men of great wisdom unwittingly suffer ridicule without coming to their senses. What then? (2, 5, 6)

2.32   GOING TO EXTREMES

If you curse someone but he does not reply, it is because he is tolerant. Do not assume he is afraid of you and keep at it, seeking to humiliate him further.[33] If the other person rises up and you respond, I am afraid that you might be struck dumb and be unable to speak.[34]

If you accuse someone and he declines to defend himself, it must be because he knows where he stands. Do not assume he is afraid of you and persist, trying to attack him even harder. If he then makes his case and you dispute it, I am afraid that you might end up in the wrong and be unable to escape punishment yourself. (1, 4)

2.33   THINKING BEFORE SPEAKING

Even when you are on close friendly terms with relatives and old friends, do not tell them all your secrets. I worry that someday you might take a dislike to each other; then the other person will use what you said before as ammunition in

---

[33] That is, do not act like the "average person" in 1.3 who tends "to retreat when he runs into strength and become reckless when he encounters weakness."

[34] Apparently as retribution.

his quarrels with you. Likewise, when you are not on good terms with someone, do not make things worse by telling him the naked truth. I fear that after you have made up and have become friends or contracted a marriage, your former words will be a source of embarrassment.

As a general rule, the worst time to point to a person's hidden flaws or to expose his ancestor's bad deeds is when you are angry. Aroused by a momentary rage, you want to state the unvarnished truth and give no thought to how the anger and resentment will deeply enter into the other person's bones and marrow. This is the reason the ancients said that words cause deeper wounds than spears and lances.[35] There is also a proverb, "When hitting a person do not hit his knees, when talking to a person, do not mention his true failings."[36]   (2, 4, 4, 5, 6)

2.34 FACIAL EXPRESSION

When conversations bring friends and relatives to take a dislike to each other, it is not always the words that cause the injury; often what arouses one person's anger is the other's harshness in facial expression or manner of speaking. If you are able to keep a warm expression and subdued manner when you criticize a person's shortcomings, then even if what you say is cutting and direct, the person will at least not resent you, whether or not he takes your advice. But if in your ordinary conversation your manner and expression are severe, then even if you have said nothing to hurt him, you will surely make him suspicious, whether or not you make him angry.

[35] From *Hsün Tzu*, "Jung-ju" (Shih-chieh shu-chü ed. 4, p. 33).
[36] Compare the proverb quoted by Arthur Smith, "When hitting a man do not hit his face, when cursing a man do not mention his shortcomings" (*Proverbs from the Chinese*, p. 294).

The ancients said that when you are angry at home it shows on your face in the market place.[37] When you talk to someone while angry, you will not seem agreeable. The other person will not know the reason for your temper and cannot help considering it odd. Therefore, when you temper is aroused you must watch yourself with extra caution during conversations with others.

One of my elders had a saying, "Be cautious about speaking after drinking wine; avoid scolding during meals; endure what is hard to bear and be patient in what matters; go along with people who are determined." If you can stick to these principles all the time, you will have much to gain.

(2, 4, 4, 5, 6)

2.35   HONORING ELDERS

The members of a community ought to respect people of advanced years because they are close to parents in age. But a community may have a person long in years but short in virtue who, claiming that he is immune from punishment, shamelessly curses and humiliates others on little or no grounds.[38] In such a case the superior man ought to tolerate him and refrain from trying to reason with him.   (4)

2.36   CORDIAL RELATIONS

In social relations, you must always be pleasant and relaxed, regardless of whether those you are dealing with are higher or lower than you in status. Do not presume to give yourself

[37] Paraphrase of *Tso chuan*, Duke Chao 19 (see Legge, trans., *Classics* 5, pp. 674–75).

[38] According to *SHT* 4/3a, those over seventy could have punishments for noncapital offenses commuted to fines, those over eighty could commute even capital offenses, and those over ninety were not subject to penalties at all.

airs or put a lot of effort into clothes or appearance. If your words and conduct are visibly unusual, how will people be able to stay close to you any more?

On the other hand, you should not be too casual or familiar. At banquets and parties where wine is served, you should certainly sing and laugh and have a fully enjoyable time, but beware of making fun of others, for you might hit someone's sore spot and spark a quarrel.   (2, 3, 4)

2.37   LOFTY TALENT AND CONDUCT

People naturally value conduct that is lofty; there is no need for the person's appearance also to be superior. People naturally esteem talent that is lofty; there is no need for the person's speech also to be superior.   (3)

2.38   HEAVEN'S PUNISHMENTS

In rural communities there sometimes are high-ranking families who maltreat people, taking advantage of the local official's hesitancy to take action against them. There may also be families with substantial economic resources who openly give and receive bribes in order to harm others. When these people gain sway, the county and prefecture can do nothing about it; even the gods and ghosts get out of their way. How in the world could a poor person try to reason with such bullies? Out of perversity they will surely prove a menace to any property adjoining theirs—houses, grave plots, hills, forests, fields, or gardens—stopping only when they possess them. They will seize whatever they take a fancy to, clothes, food, furnishings, small as such items may be. You must keep out of the way of people like this. Wait until their wrongs have piled up and Heaven punishes them. In addition, the family's sons and grandsons will be able to destroy the fathers and grandfathers, thus avenging their neighbors.

Rural communities may also have people skillful at law-suits who manipulate the strengths and weaknesses of a case and falsely argue for litigation. Thus they disturb the county and prefecture authorities who do not dare punish them for their offenses. There are also those who rely on having many relatives—fathers, brothers, and sons—to form malicious gangs. They seize people's property; if the victims protest, they form a mob to beat them up. They also bribe the county and prefecture officials, who seldom put an end to their crimes. You should not try to suppress these sorts of people either. Wait until their wrongs have piled up and Heaven punishes them. In addition, for no apparent reason, they will fall into the net of the law, from which no plotting of theirs can save them.[39]

In general, those who do evil but have the good fortune to avoid punishment will surely get what they deserve at a later time for no apparent reason. This is what is meant by the saying, "The net of Heaven is all-embracing; it is coarsely woven but nothing gets through."[40]   (2, 4)

2.39 SUPERIOR AND INFERIOR MEN

There are gentlemen and officials of rural communities who are armed with special tricks in their dealings with others. You cannot let these people too near you, but it is hard to keep them away. These men are what are called "the inferior people among the superior ones." You must be on your

[39] The existence of these sorts of people is also well attested in *CHTK*. The author of that work, however, does not seem to have shared Yüan Ts'ai's confidence in eventual retribution. Unless magistrates and prefects kept close control of the situation, he thought it was all too easy for these bullies to thrive.

[40] *Tao te ching* 73 (Waley, trans., p. 233).

guard, lest through their deficiencies in faithfulness and principle they get you into trouble.

Among the class of peasants, artisans, merchants, and bondservants there are some whom Heaven endowed with honesty and sincerity and who can be entrusted with business and assets. They are called "the superior men among the inferior people." Be sure to get to know them. It is best to show them some kindness and then you will never need to worry about them cheating you.   (4)

2.40   THE COMMON PRINCIPLE UNDERLYING OFFICE-HOLDING AND FAMILY MANAGEMENT

When gentlemen and officials (*shih-ta-fu*) live at home, if they could reflect on the time they spent in office, then they would not intercede with requests, seize power, and upset current practices. When they are in office, if they could reflect on their time at home, they would not provoke resentment through harshness and cruelty. Anyone incapable of such reflection will make these mistakes. Thus those currently in office will talk of the deplorable deeds of officials temporarily residing there; and the latter will often talk of the improprieties of those currently in office. Both sides fail to mention the merits of the other.   (2, 5)

2.41   EXPECTING GOOD FAITH AND TRUSTWORTHINESS FROM INFERIOR PEOPLE

Superior men seldom fail to preserve the two virtues of good faith and trustworthiness, but inferior people often lack them. For instance, when an inferior person tries to sell things, he dresses up worn or poor objects to look new and wonderful and phony ones to look genuine. Having applied glue to the satins, moistened the grain, put water into the meat, and substituted other things for medicines, he then uses clever language to get them sold. He has no consideration for those who eat or use these articles by mistake. These are examples of their lack of good faith.

There are people who take on debts and do not pay them back for a long time. When you demand payment, they promise it will be ready in one month; but when you ask for it at the stated time, you get nothing but another promise for the next month. When you come again to ask for it, you again get nothing. This can go on with ten or more promises without your ever getting anything. Also, there are crafts-men who insist on a deposit before fashioning something. They may promise the finished piece in a month, but when you ask for it in a month, you don't get it. They promise it will be ready in another month, but when you return, you still don't get it. This can occur more than ten times without your getting the object. Such behavior illustrates lack of trustworthiness. Other examples are too numerous to relate.

Inferior people act these ways day in and day out without the slightest compunction. But superior men are frequently angered and offended. Wanting to show them a lesson on the spot, they will sometimes go so far as to beat them or sue them. The superior man should reflect on his own person: Has he avoided all insincere or unfaithful acts? If he could have pity on the inferior person's ignorance and the pressures that lead him to self-serving expediency, then he could calm down a little when these annoyances occur. (5)

2.42   COUNTERFEIT MEDICINES

When the superior secretary Chang An-kuo[41] was prefect of Fu-chou, he heard that someone was selling counterfeit

[41] Chang Hsiao-hsiang (1129–1170).

medicine. He issued a placard with injunctions as follows:

> Recluse T'ao and Sage Sun, on the basis of the *Pharmaceutical*'s thousand golden prescriptions, organized the materials that are beneficial to people.[42] They performed many acts of unobtrusive virtue and their names are among the ranks of immortals. Since then there have been numerous people who have received blessings as a reward for conscientiously saving people in their practice of medicine or pharmacy. Even excluding those recorded in the pharmaceutical books, there are a great many cases in recent times. Some people have become millionaires by merely selling one effective medicine; others have gained personal glory that they enjoyed to old age; others have had their sons or grandsons pass the examinations so that their family was transformed into an official household. These rewards are like shadows following forms: they never falter. I have also with my own eyes seen people who sold counterfeit medicines. At first they accumulated a modest estate, which convinced them that their strategy was working. They were not aware that in the unseen world their family's apportioned happiness was being reduced or eliminated. Some later suffered repeated misfortunes, while in other cases it was their descendants who went bankrupt for no apparent reason. There were even some who were struck by Heaven's fire in storms or earthquakes.[43]

[42] T'ao Hung-ching of the Liang dynasty (502–556) is credited with supplementing Ko Hung's collection of prescriptions, the *Chou-hou po-i fang*. Sun Ssu-mo of the T'ang (618–906) wrote the *Ch'ien-chin fang* (*Thousand Golden Prescriptions*) in thirty chapters. Both were in circulation in the Southern Sung. See *Chih-chai shu-lu chieh-t'i*, 13, p. 371.

[43] Lightning as an especially appropriate form of punishment by Heaven appears often in *ICC* stories. See, for instance, *ICC ting* 9, pp. 615–16.

How often people, faced with a medical emergency, have proffered their money and asked the pharmacist for a remedy! Filial sons and obedient grandsons hope for a medicine that will cure in one dose. But when they are swindled into taking counterfeit medicine, it may not merely prove useless but may even do harm. If in everyday life a person accidentally kills a bird or beast, he still receives the karmic consequences. How much more true this must be for taking a man's life, since among the myriad beings men are the most valued. Those who endanger the life of innocent people will incur endless pain.

His text is lengthy, so I will not record any more. These words of the secretary do not apply exclusively to those who counterfeit medicine. Perceptive men ought to be able to think of analogous situations. (4, 5)

2.43 DIGNIFIED SPEECH AND DEPORTMENT

Market areas, streets and alleys, tea houses and wine shops are places frequented by all kinds of inferior people. When our sort has to pass through them, we must be dignified in speech and deportment. That way we can avoid the problem of being casually insulted by them.[44] If you encounter an uncontrollable drunk, it is best to get out of his way. Definitely do not get into arguments with him. (3)

2.44 CLOTHING STYLES

In the market, do not wear unusual clothing or behave in exceptional ways. If you do, inferior people will ridicule you for it.

[44] *PYT* adds the phrase, "There is also no need to listen if you are criticized."

Improving Personal Conduct

2.45 INCONSPICUOUS APPEARANCE

When living in the countryside, your carriage, horse, and clothes should not be new or splendid. The reason is that many of your relatives and old friends in the countryside are poor. If you show yourself to be special, the poor ones will be ashamed and will not dare approach you. How would you feel at ease with this? Explaining this to youngsters who still smell of milk is impossible. (4)

2.46 WOMEN'S CLOTHING

In women's clothing and ornaments, strive only for cleanliness, for it is especially important for women not to stand out. If one woman among ten others is wearing conspicuous clothes or jewelry, the others will point and take note of it. Will the odd one then feel comfortable in anything she does? (4)

2.47 RITUAL AND DUTY

Food and drink are something people want and cannot do without; but to seek them unreasonably is gluttony. Male–female relations are something people want and cannot do without; but to force them unreasonably is adultery and debauchery. Material goods are something people want and cannot do without; but to obtain them unfairly is theft and extortion. Once people let loose their desires, quarrels begin and lawsuits arise.

Because the sage kings were concerned about this, as a means of regulation they set up rituals to moderate men's food, drink, and sexual relations, and established moral principles to limit how much people take and give.[45] The superior

[45] The idea that desires are natural but their satisfaction must be regulated by the rules of ritual and duty was first elaborated by Hsün Tzu (3rd c. B.C.). See Watson, trans., esp. pp. 24–32, 89–96, 157–71.

man may know that he desires these three but he doesn't lightly give oral expression to his thoughts, much less let them grow in his heart! The inferior person is just the opposite.

2.48 TEMPTATION

The sages said that so long as you do not see desirable things, your emotions will not become confused.[46] This is a major way of keeping out of trouble. For if you see some delicious food, you will surely gulp it; if you see great beauty, you will surely stare at it; if you see money and valuables, you will surely want to get them. Unless you make determined efforts, you will not be able to escape these reactions. Only by stopping the desires at their source—by not looking when the temptation is before you—can you avoid reckless thoughts and thus make no mistakes.

2.49 PASSIONS

There are sons and younger brothers who are so mired in their passions that they lose their way permanently, in the end feeling no regret when they ruin their families. Such young men generally began by "giving it a try." Since they had had little experience, they were not able to see through to the consequences of their actions and reached the point of no return.   (3)

2.50 SELECTING FRIENDS

Some contemporaries worry that their sons and younger brothers, being immature and unsettled, could become fool-

---

[46] *Tao te ching* 3 (Waley, trans., p. 145). In all other cases where Yüan Ts'ai attributes a saying to the sage or sages, it turns out to be by *the* Sage, Confucius. Perhaps in this case he forgot where this quotation came from and thought it was found in the *Analects*.

ishly addicted to wine, women, or gambling to the point where they become confused in their goals, lose their virtue, and ruin their family. Therefore, the elders confine them to the house, restrict their coming and going, and sever their social relationships. The consequence is that the young men have no experience; they are unsophisticated, awkward, and do not understand people's feelings. Still the elders do not see the flaws in their strategy. Once you relax these prohibitions, the young men's passions will find a hole to break through and will be as irrepressible as a prairie fire. It's even worse when the young men are confined to the house where there is nothing for them to employ their minds on except secretly dreaming up ways to be unworthy. Is this any better than going out?

The best course is to have the young men come and go at reasonable intervals while choosing their friends carefully. Then they will become familiar with the unworthy activities they take part in and will learn to size up situations. They will develop a sense of shame and learn restraint, and even if they try something out, they won't be so naive and awkward that inferior people are able to manipulate them easily.   (4)

2.51   THE RISE AND FALL OF FAMILIES

Men who establish their families not only produce riches in abundance, but also day and night they make plans, worrying about how to avoid slipping back to hunger and cold. Sons who ruin their families not only cause trouble and waste their time, but also they boldly indulge themselves, saying there is nothing more to worry about.[47] This is proof of the

---

[47] Cf. the conclusion to Liu Tz'u's (9th century) family instructions: "I have observed that all of the famous and eminent families achieved their position because their ancestors were trustworthy, filial, diligent, and frugal, and they lost it because their descendants were stubborn, willful, extravagant, and proud" (*CTTL* 2/23b–24a).

saying, "The fortunate person, running into trouble, will turn it into something fortunate; the unfortunate person, even when running into good luck, will turn it into misfortune."[48] This is often seen in the middle-aged and elderly. Those who recognize this principle will understand without comment. (3, 4, 5)

2.52   FLOURISHING AND DECLINE

The man who establishes his family's fortune sees that whatever he starts turns out as he planned and concludes that this is due to his knowledge, skill, and cleverness. He does not recognize that this just happens to be his fate. As his ambitions grow, he becomes greedy and scheming. He also thinks that his family, unlike any other, will achieve long-lasting success and prove indestructible. Surely the Creator secretly laughs at such men![49] Probably the person to ruin his family has already been born. A son or grandson who morning and evening is in his company will someday cause his father or grandfather trouble and bankrupt them. The pity is that the father or grandfather does not see this with his own eyes.

One of my senior friends built a house. He entertained the builders in the east wing and said, "Here are the people who built the house." He entertained his sons and brothers in the west wing and said, "Here are the people who will sell the house." Later it turned out just as he predicted.[50]

[48] From Yang Hsiung, *Fa yen* 6 (*Fa yen i-shu* ed. of Shih-chieh shu-chü, 9/10b).

[49] Overconfidence in one's plans, which seems to deny the power of Heaven and the Creator (cf. 2.7), is a type of arrogance or self-satisfaction, to be distinguished from prudent, cautious planning, discussed in the previous item and in many others, such as 2.54 and 2.56.

[50] This story is also in *P'ing-chou k'o-t'an*, 3, p. 44.

Today's scholar-officials have a saying: "What you see before your eyes you should take steps to manage. Don't worry about things your eyes cannot see."[51] Gentlemen of perception know that the future is beyond human control, and in their own hearts they are at ease. How superior they are to the deluded! (4, 4)

2.53. BUDGETING

The person who builds up the family fortune finds it easy to make progress toward a solid position. The reason is that his clothing, food, and furnishings, as well as the miscellaneous expenses for weddings, funerals, and other rituals, are on a low and scrimpy scale, in accordance with his old habits. Therefore, every day his income exceeds his expenditure, so he always has a surplus.

The son of a rich family easily falls into bankruptcy. For, in his clothing, food, and furnishings as well as the miscellaneous expenses for weddings, funerals, and other rituals, his scale is lavish, in accordance with *his* old habits. He also may divide the property to establish several households with the result that expenses increase several-fold. When sons and younger brothers recognize their situation and make long-term plans to reduce and economize, I still worry that their efforts will be inadequate. How much worse it is with those who are not aware: How can they manage? The ancients were referring to this phenomenon when they said that to go from frugality to extravagance is easy but to go from extravagance to frugality is hard.[52]

The families of great personages of high rank are especially

---

[51] That is, do not plan too far into the future, or too ambitiously.

[52] Ssu-ma Kuang in his letter to his sons attributes this saying to an early Sung man, Chang Chih-po (*SMCC* 67, p. 840).

difficult to preserve. When they first attain position and prominence, even during inactive periods, their salary will be substantial and they will receive many gifts. They will have many people at their beck and call, and the province or prefecture will provide clothing, food, and furnishings. These may well be splendid and costly, but the money for them will not come from the family assets. But after the great man's death, the salary, gifts, and servants all cease. Daily expenses will have to be met from family assets. It is even worse when the family then divides into several families but the standard of living remains as before! How can they escape bankruptcy? Such is the force of circumstances. Heirs ought each to economize. (2, 4)

2.54   THINKING AHEAD

Some people living in our society give no thought to the obstacles their ancestors faced in establishing the family; they only think of continuing the sacrificial offerings to them.[53] They also give no thought to their descendants' need for something to rely on to protect them from hunger and cold; they give birth to numerous boys and girls and then treat them like strangers. They indulge in wine and women, gamble, and get up to no good, depleting their family property for the sake of momentary pleasures.

Such people are the misfortune of families. Nevertheless, since they do not even show concern when they risk legal punishment, there is no way you can turn them around through lecturing, cajoling, or scolding. Just leave them alone as there is no way of helping them. (4, 4)

[53] The implication here must be that one owes more to one's ancestors than mere continuation of the sacrifices through perpetuation of the blood line; one also owes efforts to maintain the family's status by careful management of its property.

2.55 FRUGALITY

Wealthy people worry about theft, so they always tie up their valuables and secure them with locks and knots. They seal and label the boxes with extreme carefulness. Out of worry that their money will be frittered away through unregulated expenses, they always budget and make estimates, spending with extreme frugality. But some who are very cautious still suffer losses. If in a hundred days of cautiousness there is not a single day of laxity, there can be no losses; but if for a hundred days you are cautious and then for one day you are not, the loss on that one day is the same as if you had been careless for a hundred days.

There are also people who are extremely economical yet deplete their resources. If in a hundred matters you are frugal and never are wasteful in even one matter, then you cannot end up depleting your reserves. But if in a hundred matters you are frugal but in one you are not, then the waste on that one can have the same effect as being casual about all matters. What I mean by the "hundred matters" include food, drink, clothing, houses, gardens, halls, carriages, horses, servants, furnishings, and hobbies; the causes of waste are diverse.

A degree of luxury in accord with your financial resources is not what I am calling wasteful. But you have reached reckless waste when you do things without calculating your financial capability, or when your actions exceed extravagance or you buy things for which you have no current need, even if you can afford them. Young men who have responsibility for their family's affairs need to acquire a profound appreciation of this.[54]   (4)

[54] Yüan Ts'ai seems to be referring to cases where a young man other than the family head might be assigned responsibility for financial affairs in a large complex family. Ssu-ma Kuang's remarks about his relatives who served as managers are given above in Part One, chap. 2, "The Family as a Corporate Unit."

Part Two

2.56   ADVANCED PLANNING

If your family property is in the middle range, you must start to worry early about all affairs. Careful thought must be given early to preparing a livelihood for your sons by teaching them an occupation or profession. You should also accumulate your daughters' dowry clothes, bedding, and jewelry in advance. Then when you send them off as brides, you will not be hard put.[55] If you set these matters aside and do not think about them, simply calling them exigencies to be handled as they occur, then what choices will you have? You will either have to sell land or buildings as temporary expedients, or callously watch your daughters' humiliation in front of others.[56]

When a family has elderly members but the items needed for the funeral and burial have not been prepared, they also call it an exigency. The only alternatives are provisionally selling land or houses or callously allowing the funeral and burial to fall below the ritual norm.

Recently there have been people who plant ten thousand pine trees when each daughter is born. After the girl is grown, they sell the trees to cover her marriage expenses, thus assuring that the girl will not miss the best time for marriage. There are also those who in their youth or middle age prepare the clothing, utensils, and tomb needed for their burials. Such people will not be left for several days without burial robes or coffins to be set out in, nor for several years without a plot to be buried in.   (4, 4)

[55] Cf. 3.64 where Yüan Ts'ai mentions having to sell land to pay for a marriage.
[56] By calling the sale temporary or provisional, Yüan Ts'ai probably means *tien* sale with the full intention of redemption.

2.57 SERVING IN OFFICE AND MANAGING A FAMILY

Serving in office should involve consideration and aid the way managing a family does. Managing a family should have rules the way serving in office does.[57]   (4, 4)

2.58 OCCUPATIONS FOR YOUNGER RELATIVES

Assuming they have no hereditary stipend or real estate to depend on, the sons and younger brothers of gentlemen-officials (*shih-ta-fu*) will need to plan for their means of supporting their parents and children.[58] In such cases, nothing is better than becoming scholars. Those with superb natural abilities can study for the *chin-shih*: the best of them can take the degree and gain wealth and official rank; the next best can set themselves up as teachers, thus receiving tuition income. Of those without the ability to pursue the *chin-shih*, the best can become clerks and work with documents, the next best can practice punctuating reading for children and become their tutors.[59]

If the profession of scholar is not possible, then the arts and skills of medicine, Buddhism and Taoism, gardening, and commerce can all provide support for your family without bringing shame to your ancestors.[60] All are acceptable. What

[57] The similarity between the rules for managing a family and managing a county or prefecture can be seen by comparing Yüan Ts'ai's advice with that of the author of the *CHTK*. For instance, his advice on controlling underlings (1, pp. 3–6) is much like Yüan Ts'ai's on controlling servants, and his advice on balancing income and outlay (1, pp. 2–3) is like Yüan Ts'ai's on household budgeting. See also Part One, chap. 7, pp. 159–61.

[58] The phrase used echoes *Mencius* 1A:7 (see Lau, trans., p. 58).

[59] It is interesting to note that in Yüan Ts'ai's hierarchy, being a clerk was better than being a tutor.

[60] Instead of "monks," *SK* has "diviners, astrologers, and physiognomists." In 1.65 the *SK* also omitted references to monks, so this change was presumably deliberate on the part of the *SK* editors.

brings the most shame to your ancestors is for your younger relatives to waste their energies in dissipation and end up as beggars or thieves. Indeed, the greatest condemnation is due those incapable of becoming scholars but unwilling to be trained as doctors, monks, farmers, or merchants, and so on, preferring to become beggars or thieves.

By beggars I mean those who go in front of a high-ranking person and with a forceful demeanor ask for assistance, or who bow before rich men and use a pretext to ask for a loan, or who sojourn at Buddhist or Taoist temples where people point to them as men of the clouds. By thieves I mean those who occupy office and conceal their embezzlements, or who while living in the countryside take advantage of the stupid and weak, seizing their possessions or privately dealing in contraband tea, salt, or wine.

How is it that there are people in our world who do these things without feeling ashamed of themselves?   (1, 4, 4)

2.59   LAZINESS AND DISSIPATION

People with no occupation, and those with occupations who are too fond of leisure to be willing to work, will get used to indecent activities if they come from rich families and will become beggars if they come from poor families. People who drink without limit or eat meat without moderation, who love to have affairs with women or are given to chess playing, will bankrupt their family if it is a rich one or become thieves if it is a poor one.   (1, 4, 4)

2.60   EMERGENCY ASSISTANCE

When people suffer a misfortune they cannot cope with, when they run into hardships and have nowhere to turn, when they are too poor to support themselves but because their character is straightforward they are too mortified to mention it to other people, in all these cases you ought to do as much as you can to aid them, even if you have little surplus yourself. Even if such people are unable to repay your kindness, they will surely be grateful.[61]

There are also people who are not actually destitute but who make a profession of calling to ask for favors. Skilled in the arts of flattery,[62] they visit all the houses of the rich and high-ranking and make requests at every prefecture or county office they pass through. Whenever they acquire something they take it as a sign of their own ability, but they get angry and bitter if they fail. They will feel no gratitude today nor return the favor in the future. The proper course is to show no pity on them and refuse to help them. How can you deprive yourself of resources you wouldn't dare squander to supply them with things they don't deserve to have!

(5, 6)

2.61 ACCEPTING FAVORS

Whether living at home in the countryside or traveling, do not accept favors from others too readily. Until you are successful yourself, you will always be conscious of having accepted the favor. Whenever you see the person who gave it, you will be deferential, and the person who extended the favor to you will look condescending. After you gain glory and success, you may not be able to repay everybody, and should you not, you may seem to have failed in your duty. Therefore, do not lightly accept even one meal or one roll of silk.

When one of my seniors used to see someone in office

[61] On repayment of kindness, see Lien-sheng Yang, "The Concept of 'Pao' as a Basis for Social Relations in China."
[62] *YCL* has "Skilled in the arts of spreading rumors and flattery...."

Part Two

trying to gain numerous patrons, he would warn him, "If you receive too many favors, it will be difficult to stand at court." It is well worth thoroughly musing over this point.

(5, 6)

2.62 REMEMBERING FAVORS

Nowadays when people receive gifts or favors they often do not remember them, but when they do anything for someone else, no matter how minor, every detail remains vivid in their memory. The ancients had a saying, "Do not remember the favors you do; do not forget the ones you receive."[63] Take this as a challenge. (3, 5)

2.63 HOW OTHERS TREAT YOU

People who were ignored by their fellow residents when they were poor and struggling will treat those townsmen like enemies after they attain glory and success themselves. This is unperceptive. If a fellow resident was unfriendly to you, and you, taking offense, are unfriendly to him in return, won't he surely also later remember your behavior?

Don't be warm with those who slighted you in the past, but also don't make them resent you. If it becomes possible to assist someone who in the past did not associate with you, you must do it. (4)

2.64 JUST RETRIBUTION

The Sage said to repay wrongs with justice.[64] This is the best course and is always appropriate. To repay a wrong with

[63] From an inscription by Ts'ui Yin (d. 92), included in *Wen hsüan* 56, p. 1206.
[64] *Analects* 14:36 (Waley, trans., p. 189).

another wrong is outside consideration. But gentlemen-officials (*shih-ta-fu*) who wish to attract a name for generosity, or who hold an old grudge, may deliberately let the other person continue doing the wrong thing.[65] This is just false show and is unreasonable.

What the sages meant by fairness is this: If the person is worthy, you do not discard him because of your personal enmity; if the person is unworthy, you do not cover it up because of your personal enmity. Right is chosen and wrong rejected according to the facts of the case. If this is the way you act when you have been wronged, you will never get caught in an endless series of reprisals.

2.65 DRAWN-OUT LAWSUITS

When you live in the countryside, whether you like it or not, you will eventually be unable to avoid getting into a dispute with someone, and much against your wishes you will find it impossible to avoid being party to a lawsuit. If the other party will admit some fault in the areas in which he is wrong, let it go at that. Then you will not have to put out money and associate with court clerks to bring down on him the maximum penalty.

When it comes to disputes and lawsuits over property where you have no case and twist the truth to appear in the right, you may attain your objective if the officials are greedy and careless, but won't you be ashamed before the gods? Besides, the one who was wronged will not take it lying down but will countersue. The expenditure will be ten or more times what it is worth. And what if you encounter a worthy and intelligent judge! How can you make wrong seem right then?

[65] That is, those with grudges purposely give him "enough rope to hang himself," as the English expression puts it.

Generally speaking, each side of a lawsuit has its strengths and weaknesses and publicizes its strengths while concealing its weaknesses. With an unperceptive judge, the case can get complicated and fail to be resolved, or a decision can be reached that doesn't cover all the particulars. In such situations the clerks may take bribes to manipulate the law. This is how the deceptive destroy their families. (2, 4, 4, 5, 6)

2.66   OPPRESSIVE OFFICIALS AND CLERKS

When the officials are greedy and cruel or the clerks high-handed and oppressive, men of wisdom and courage, unable to bear watching the populace of their locality suffer, use their power to bring charges against them. But cruel and greedy officials certainly have some backing they depend on. Perhaps they have relatives in high places or are the favorites of the prefectural authorities. Hence it is hard to have them removed. Oppressive clerks also have backers. It may be that they are loved by the officials who employ them or have old ties to the clerks in the prefecture, which makes them afraid of nothing. When a resident brings a charge, the accused official will get letters from the high and mighty pleading for protection; the accused clerks will use government funds to pay bribes, will destroy records, and will alter the legal dossiers. Even if the resident is skilled in litigation, winning is never easy.

There are also people who bring charges against officials just because they want to intimidate the officials into treating them with special caution. These people start their lawsuits without any notion of ridding the populace of an evil. I have often noticed that people who bring charges against county and prefectural officials then take advantage of the officials' fear of them to put off payment of their taxes. Ordinary households have to pay some converted taxes; these people decline to do so. Ordinary households have to pay special assessments; these people refuse to. They stand in court with their eyes askance, answering the officials with no sense of deference. They assume a formal posture when sitting in the county offices where they curse and humiliate the clerks. They boldly appropriate official property but are unwilling to pay taxes. They cheat and insult good but weak people, yet demand penalties against others. In their constant pursuit of subverting justice, they ask for favors in government matters. Some of them conspire with the clerks in their evildoings. They manipulate the official staff to make them tolerate whatever malicious acts they want to do against the local people. Anyone—official or commoner—who is so wicked will in due course be punished by Heaven, even if he avoids suffering at the hands of men.

2.67   POPULAR CUSTOMS

When gentlemen and officials (*shih-ta-fu*) meet, they often say that the commoners of such-and-such county are peaceable, and the commoners of such-and-such another county are unruly. If you look into the grounds for these characterizations, you will see that if local commoners dare not utter a word, swallowing their sounds and sucking in their breath when they suffer from corrupt officials, then they are called "peaceable." If they make lists of their official's wrongs and bring charges to the prefecture or circuit intendants, then they are "unruly." Isn't this a distortion of the meaning of unruly?

People today often point to Feng-hua county as unruly.[66] If you ask the residents of Feng-hua, they say, "The officials we accused had all taken bribes. What is this talk of Feng-hua

[66] Feng-hua was in eastern Chekiang, near Ningpo.

being unruly!" Their version is entirely accurate according to what is said by people from nearby places like Huang-yen.[67] Such behavior is just what the Sage meant when he said, "The people supplied the means by which the Three Dynasties walked the straight path."[68] How is this unruliness!

Let me itemize the conduct that is unruly. If people do not pay taxes or imposts or additional assessments they owe, they are indeed unruly. But if the county on some grounds expands the additional assessments, concealing the breakdown, then if the people are unwilling to pay them it is not unruliness. When officials in their judicial decisions base themselves on the utmost impartiality and are in accord with the meaning of the law, then it is unruliness to follow selfish interest and angrily seek to overturn a decision. But when the officials take bribes and declare right to be wrong, then if those who suffer the injustice appeal or bring charges by turns, they are not unruly. When the officials are pure and upright and decide cases themselves, and local bullies have no one they can bribe nor any way to lay plots, then it is unruliness to connive with the clerks to coordinate the written and oral evidence and to embellish matters in order to start unreasonable lawsuits. But if the officials are in league with the clerks to devise schemes of all sorts, which they conceal from scrutiny while accepting bribes and stealing the office funds, then those who are able to put forth the effort to cry injustice on behalf of the populace are not unruly.

[67] Huang-yen was a county in eastern Chekiang, near T'ai-chou and Kuei-chi.

[68] *Analects* 15:24 (Waley, trans., p. 198), "The Master said, 'In my dealings with men, which do I slander, which do I glorify? If I sometimes seem to glorify someone, it is because I found reason to do so from examination. The people supplied the means by which the Three Dynasties followed the straight path (i.e. the path of uprightness).'" The Three Dynasties are the Hsia, Shang, and Chou,

2.68   TAX FRAUDS

When counties or circuits have officials who arbitrarily impose additional taxes or take them in advance under the pretext of borrowing government funds, people will urge one another to bring charges. For the twice-a-year tax has its own fixed quota, sufficient to furnish what is due the court and what is needed for the prefecture and county. The labor service tax also has a fixed quota, adequate to cover expenditures and hiring laborers for dispatching and delivering the revenues. When the county officials rectify themselves, thereby guiding those below them, the people will not hide their obligations and will pay up. If officials never steal and never waste anything, they cannot expect a surplus, but neither will they have to worry about deficits.[69]

Now, unscrupulous county magistrates have the canton officers supply every item of their food, clothes, and daily necessities, their conveyances for social visits, the presents they send to ask for favors, the articles they have made, the goods they store in boxes, as well as all sorts of other needs.[70] How can those who serve as canton officers use their own assets to supply the county officials? Consequently, those in these positions must play tricks with the files and documents. Some divert the people's tax payments and do not deliver them to the government. Others misappropriate money in the treasury. Some counterfeit receipts to show that an army passed by or that they entertained guests in transit. Or surreptitiously they may repair the office buildings but publicly ask for funds to cover damage. Or in the open they may act as though they are forwarding goods but on the road intercept

[69] This item is apparently addressed to active local officials and seems somehow misplaced in his book. Its general tone is similar to *CHTK* 4, pp. 35–39.

[70] On canton functionaries (not regular officials), see Brian E. McKnight, *Village and Bureaucracy in Southern Sung China*, passim.

and appropriate them. The variety of frauds they practice defies enumeration.

As the county officials are used to their corruption, they ask no questions, even though they know what is going on. It is even worse when those involved are dull-witted and do not understand the fine points of finance and taxes, or when they conspire in the frauds. Then within a year even a small county can be short several thousand strings of cash without anyone even noticing.

For these reasons, when an official has had trouble due to arbitrary increases or improper loans so that on completion of his term of service there is still an outstanding debt to the prefecture, he will try to bribe his way out, just to get free from his post. The prefecture then takes the accumulated deficit and forces the next administration to make it up. Now, if the prior administration found that one year's tax revenue was inadequate for one year's expenditures, how is the succeeding administration going to be able to make up the deficits of several years' taxes out of one year's revenue? Therefore, often they will refuse responsibility for what was borrowed by the previous administration. Or they may devise other schemes to extract the people's wealth covertly to make up for the old shortages. Imagine the disaster this causes! [71]

Those who occupy an office and oversee its affairs must be meticulous. They must search fully for any signs of crafty clerks or treacherous local people. If they trust the clerks too easily, then the clerks will accept bribes from the local people. All sorts of forgeries and lies will be perpetrated, and right and wrong will be confused. If the magistrate makes his decisions on the evidence they supply, how can he help but pervert justice?

[71] The remainder of this passage is found only in the *CPTC*.

Sometimes youngsters become officials and prove dull-witted and ignorant of how affairs are handled. They may share the greed of the clerks, and even when they know who is in the right decide to the contrary. In such cases, the grievances the commoners suffer never get redressed. This is why so many of those who serve in office have no descendants. If you are in this situation, shouldn't you also think about the reason your superiors entrusted you with this position, and why your subordinates are making appeals and bringing charges to you? Isn't it because they hope that you will redress the wrongs they've suffered? How can you not be fully impartial in your spirit!

The general rule is that as an official you should place the highest emphasis on the spirit of impartiality. Doing so will not only allow you to avoid bringing shame on yourself; it can also bring benefits to your sons and grandsons.

CHAPTER 3

Managing Family Affairs

3.1   SOLID HOUSES

In managing a family, you should see to it that the fence walls around your house are high and sturdy, the hedges dense, and the windows, walls, doors, and gates secure. Repair any damage promptly. If there are drainage outlets for water, put grates over them. Keep them new and strong and do not neglect them. Even though clever thieves will be able to find ways to enter in a moment by boring holes in fence walls, cutting through hedges, knocking holes in house walls, and breaking open doors, you will at least not be inviting them in as you would be by allowing dilapidated fence walls, broken hedges, rotten house walls, and worn-out doors. Moreover, through these maintenance efforts, you will avoid the problems caused by slaves running off or unworthy sons sneaking out at night. Although the authorities can deal with robberies, runaways, or trouble caused by unworthy sons, the cost will be high.   (2, 3, 4)

3.2   ESTATE TENANTS

Your residence may be off by itself in a quiet, rustic spot in a mountain valley. If so, be sure to set up estate tenant houses at strategic spots in a circle around the house. Recruit families with several adult men to live in the houses. Then if there is a fire or an intruder, the tenants can come to your aid when you call for help.   (2, 4, 5, 6)

3.3   RAISING ALARMS AT NIGHT

The barking of dogs at night is not always a sign of the arrival of intruders. Yet because there could be a thief making a test, you must not assume an innocent explanation and fail to raise an alarm. The same holds true for strange noises heard at night; do not simply attribute them to mice and fail to raise alarms.   (2, 4, 5, 6)

3.4   PATROLS

You ought to see that there is a passable road in a full circle around your house. At night have ten or more patrols on this path. Careful planners live near the city wall and away from empty lots. In addition they have a double set of walls and send someone to patrol in between them. Within the house itself, you can have the young men and the bondservants take turns making patrols.   (2, 3, 4, 5)

3.5   CHASING THIEVES AT NIGHT

If you hear a thief at night, you should immediately shout "There's a thief" and then proceed to catch him in a deliberate fashion. The thief will surely try to escape. You should not try to hit him in the dark, for there is the danger that the thief's panic will lead him to wound you with a knife, or by mistake you might hit someone in your own family.[1] If you take a candle to look at the thief, there will still be time to strike him. When a thief is captured, naturally you should abide by the law. Do not beat him excessively.

(2, 3, 4, 5)

[1] *ICC ting* 6, p. 590 tells the story of a man who killed his own son in the middle of the night, thinking he was a thief. This led to his wife, then him, and finally his son's wife all hanging themselves. This is supposed to have happened in 1172, so perhaps Yüan Ts'ai remembered it.

(279)

3.6   TEMPTING THIEVES

Families with great accumulations of goods are the ones thieves love. And because the people in these families often like to display their magnificence, they set out their treasured articles; this makes the thieves salivate even more! Rich and substantial families may store money and grain but should not collect precious objects or gold, jewelry, or silk. That way, even if they are robbed, their losses will not be large.

One of my elders warned his family that, outside of summer and winter clothes, they should keep on hand as a precaution against the unexpected not more than one hundred bolts of silk.[2] This is the view of a profound person. But is there any point in trying to explain this to the ordinary person?   (2, 4)

3.7   IN CASE OF ARMED ROBBERY

Some robbers come in the middle of the night; with torches and unsheathed knives, they force open the door and enter the house. It is essential that you be prepared for such incidents. You should send people to keep a lookout at the entrance to nearby roads. If anything out of the ordinary occurs, they can warn you. Also, arrange for a side exit that the old, the young, and the women can use for escape in case of emergency.

You should also, as a routine matter, have the young men in your family and the male servants maintain the weapons and know what steps to take to defend against attack. If they can withstand an attack, they should do so; if not, they should avoid confrontation. But by no means let the robbers capture

[2] Silk had regularly served as a medium of exchange and tax payment in the T'ang, and some tax was still collected in silk in the Sung. See D. C. Twitchett, *Financial Administration under the T'ang Dynasty*, pp. 25, 70–71. See also 3.70.

any family members. If someone is taken, he or she will be made a hostage, and the local mutual security group and the police will not dare pursue the robbers.[3]   (2, 4, 5)

3.8   OPPRESSION AS A CAUSE OF ROBBERY

Although robbers are inferior people par excellence, they also have rationales. Rich families who normally are not oppressive and moreover are able to be charitable and to do good deeds will be spared during disturbances created by fighting or fire. The robbers will be merciful to them and not burn down their houses. Generally the families robbers derive satisfaction from burning, looting, or debauching[4] are those of people who have done many evils. Rich families each ought to examine themselves in this regard.

(1, 2, 3, 4, 6)

3.9   MISSING OBJECTS

In a family house, should an object be missed, begin a search promptly. Knowing there is to be an immediate search, the culprit may toss the object in some out-of-the-way spot and you can regain it without an incident. If the search is not prompt, the object can be passed to someone outside, making recovery impossible.

At the same time, do not suspect a person without evidence. If your suspicions are well placed, the culprit may suspect your suspicions and do something unfortunate. If

---

[3] At the lowest level a single mutual security group (*pao*) was composed of ten households, five such *pao* formed a large *pao*, and ten large *pao* a general *pao*. Each level of *pao* had a *pao* head with responsibility for reporting crimes. On this system see Brian McKnight, *Village and Bureaucracy*, pp. 33–72.

[4] This and the previous sentence follow the reading of the 1179 editions.

your suspicions are misplaced, then the true thief will be getting just what he wants.

What is worse, once suspicion has been aroused, you will interpret every action or expression of the one you suspect as related to the theft, when actually he never stole anything. Sometimes your suspicion has already been put into words, or the suspected party unreasonably punished, when the lost object accidentally turns up or the real thief is captured. Regrets are then too late. (2, 4, 5, 6)

3.10 KINDLY RELATIONS WITH NEIGHBORS

You must have neighbors near where you live, for otherwise there will be no one to rescue you in case of fire. If there is no stream in the area immediately around your house, you should dig a pond or well, for otherwise there will be no water for extinguishing fires. In addition, in normal times you must assist and succor your neighbors with kindness.

There are gentlemen-officials (*shih-ta-fu*) who in ordinary times use their official influence to maltreat and bully their neighbors.[5] One day an enemy may come and attack their family or burn their house, but the neighbors will warn each other, "If we put out the fire, afterwards not only will we receive no reward, but that man will bring charges against us, saying we stole his family's goods. Who knows how long the case will be at court? If we do not go to his aid to put out the fire, all we'll receive is one hundred blows."[6]

The neighbors would willingly take the beating to enjoy watching the mansion burn to the ground, with none of the

---

[5] Cf. 1.39 and 1.40 on bullies who came from *shih-ta-fu* families.
[6] *Ch'ing-yüan t'iao-fa shih-lei*, pp. 606–608 has a long series of punishments for fire-related offenses but does not list this one expressly. The punishment, however, for failing to aid the firefighters when a government building was on fire was one hundred blows.

furnishings passed down to the surviving generations. Such are the consequences of the owner's previous cruelty.

(2, 4, 4, 5)

3.11   KITCHEN STOVES

Fires usually start with the kitchen stove. One reason is that the kitchen is not swept for long periods and the dust and soot easily catch fire. Fires also start because embers are left in the stove and ignite a stack of firewood left beside it. During the night be sure that the stove is checked during patrols.

(2, 4)

3.12   DRYING THINGS OVER FIRES

Drying things overnight often leads to a fire. At home people may put a cover over a smoldering fire and place clothes or baskets on top. These items are highly inflammable and must be constantly watched.   (2, 3, 4)

3.13   FIRES IN TENANTS' HOUSES

Because the houses of silk workers are low and cramped, when it is time to set the cocoon frames over the fire, precautions against fire are essential.[7]

Peasant families are in danger of fire because they collect manure and often build thatched houses. Moreover sometimes ashes are dumped near them. Caution must be exercised to be sure there are no live embers in the ashes capable of starting a fire.   (2, 4)

---

[7] The frames with the silkworms were set over fires to keep them warm during spinning. See *T'ien-kung K'ai-wu*, trans. E-tu Zen Sun and Shiou-chuan Sun, p. 42.

3.14 OTHER CAUSES OF FIRES

With thatched-roofed houses, you must be on constant guard against fires. During wind storms you must be on constant guard against fires. If you store oil or coal,[8] you must be on constant watch against fires. Situations like these that call for careful supervision are numerous.   (1, 2, 4)

3.15 ADORNING CHILDREN

Rich people who dote on their little children deck them out with gold, silver, pearls, and jewels. Covetous inferior people will waylay the children in some quiet out-of-the-way spot and kill them to get the jewels. Even if the culprit is reported to the government and sentenced by the law, what good is this to you?   (1, 2, 4, 4, 5)

3.16 LEAVING CHILDREN UNATTENDED

In the city, because of the danger of kidnappers, do not allow little children out in the streets and alleys unless an adult male is carrying them or holding their hands.   (2, 4, 4)

3.17 CHILD SAFETY

Wells in people's houses should have railings around them, as should ponds. Care is needed at spots with deep ravines and rapid streams, high points where one could fall, and near machines that can be set off by a touch. Do not let little children get right up to them. If by any chance someone is careless, it will be too late to place the blame elsewhere.

(2, 3, 4, 5, 6)

[8] Reading "coal" for *hui* "limestone."

3.18 MAKING PEOPLE DRINK

When relatives and guests come to visit, do not pressure them to drink. Some may fall asleep for the night from the wine, and you will have to order someone to look after them.

Once in Kua-ts'ang[9] someone plied a guest with wine. Afraid that the guest might leave without saying good-bye, he put him to sleep in an empty room and locked the door. When his hangover made him thirsty, the guest called out for something else to drink; when he got no response he drank the water in the flower vase. The next day when the host opened the door he found that the guest had died. The guest's family brought the case to court. The prefect, Wang Huai-chung, thoroughly searched the room, and saw the flower vase and the soaking dried lotus flower. Wang put a dried lotus flower into the vase water as a test, then had a criminal under a death sentence try it. This proved that it was poisonous, and the host was released. In another case, someone left water on a table without covering it. There was a snake in the room which left poison in the water. A guest, by drinking this, died. See how careful one must be in all matters!

(2, 4, 4)

3.19 UNDESIRABLE ACTIVITIES OF SERVANTS

Having them rise at daybreak and go to bed promptly at sundown is the way to stop illicit sexual relations, theft, and other undesirable activities among male and female bondservants.[10]   (1, 2, 4, 4)

---

[9] A county in Chekiang.
[10] Following the reading in the 1179 editions. *CPTC* omits "male and female bondservants."

3.20 SEGREGATION OF THE INNER AND OUTER QUARTERS

Ssu-ma Wen Kung's[11] "Miscellaneous Forms for Managing a Family" requires that male servants stay outside the gate to the main hall except in emergencies or to make a repair. Wives, daughters, maids, and concubines likewise do not go through the gate to the outer courtyard without good reason. Instead, they use a bell to call a serving boy to carry messages between the two areas.[12] This is over half of what is needed to manage a household.   (3, 4, 4)

3.21 PRECAUTIONS FOR MAIDS AND CONCUBINES

Maids come into close contact with their masters, and some make use of this to form an illicit relationship. When the servant class bear children, they attribute them to the master. As a result people often raise stupid and vulgar offspring who end up ruining the family.

The general rule with maids and concubines is to be careful of what is begun and to take precautions concerning how things may end.   (1, 2, 3, 4)

3.22 RESTRICTING THE MOVEMENTS OF MAIDS

When men do not prohibit their maids and concubines from freely coming and going, sometimes a woman may have relations with an outsider and get pregnant. If the master simply drives the woman away without clearly establishing her guilt, often after he has died she claims that the child was his and tries to get the boy accepted into the family. This easily gives rise to lawsuits.

Take warning from this so as not to burden your descendants with trouble.   (1, 4)

[11] That is, Ssu-ma Kuang. See Part One, chap. 2.
[12] *SMSSI* 4, p. 43.

3.23 SETTING UP MAIDS AND CONCUBINES

Some men with jealous wives set up maids or concubines in separate houses. Some even support prostitutes as their concubines, ordering them to stop seeing anyone else. Such men set up very tight precautions and arrange for very thorough supervision. Yet the man entrusted with the task of supervising may be bribed to turn around and serve as the lookout for some outsider who wants to come and go without the master's knowledge. This can reach the point where the master rears the outsider's son as his own heir.

Another problem occurs when the woman gives birth while the master is away. She then can discard the girl she bore and substitute someone else's boy. The master then rears him without knowing he is not his own son. How naive and stupid these men are!   (2, 4, 4)

3.24 TAKING CONCUBINES LATE IN LIFE

Most women are jealous, so men with wives seldom keep concubines, and those who do keep them usually are without wives.[13]

If you keep maids and concubines, precautions and restrictions are needed both with regard to your sons and younger brothers within the family and with regard to servants outside it. Even when you have a wife to act as mistress there is sometimes trouble, so naturally there is more when no one is in charge.

If only one person is keeping an eye out, deception will be easy. Therefore, doing this late in life is especially unsuitable. What would you do if an unexpected disaster happened?

                                                          (1, 2, 4, 4)

[13] Here Yüan Ts'ai is speaking of "favored concubines," not women closer to maids, whom he routinely mentions as under the supervision of wives.

3.25   GUARDING CONCUBINES

Families that keep concubines sometimes are so foolish as to house them in side rooms no one else ever passes or rooms with side doors to the outside. Sometimes the toilet is next to the kitchen and a man manages the kitchen. Sometimes at night there is drinking in an inner room and male servants help in the service.[14]

Some of the deceptions are beyond anyone's ability to prevent because concubines plan carefully to keep the master from getting suspicious. Since they will take turns keeping a lookout for each other, the master has no means of learning what is going on.   (2, 4)

3.26   ATTRACTIVE CONCUBINES

For the amusement of their guests, some men teach their maids and concubines to sing and dance or to serve food and wine. In such cases do not select women of striking beauty or superior intelligence, for there is the danger that such a woman will arouse feelings of lust in some evil guest. On seeing such beauty he will want to get a hold of it and will chase after it with such singlemindedness that he ignores all obstacles.[15] If the guest has authority over you, anything can happen. The affair of Lü-chu is an example from antiquity,[16] but there are also plenty in recent times that I'd prefer not to mention by name.   (1, 2, 3, 4)

---

[14] The idea here is apparently that any contact with male servants is dangerous.

[15] Literally: like one who, chasing an animal, does not see Mt. T'ai.

[16] Lü-chu was a favored concubine of Shih Ch'ung (d. 300). When the prince Sun Hsiu saw her, he wanted her; when he couldn't get her easily, he arranged to have Shih executed. Lü-chu committed suicide rather than be taken. In the end Shih's whole family, fifteen people in all, lost their lives. See *Chin shu*, 33, p. 1008.

3.27   GAMBLING IN THE WOMEN'S QUARTERS

In the families of gentlemen-officials (*shih-ta-fu*) sometimes at night men and women get together in a group and noisily play at dice until dawn. In such cases why not make excuses and leave? Try to give it some calm thought.   (2, 3, 4)

3.28   SELECTING SERVANTS

Families with menservants ought to choose ones who are simple, straightforward, careful, honest, and willing to apply themselves to their tasks. You should not pick those who have a pleasing way of responding to orders or moving about. Otherwise your sons and younger brothers, who know nothing about where their food and clothes come from, will have no ambition to excel in virtuous endeavors; instead they will want their servants to excel in appearance and cleverness.

Wasting money on supporting these useless men is not the worst thing you could do, but when the younger members of your family get into trouble, it will be this type of servant that led them there.   (2, 4, 5)

3.29   OVERLY SMART SERVANTS

Do not keep servants who look like the frivolous young men in the market place, who wear unusual hats and attractive clothes, or whose speech is deceptively persuasive.

If you have kept a servant for a long time and suddenly he acts this way, you should be suspicious about the goings-on in the women's quarters.   (2, 4)

3.30   LENIENCY TOWARD BONDSERVANTS

Bondservants are inferior people (*hsiao-jen*) who labor for others. Heaven has usually endowed them with dull intellects. In their work they make stupid mistakes and are disobedient. They make no effort to save you trouble. For instance, in arranging goods, they will let the crooked pass for straight, or in cutting up things, they will try to let the long pass for short.

The reasons for this sort of behavior are varied. Some bondservants are very forgetful by nature; you charge them with some matter and they remember not a whit of it. Others by nature are overly obstinate; they show you something that is not right but claim it is right. Still others by nature are overly irascible; they answer back lightly and do not know their place. For these reasons, the master often shouts insults at them when giving orders. When the servants respond by becoming more quarrelsome instead of by reforming their ways, the master loses his temper and may start to beat them. Sometimes, through a slip of his hand, he ends up killing them.

Family heads, when giving orders if something displeases you, say to yourself: "The natural stupidity of inferior people is like this." [17] You should deal with the servants leniently and teach them more thoroughly, to save having to reprimand them again. If you follow this course, the servant can avoid punishment and you as the master can attain greater tranquillity. You can also save a lot of trouble.

As for maids and concubines, they are even more stupid than male servants. Besides, your wives and daughters are often petty, quick-tempered, quarrelsome, obstinate, cruel, oppressive, and ignorant of the ancient and recent moral truths. Therefore, in rebuking the maids and concubines they go much further even than their husbands. As the family head, you ought regularly during times when nothing is

[17] Cf. 1.6 on dispelling anger.

happening to explain to your wife the way to deal with bondservants in the hopes of enlightening her.   (2, 4, 5, 6)

3.31   DELEGATING SUPERVISION

In managing a family, some men make the decisions for themselves on what should be done in all matters, from putting things where they belong to the work of fields, storehouses, kitchens, privies, and so on. Afterwards they issue repeated orders to the bondservants to get the work done but still continually worry that they will be neglectful and things will not be done as planned.

Other family heads nowadays give personal attention to nothing; the bondservants are allowed to decide what to do in all matters, large or small. When the family heads are not satisfied with the results, they angrily curse and beat them over and over. Those stupid servants are only able to do physical work and to follow orders. How would they be able to make good plans that in every regard match the master's unstated goals? If you do not understand this, you will bring a lot of trouble on yourself.

The best course is to have one person who is not engaged in toil act as supervisor just the way craftsmen do. Call him the Worker in Charge. The rationale for this is that when a person has his own tasks to perform he does not have the time to observe others. So you must order one person who has no task himself to observe and lay plans for the others. It will not be much trouble, and the success of the work will double.

(2, 4, 5)

3.32   OBSTINATE SERVANTS

Bondservants, male or female, who are obstinate and completely incapable of following direction should be amicably sent away. Do not retain them or else unpleasant incidents will occur. The master might go overboard in beating them and cause injury; their type, resenting this, might make trouble, some of which is unmentionable.

Servants, male or female, who commit adultery or theft or who run away should be dispatched to the authorities and dealt with according to the law. Do not beat them yourself as a private punishment, for there is a danger that something unintended might happen.

In cases where running away was not the servant's own wish, or what was stolen was merely some food, drink, or trifle, you should remember his or her diligence in the past and merely inflict light punishment. You may retain him or her as before and continue giving orders.   (1, 2, 4)

3.33   BEATING SERVANTS

When your servants commit misdemeanors, do not beat them yourself. The reason is that, at the moment of anger, you will not keep count of the number of strokes you inflict. Your efforts will be in vain and merely tire you, and your servants will not necessarily hold you in greater awe. You should reproach them calmly and order someone else to beat them, setting the number of strokes in accordance with the seriousness of the offense. Contradictory as it may seem, by not showing excessive anger you will gain authority; your maids and concubines will come to hold you in awe and trepidation.

In the family of prefectural assistant Hu Yen-t'e of Shou-ch'ang,[18] the young men are not allowed to beat male

[18] Shou-ch'ang was a prefecture in Chekiang, less than 50 miles from Yüan Ts'ai's native place. The *CPTC* ed. does not give the title "prefectural assistant," merely saying "Mister." The 1179 editions include it.

bondservants themselves, nor are the women allowed to beat the maids and concubines. If any of the servants does something wrong, the family members report it to the family head, who deals with the case. If a woman beats a maid or concubine on her own, one of the young men is beaten.[19] These are the family rules of a wise man.   (1, 2, 4, 5, 6)

3.34   TIMES FOR CORRECTING SERVANTS

Once you have finished beating a male or female servant who did something wrong, give orders in exactly the usual way to avoid further problems. The reason for this is that an inferior person (*hsiao-jen*) who has just been beaten will be resentful; if the master's anger does not let up, there is a danger that he or she might commit suicide [to get back at him].   (1, 2, 3, 5)

3.35   PERVERSITY ON THE PART OF SERVANTS

In cases where servants hang themselves for no reason, they can be saved if the body is still warm. Do not untie the rope [from the rafters]. Grasp the body and raise it a little so that the noose becomes a little looser. Then have someone else slowly loosen the noose with his fingers. When you see that the breath is gradually coming back, then you can let the body down. Next quickly get someone to suck air out of the servant's nose to make his breathing continuous.[20] This way

---

[19] As her punishment. The family head cannot beat his sisters-in-law or daughters-in-law, so he has their husbands beaten instead.

[20] Apparently a kind of artificial respiration is meant. See also McKnight, trans., *The Washing Away of Wrongs*, pp. 155–56, where a wider variety of methods of reviving hanging bodies is given, including ones supposedly useful even for bodies already cold.

the servant can be revived. Sometimes out of ignorance of these principles, people start by untying the rope where it is attached. Because of the weight of the body, the noose becomes even tighter. Within the time elapsed by a breath, rescue becomes impossible.[21] Therefore you must know in advance what to do.

When the body is already cold, rescue is impossible; if tried it will not lead to revival. In such cases, you should keep the body where it is without moving it. Call for the local mutual security group to have the matter reported to the government.[22] Order a dependable person to keep watch day and night, lest dogs or rats desecrate the corpse.

Cases of self-inflicted wounds are no different. You should cover the wound with something. If life is already ended, do as described above.

Houses with wells should have steps made in the side of the wells by gaps in the brick work; this will allow people to go up and down. If someone falls into or jumps into the well, a person can be sent in to save him or her. If the rescue attempt is unsuccessful, proceed as outlined above.

In cases of drowning (intentional or not), if the water is too deep for someone to walk in and pull the person out, you should throw a bamboo pole and something that floats like a wooden board, which the drowning person can grab and use for flotation. That way rescue is possible. If unsuccessful, proceed as outlined earlier.

In case of death from nightmares while sleeping or other

[21] Probably what actually occurs is that the neck breaks and severs the spinal column. An ordinary hanging leads to death by strangulation, a process that takes some time. In modern execution by hanging, by dropping the body and breaking the neck, death is nearly instantaneous.

[22] See n. 3 above. On the official inquests that follow, see McKnight's introduction to *The Washing Away of Wrongs*. On the specific problem of suicides by servants, see pp. 111–12 in the same book, where the importance of not moving bodies is stressed.

sudden deaths, do not move the corpse, as already explained.[23]   (1, 2, 4)

3.36 SERVANTS' ILLNESSES

When servants who have no relatives get sick, have them go to a neighbor's house to be treated. Also have the local mutual security group record their statements and inform the government of it. Then if they die there will be no complications.[24]   (4)

3.37 PROVIDING THE NECESSITIES FOR SERVANTS

If you want servants to work hard for you, you must provide them with the wherewithal to stave off hunger and cold. The family head must constantly keep this fact in mind and see that their clothes are warm and their food filling.

The gentlemen-officials (*shih-ta-fu*) have a saying: "Do not be vexed that you keep too many maids: Teach them to spin and weave and they will be able to produce clothes for the body. Do not be vexed that you keep too many menservants: Teach them to plow and plant and they will be able to produce food for the stomach."

As a general rule, lesser people (*hsiao-min*) have enough strength to manage their own food and clothes, but because they lack the resources on which to apply their strength, they

[23] Death from nightmares and sudden death were officially recognized causes of death. See McKnight, trans., *Washing Away of Wrongs*, pp. 158, 161.

[24] In general the authorities were supposed to investigate all deaths of people who did not live among relatives who could testify that they died of natural causes. One way to avoid an inquest in the case of a servant with no nearby relatives was to have a deposition concerning the illness made before the death occurred. See McKnight, trans., *The Washing Away of Wrongs*, pp. 10, 43, 142.

cannot maintain themselves and must seek to work for others. Rich families must try to have compassion for them. If they keep servants, then they should take care of their physical needs in return for the labor they perform. The virtue in this is great. And their sort will gladly perform strenuous toil for you so long as you keep them warm and fed. (2, 4, 5, 6)

3.38 PLACES FOR EVERY PERSON AND ANIMAL

The places where the male and female bondservants sleep should all be checked out. You should make sure that they are protected from the wind and cold in the winter. This even applies to the likes of oxen, horses, pigs, sheep, cats, dogs, chickens, and ducks: each should have space in a pen or enclosure to rest in during periods of cold. This thoughtfulness characterizes the benevolent person who recognizes the underlying similarity between us and other beings.

(1, 4, 5, 6)

3.39 THE DESIRE FOR LIFE

Birds and animals may differ from man in their physical and moral make-up, but they share with man a preference for community and a distaste for isolation, a greediness for life and a fear of death. Therefore birds and animals cry plaintively when they are separated from their flock or herd and wail when they are brought to the kitchen. People have become hardened to this and pay no attention: indeed some get angry at the noise.

Why not ponder this for a moment of self-reflection? What birds and animals want from man is the same as what man wants from Heaven. When animals cry out, they are appealing to men, but the men have no pity on them. Now, when men are in situations of distress, danger, and suffering, how can they look up and wail in hope of gaining Heaven's pity? As a rule, men who are seriously ill and unable to go on any longer and ones imprisoned and unable to get out invariably reflect on their past actions, saying to themselves, "such was bad, such was wrong." Those who through remorse decide to begin anew call on Heaven and the sun as witnesses to their vows. Yet once they have recovered or gained their liberty, they give no more thought to the vows. They commit sins and do bad things, just as before.

If I repeated the above to someone going through a time of trial, he would concur with it.[25] Yet I still worry that after his suffering ends, he would forget it. What chance is there that anyone ignorant of suffering will see my remarks as other than farfetched? (5, 6)

3.40 WET NURSES

My seniors have stated how wrong it is to employ someone to suckle your child instead of having the mother do it herself.[26] It is particularly bad to seek a wet nurse before the baby is born and to make a woman abandon her own child to suckle yours. Indeed, when the nurse's child is still an infant and she sets it aside to nurse yours, her baby will cry and will even sometimes die of starvation.

[25] Following the reading in the 1179 editions.

[26] Hung Mai, in *Su-k'ao*, 7b, also says his seniors made such a remark but does not identify his source either. *CSL* 6, p. 195 (Chang, trans., p. 178) includes a passage by Ch'eng I saying that it is wrong to make a mother abandon and thereby kill her child to suckle yours but does not condemn the practice of using wet nurses as strongly as Yüan Ts'ai does, saying it is often necessary because the mother is unable to nurse her own child. Ssuma Kuang mentions nothing against employing wet nurses. In *SMSSI* 4, p. 44, he says, "When one seeks a wet nurse for a newborn son, take care to choose a woman from a decent family who has a gentle and modest nature."

There are also cases where an official assigned away from home will pressure a broker into trapping the wife of a commoner into giving up her husband and children to suckle his baby. Later he forces the nurse to come home with him, thus breaking up her family, for she never sees the rest of them again during their lifetimes.

Gentlemen and officials cover up for each other in this matter, and the laws have not been able to put a stop to it. But have the guilty ones no fear of Heaven! (2, 4)

3.41 RETURNING HIRED WOMEN

If you hire someone's wife or daughter as a bondmaid, you should return her to her husband or parents on completion of her period of service. If she comes from another district, you should send her back to it after her term is over. These practices are the kindest and are widely carried out by the gentlemen-officials in Che-tung.[27] Yet there are people who do not return their maids to their husbands, remarrying them to others instead; others do not return them to their parents but marry them off themselves. Such actions are the source of many lawsuits.

Even worse are those who have no sympathy for their maids' separation from their relatives and distance from their hometowns and who make them stay in service for their entire lives with neither husbands nor sons. Even in death these women's spirits are left unsupported.[28] How pitiful it all is!

[27] Name of a circuit, Liang-che tung-lu (where Yüan Ts'ai lived), largely corresponding to present Chekiang.
[28] A reference to the need to have sons in order to become an ancestor and receive ritual offerings.

3.42   LOCAL SERVANTS AND SLAVES

If you are going to keep bondservants, local people are best. When they become ill, their relatives can be asked to take care of them and support them. If they destroy themselves for no good reason, their relatives can look into what happened and as witnesses give testimony about whether the suicide was strictly a private act or not.[29]

If it happens that you have maids with no husbands, sons, or brothers to depend on, or male bondservants with no homes to return to, in recognition of their labors you have no choice but to maintain them. You ought to have them make statements in advance to the local mutual security group and in addition inform the government authorities.

Another alternative is to plan in advance by choosing mates for your male and female servants. That way you can avoid unanticipated problems later on.   (1, 4)

3.43   BROKERS

When hiring a male or female servant, you must use a broker-guarantor to make the selection. Moreover, do not allow someone from your own family to perform this service.   (1, 4)

3.44   THE PROVENANCE OF MAIDS AND CONCUBINES

When you buy a maid or concubine, after the contract is written you must closely look into the woman's origins. There is always the danger that she is a commoner's daughter who was kidnapped. If that turns out to be the case, report it

---

[29] See 3.35 and 3.36 on procedures with servants' deaths.

immediately to the authorities; out of concern for her safety do not return her to those who offered her to you for sale.

(1, 4)

3.45   THE LEGALITY OF SALE OF MAIDS

In buying a maid or concubine, you must inquire whether she can legally be indentured or sold. If not, do not complete the contract. Should she really be destitute and without means of support, bring her before the authorities to make a statement herself. Do not conclude the contract until a guarantor who has examined the evidence is present.

Should it happen that the girl cannot give an account of herself, have the one who offered her describe the situation in the contract. Pay the girl less than the usual wages and wait for her parents to recognize her; then return her at once.

(4)

3.46   YOUNG TROUBLEMAKERS

Among your agnatic relatives, neighbors, or relatives through marriage there may be some young troublemakers who use their strong backing to help one family at the expense of another. Rich families often make use of these young men as their strongmen and are satisfied for a time, for this type, although treacherous on the inside, are always compliant on the outside. If the young men in the rich family curse them or treat them disrespectfully, they put up with it, and the young men become fond of them. Later on, after the family head has died, the ones who lead the young men astray are invariably this sort.

Generally, the family head has had experience with these young troublemakers and has the wisdom to know how to harness their strength for his own purposes. But the sons and younger brothers must become as wise as their elders if harm is to be avoided. People of middling talents seldom escape being misled by them; thus they end up ruining their families.

Records of the T'ang dynasty mention birds and foxes capable of transforming themselves; during the day they perched or rested as usual, but at night they roamed wildly and acted with no restraint.[30] This is a fit description of young troublemakers. If you have regularly associated with honest, cordial, and upright gentlemen, even though they may say displeasing things, your family will benefit after your death due to the long time your sons and younger brothers will have spent in their company. This is what is meant by the phrase, "pleasing things often prove harmful; unpleasant things often prove beneficial." This happens so often that it deserves thorough consideration.   (2, 4, 5)

3.47   CONSCIENTIOUS AGENTS

With agents put in charge of storehouses, you should regularly check the ledgers and inspect the balance on hand. Require agents who are put in charge of grain and rice to keep strict records and conscientiously take care of the keys. In addition choose a careful and obedient person to act as guard.

With regard to agents to whom you lend capital for use in trade, be sure you have ones who are honest and frugal with their own property before you entrust them with anything. Remember that families of middling means have trouble merely meeting all their daily expenses, so naturally those who work for others are people who can barely afford to

[30] Stories of foxes are especially plentiful. The *T'ai-p'ing kuang-chi* includes nine chapters of them. See, for instance, 454, p. 3707.

keep themselves warm and fed. And since even the middling person loses balance when he sees things he wants right in front of him, one cannot expect any better from the lower sort of stupid person.

If your agent is faced with the attractions of wine, food, music, and women, how can his heart remain unmoved? In the past he may never have had enough money to satisfy his hopes or fulfill his needs; he may have shared hunger and cold with his blood relatives at home and outside had to pretend he didn't notice the temptations in front of him. As an agent he is within sight of overflowing wealth and goods. Even if day after day he tries to be strict and put his desires to rest, if the master is easygoing about his affairs, the agent will not be kept in line through fear.

Embezzlement begins with the agent taking only the slightest amount; in his heart he believes he will repay it later and so he is not yet afraid. After some time, when he sees that the master has noticed nothing, he gradually increases his peculations as the days and months go by. By the end of a year they are substantial. By now he is afraid but sees no way out except to cover up for himself. After two or three years, his depredations are too noticeable to be hidden. The master will want to deal with him harshly and his repentance will come too late.

People who use agents should take warning from this.

(2, 4, 4)

3.48   CARING FOR TENANT-FARMERS

The state values agriculture, for it is the source of food and clothing. But the plowing and planting of a family are the product of the toil of tenants. How can you then not value them?

When members of your tenants' families give birth, get

married, build houses, or die, you should give them generous gifts. If during the farming season they need to borrow, do not charge much interest. During years of floods and droughts, check the extent of the damage and quickly make reductions or exemptions from the rent owed.

Make no unfair demands on your tenants and do not impose labor service at unreasonable times.[31] Do not let your sons and younger brothers and your agents harass them on their own. Do not raise their annual rent because of something an enemy of theirs has said. Do not force them to take loans in order to receive high interest from them. Do not let greedy thoughts arise when you see that they have their own fields.[32]

If you look after your tenants and love them as though they were your relatives, you will be able to rely on their strength for your clothes and food, and you will be able to look up and look down without shame.   (2, 4, 4, 5, 6)

3.49 BORROWING BY TENANTS AND SERVANTS

In emergencies the wives and daughters of tenants and servants will come to a family's women or children and try to get loans of money or grain at heavy interest or try to pawn an article, asking that no one let the family head know. In such cases the borrower fully intends to default. If the women or children do not let the family head know of the loan, they will not dare demand repayment and will end up having to absorb the loss. Family heads ought to see that these facts are explained to their family members.   (1, 2, 3, 4, 4)

---

[31] For an example of the kind of labor that could be imposed, see 3.52, which discusses irrigation repair projects.

[32] As Liang T'ai-chi points out in "Tu 'Yüan-shih shih fan,'" p. 39, all of these practices must have been common ones in Yüan Ts'ai's time, or he would not need to discourage them.

3.50   OUTSIDERS IN THE HOUSE

Buddhist and Taoist nuns, women matchmakers and brokers, as well as women who claim to be dealing in acupuncture needles and moxa must not be allowed into your house. In general, this sort is responsible when the women's money or valuables are missing, or when wives or daughters are enticed into doing something unbecoming.

(1, 2, 4, 4)

3.51   WATER CONTROL

Ponds, dammed lakes, and diked rivers serve as reservoirs to irrigate fields. Every winter, when the water is low, have them dug deeper and reinforced. Then when there is a heat wave and drought, the crops will not be totally lost, even if there is not a full harvest.[33]

Nowadays, during a drought people think about repairs, but after the harvest they forget them again. This is what is meant by the proverb, "They think of planting mulberry trees in the third month; they think of building ponds in the sixth month." How pitiful it is to see people so shortsighted!

(2, 4, 5)

3.52   BENEFITS OF IRRIGATION

When a large number of families enjoy the benefits of irrigation from a pond, dammed lake, or diked river, the families with the most land ought to take the initiative in managing the waterworks. They should see to it that the landlords provide food and the tenants provide labor. During the winter repairs, see to it that the water capacity is enlarged.

---

[33] On advances in irrigation techniques in the Sung, see Mark Elvin, *The Pattern of the Chinese Past*, pp. 124–28.

When water is being used, all fields, far or near, high or low, must get equal shares. Remember that the water is not just for your benefit. Its beneficial powers are vast enough for everyone.

Current day men are stingy with food or labor during the repairs but when water is being used get into fights over it. People will hit each other with hoes and rakes, sometimes causing fatal wounds. Even if death does not result, the brawls can lead to imprisonment and punishment. How much harm this causes! And it is all the fault of the land-owners' uncaring stinginess. (2, 4)

3.53   TREES

In the spring it is a very easy thing to plant mulberry, fruit, bamboo, and other trees. For ten or twenty years you will benefit from them. Men nowadays often allow uncultivated hill land to go to waste; then when they divide their family property with their brothers, they fight over the slightest little root and lose all affection for each other. Should there be bamboo or trees in the nearby hills or on the boundary between two plots, then the lawsuits can drag on for years. Don't they see that if in the past Heaven had not produced those trees, there would be nothing for them to fight about? If they took the funds they used for the lawsuit to hire workers to plant trees, then for ten or twenty years "there would be more wood than they could use."[34]

There are even cases where someone has a fruit tree that borders on his neighbor's house with the result that the neighbor's children get some of the fruit, and this so angers him that he chops it down. How shortsighted this is! (4, 4, 5)

[34] Allusion to *Mencius* 1A: 3 (Lau, trans., p. 51).

3.54   GETTING ALONG WITH NEIGHBORS

If you have small boys, you must keep them under control; don't let them hurt the neighbors' trees or other property. If you have oxen and sheep, you must watch them; don't let them trample on the neighbors' gardens or fields. If you raise chickens and ducks, you must have them tended; don't let them peck at other people's vegetables or crops.

If your family owns land, you must be conscientious in all your activities. If you have graves in forested hills that you want to keep densely shady, you must make the walls high to keep others out. Your gardens, fields, and fruit orchards must have carefully maintained bamboo or wattle fences around them. By keeping people from going to and fro across your property, you will avoid the need to make accusations against them.   (2, 4, 4)

3.55   FIELD BOUNDARIES

Those who own fields, gardens, or hill land must have the boundaries clearly marked. Extreme precision is particularly necessary when relatives first divide their households and property, or when a person buys or acquires interest in a piece of property.[35] Lawsuits often start from failure in these regards.

Take the case of fields. Because of unevenness of the terrain, one plot can be made into two, or to improve convenience, two plots can be combined into one. Sometimes house sites or hill land are alleged to be fields; and sometimes fields are alleged to be house sites or garden plots. Sometimes paths or streams or irrigation ditches are moved.

---

[35] "Acquire an interest in" means to buy on a *tien* contract reserving for the seller a right of redemption.

Although the authorities have maps of the region, the documents deteriorate and disappear, making things even worse if the landmarks are altered without getting the deeds witnessed by the mutual security group and certified by the authorities. Isn't this planting the seeds for lawsuits?

People would have nothing to sue each other about if they would keep their raised fields in repair and keep others from knocking down the ridges; and if from time to time they would build walls around their house sites and garden plots, repairing them as soon as necessary; and if they would dig out ditches and moats around their hill and forest land as clear boundaries, repairing them as soon as they are damaged. It is just that through carelessness field ridges are knocked down and repairs are not timely; mere bamboo hedges are used around houses and gardens and with the passage of years they become dilapidated. Such conditions encourage encroachments.

With hill and forest land, streams make acceptable dividing lines. But every now and then a border is marked with a tree, a rock, or a pit that disappears in the course of time. When a ditch is used as a border sometimes there is another similar ditch further out. In such cases complex, unresolvable lawsuits are the inevitable result.

Divisions of family property rest on "lot-books," [36] and transfers of interest rest on deeds of sale. When you are careless and do not spell everything out clearly, neither the authorities nor private individuals can settle disputes. Take heed! From time to time someone considers himself lucky that there are ambiguities in a redeemable sale of hill land, intending to use the obscurities in the language of the orig-

---

[36] These documents, described in 3.56, were called "lot-books" because the distribution of property was supposed to be done by drawing lots, each of which described a share of property.

inal contract to occupy the land.[37] This is the type of thing inferior people do on purpose. Only when intelligent judges preside can the blame be correctly assigned.   (2, 4, 5)

3.56   DOCUMENTS OF DIVISION

In some cases the "lot-books" describing the shares in a family division[38] merely record the land and other property that the specific individual is to get; other families follow the practice of showing every share on each document. When only one person's share is recorded, a desire to conceal something is usually involved. Arguments and lawsuits then result.

When each person knows what land the other is getting, its respective size and fertility can be seen once and for all. Private arbitrators and the public authorities can easily settle claims. Furthermore, if one family member helped the others in a notable way, they may want him to be given extra land from the common property, or if one person's share is inferior, the others may wish to give him more land.[39]

When property was acquired from the wife's dowry or from official service, its origin [outside the patrimony] is clear. Sometimes property is acquired by one person from entrepreneurial business, and his relatives do not think they

---

[37] *CHTK* 2, p. 16, also mentions "crafty people" who keep their eyes out for others whose land ownership documents are not entirely in order, for instance, not being sealed or having ambiguous borders.

[38] On "lot-books" see n. 36 above.

[39] Why one person's share should be inferior is unclear. It could refer to cases where land was distributed strictly according to acreage, and one person received inferior land. Or it could refer to a situation where one person had much less by way of individual property, in which case his brothers would not be obligated to give him a larger share of the common property but might want to anyway.

should share in it.[40] In these cases the property should be listed in an appendix to the lot-books. If there still are some items not in the appendix that should be divided, have a drawing for omissions. Although this is after the formal division, each coparcener should ask for equal shares again, in order to prevent the fraudulent concealments and lawsuits that drag on for years unresolved. (4)

3.57 ASSIGNING PROPERTY TO DODGE LABOR SERVICE

People who want to dodge labor service may divide their property with scrupulous equality but in the lot-books and land-tax registers make it seem as though there is only one share so that only one person has to take on labor service. The others have the goods and resources reduced so that they are exempted.[41] But sometimes their descendants try to stick to the letter of the text and hide the true possession. This gives rise to lawsuits.

If the authorities want to accord with reality in their decisions, they are blocked by the text; if they want to decide according to the text, then sentiment is against it.[42] This is an example of how vulgar people give no thought to the future consequences of their actions: before their eyes they escape the regulations, but they leave a dispute for their posterity! This deserves consideration. (4, 5)

[40] Cf. 1.25.
[41] The grade a family was assigned according to its wealth determined the type of labor service it would be required to do. Wealthy households had to take on onerous and often costly duties like tax collection. See McKnight, *Village and Bureaucracy*, pp. 38–72 and passim. Land-tax registers are explained in pp. 51–52.
[42] Cf. 2.64 and 3.59 on the opposition of the text of the law and sentiment. Judges also often spoke of the opposition or complementarity of human feelings and the text of the law in reaching decisions. Cf. *CMC*, p. 201.

3.58 FALSIFYING HOUSEHOLD COMPOSITION

People who have already divided their wealth and property but want to avoid doing labor service will sometimes try to get registered as members of the household of one of their agnatic kinsmen who is an official.[43] These actions give rise to lawsuits later on. (4, 5)

3.59 GETTING SEALS ON LOT-BOOKS

When the county or circuit authorities are greedy and corrupt, they insist on heavy payments before putting seals on family division lot-books. Some families, begrudging the expense, conceal the act and do not get seals, though privately they have divided. After many years have passed, the wealth of the parties will no longer be the same, and feelings of moral obligation will be much diminished. Should a lawsuit result, one party will state that division has already taken place but the lot-books were lost, whereas the other will claim that the property has not yet been fully divided and no lot-books have yet been prepared. If the authorities follow the text, feelings go against it; if they base themselves on feelings, the text will be against it. The result is usually the misfortune of a long unresolved law case. Thus households undergoing division should get seals on their lot-books to prevent potential problems. (4)

---

[43] Officials' households were exempt from labor service, with certain limitations. The lowest grade regular official (grade nine) could hold ten *ch'ing* (that is, 1,000 *mou*) of land without any labor service obligations on it, and higher officials could hold more. After the death of the official, his household could still claim exemption for half that amount. The problems of fraud referred to by Yüan Ts'ai were recognized by the government, and measures were repeatedly taken to deal with them. See McKnight, *Village and Bureaucracy*, pp. 109–121.

3.60   GETTING SEALS ON DEEDS OF SALE

When carrying out a transfer of property, start by using a broker who will check the family division lot-books and the land-tax register and point out the boundaries and the names of the plots and sections.[44] Go and inquire of the tenants to find out if the borders are marked and whether this is a repeated mortgage or sale.[45] Next inquire of the relatives to find out whether there are any coparceners who have left and not yet returned, or are still young and so a division has not yet taken place. If someone has abandoned his claim to the property, be sure to ask why this happened and whether or not the property should be received. If the seller is a widow or a person of inferior status who brings evidence of a claim to the property, be sure to ask how this came about and whether or not it has ever been verified by the government.[46]

If the land has been sold with right of redemption, be sure to ask for the original deed and see whether it has been sealed and whether it has any sort of illegalities or hindrances: only afterwards can a contract be written up.[47] If widows or children have to sign or seal the contract, be sure that someone witnesses their marks. And be sure that the price in strings in cash, the date, the four boundaries, and the size are all filled in completely. Because it is not a good idea to use promissory notes or commodities for payment, be sure to pay cash. Also be sure that the place where the money came from and the porter who delivered it are specified.

[44] This item is replete with legal terms also common in *CMC*.

[45] That is, whether one person is trying to sell the same property twice. See examples in *CMC*, pp. 260–64, 253–56.

[46] Probably because a widow cannot sell her children's property without authorization from the government. See *CMC*, pp. 249–53. People of inferior status would include children and servants.

[47] See 3.62 on illegalities.

Once the contract is completed, be sure to get it sealed immediately; I worry about having the payment come after getting the seal. Once the contract is sealed, be sure the seller leaves the property; I worry about having the payment come after taking over management. Once the seller has left the property, the taxes must be reassigned; I worry about a failure to reassign the taxes out of laziness, which can result in being sued by someone and having the property confiscated.[48]

The laws and statutes of the courts are extremely detailed on the matter of transfers of property. The reason is that the court wishes to prevent disputes. But people, out of ignorance, sometimes end up violating these laws. They do not get seals on the deeds, or do not quit the property, or do not reassign the taxes. When the piece of property is sold over and over again, the lawsuits can drag on for years. Isn't this a case of people hastening their own destruction!   (1, 4)

3.61   PURCHASING NEIGHBORING PROPERTY

You should pay a little extra for property that you wish to acquire because it is nearby and offers benefits. Do not offer a low price because you are a relative or neighbor,[49] or because you are going from a partial to a full purchase,[50] or

[48] Four stages of transfer seem to be implied here: the transfer of money, getting the contract sealed, the transfer of occupation and management of the property, and the transfer of tax obligation. Yüan Ts'ai's point seems to be that there should be no delay in completing all four parts and that the money should not be paid until the seal and occupation are acquired. On the legal procedure involved in the sale of land, see also Niida Noboru, *Tōsō hōritsu*, pp. 89–138, and Jacques Gernet, "La Vente en Chine d'Apres les Contrats de Touen-Houang (IXe-Xe Siecles)."

[49] Referring to the prior option rights of relatives and neighbors. See Part One, chap. 6, n. 3.

[50] That is, use had already been acquired on a *tien* contract, but now full rights are being acquired.

because no one else dares buy it. Should by any chance someone else buy it, your regrets will be too late and lawsuits may result. (1, 3, 4)

3.62   ILLEGAL PURCHASES

Transactions in land or other property that are in violation of the legal articles should not be undertaken, even at bargain prices.[51] If later on the matter comes to the attention of the authorities, the expenses will be ten times the savings. Nevertheless, rich people often want to buy this type of property, saying to themselves that later they will raise the money to take any challengers to court. Those who suffer from this mania are beyond salvation. All too many create trouble for themselves or their descendants this way.

(4, 5, 6)

3.63   LEGAL TRADE

Transactions must be in accord with the legal articles in every single particular in order to avoid later complications. You should not neglect this and let your guard down, depending on your friendship with the other party. Should there be a falling-out, these ambiguities could become the basis for disputes.

When making a transaction, if you accept less than the full payment, or if you redeem property without taking the note back, you ought to let it be known immediately or even

---

[51] A transaction could be illegal for a variety of reasons. As mentioned in 3.60, the seller might no longer be the owner, having already sold it to someone else; or he could be at best a part owner, having sold the right to use and enjoy the fruits of the property to someone else under a *tien* contract; or he could have coparceners who have to agree to any sale. A section of the *CMC* has twelve cases of "illegal transfers of property" (pp. 311–70).

inform the authorities, in order to nip in the bud the possibility of subsequent accusations. Be warned!   (1, 4, 5, 6)

3.64 KINDNESS ON THE BUYER'S PART

Poverty and wealth are not permanent circumstances. No
house or field has a permanent owner. When you have
money, you buy; when you lack it, you sell. Aware of this
truth, the party buying should not be cruel to the party
selling.

When someone sells his property, it is because he is short of
food, or owes a debt, or has an illness or death in the family,
or a marriage or lawsuit to pay for. As his expenses amount to
100,000 cash, he sells 100,000 cash worth of property. If the
buyer pays the price at once, even if it passes immediately
through the seller's hands, the business of selling property to
meet expenses has been concluded.

Inhumane wealthy men, when they see how pressing the
seller's need is, will ostensibly resist the purchase while secretly trying to hook it, in order to pull down the price.
Once the deed is signed, they turn over only ten or twenty
percent at first, promising to give the rest in a few days.
When the seller comes to ask for it in a few days, they make
excuses, saying the money is not yet ready. If the seller asks
again and again, he may be given a few strings of cash, or the
buyer may give rice, grain, or other goods as part of the
payment, which then are subtracted from the balance owed
at inflated values.

The seller certainly by now is in terrible straits. The little
he has gotten has been spent in various ways. The way he had
previously planned to use the money is no longer possible.
And if he keeps sending someone to ask for the payment, the
cost of such services must be counted.

The rich man at this point is secretly delighted, believing

his strategy excellent. He does not know that the way of Heaven favors recompense. He will receive retribution in his lifetime, or his sons or grandsons will receive it. Few rich families are aroused to this truth. How deluded they are!

(1, 4, 5, 6)

3.65   INTEREST

When you lend money or grain, you expect the return of interest. This is how the rich and poor supply each other, and the practice should not be omitted.[52] In the Han dynasty, someone with a thousand strings of cash was comparable to a Marquis with a thousand households, which meant that in one year he could earn 200 strings of cash.[53] If that is compared with current practice, it is not even two percent a month. Nowadays, if we talk in terms of the average system, a pawnshop's monthly interest is from two to four percent, a moneylender's monthly interest is from three to five percent, and grain lent until harvest is from thirty to fifty percent for the term. Demanding this is not considered extortionate, and those who pay it do not object.[54]

Some of those who lend money against pawned goods charge ten percent a month. In Chiang-hsi some money-lenders can double their investment in a year; the practice of "joint-contract" refers to agreeing to pay back two strings for each one you borrowed. In Ch'ü-chou's K'ai-hua county,

---

[52] On the interdependence of the rich and the poor, compare the ideas of Yeh Shih (1150–1223) discussed in Winston Lo, *The Life and Thought of Yeh Shih*, p. 119.

[53] *Shih chi*, 129, p. 3272 (Watson, trans., II, p. 492).

[54] On interest rates, see also Lien-sheng Yang, *Money and Credit in China*, pp. 92–103. Yüan Ts'ai speaks of *fen* or parts. Two parts per month means two percent per month, but according to Yang a *fen* could also mean ten percent, and on p. 98 he interprets a rate of from three to five *fen* until harvest to mean from thirty to fifty percent for the term.

(315)

those who lend one unit of grain take back two; in Che-hsi when upper households lend one picul of rice they take back one and eight-tenths.[55] These are all extreme cases of inhumanity.

When a man has extorted people in this fashion his descendants will be paid back the same way. What is meant by "the way of Heaven favors recompense"[56] can be seen in these cases.　　　　　　　　　　　　　　　　　　(4)

3.66　TECHNIQUES OF ACQUISITION

When familes intent on acquiring more property[57] see a property-owning family with a young man who is stupid, ignorant, or unworthy, they try to force loans on him when he faces a special need. Sometimes, when the loan is first made, they may set out wine and food to coax the young man along. Sometimes, for several years afterwards, they may not ask for repayment, waiting for the interest to mount up. Then they set out wine and food again and invite him to visit. On this occasion they reschedule the debt. They add up all the interest and make it part of the capital, so it brings interest itself. Some people will encourage or compel the debtor to sell his land to pay the debt. Although the law strictly forbids this, many get away with it.[58] But "the net of Heaven lets nothing through."[59] There is a proverb,

[55] Chiang-hsi was a circuit, largely corresponding to modern Kiangsi. K'ai-hua was a county neighboring Yüan Ts'ai's native county. Che-hsi was another circuit (Liang-che hsi-lu), corresponding in large part with current Kiangsu.

[56] Quoted from 3.64.

[57] *Chien-ping chih chia*, literally "absorbing families," were an outgrowth of unrestricted buying and selling of land and a frequent source of bitterness since the Han dynasty. See also 1.52.

[58] On the basis on which the law forbade it, see Part One, chap. 6, n. 12.

[59] *Tao te ching* 73 (Waley, trans., p. 233).

"People take turns being the sons of the rich." This means that retribution will reach them. (1, 4, 5)

3.67 LOANS

Do not make loans to those who take on debts too lightly: they are certainly unreliable people who from the start intend to default on their obligations. In lending people money or grain, remember that small amounts are easily repaid and large amounts easily repudiated. When a loan reaches one hundred piculs of grain or one hundred strings of cash, even those able to repay may not want to do so. All too many would rather use their resources to pay for a lawsuit than to repay their loan! (1, 2, 3, 4, 5, 6)

3.68 DEBTS

Those who take on debts do so in the belief that they will be able to repay out of a future surplus. They do not perceive that if they have no surplus today, it's not very likely they will have one in the future.

Think of a road one hundred *li* long. Divided into two one-day trips, it can be managed in two days. If you leave the first day's portion for the second day, no matter how hard you push yourself that day, you won't be able to reach your destination.

People without foresight, who want to have plenty today, will tranquilly assume that they will have a surplus later and thus invariably ruin their family estates. Take heed from this! (1, 2, 3, 4, 4, 5, 6)

3.69 PLANNING FOR TAXES

Where there is family property there will be taxes. You should set aside what you will need for the taxes in advance and divide the remainder for daily expenditures.[60] If the income that year is poor, your only alternative is to economize. You must not encroach on the money set aside for taxes. If you do and the officials press you for some urgent impost, you will have to take on a debt with interest, or deal with a tax broker who will make you repay at a high rate.[61] These are the ways to waste away the family estate.

The terms "poor" and "frugal" indicate wisdom and virtue and are compliments. You should not be ashamed of them. If you understand this, you need not worry about ruining your family. (1, 2, 4, 5)

3.70 PROMPT TAX PAYMENTS

Although there are due dates for paying taxes, you should pay early to be safe.

For instance, in paying the summer tax of early ripening rice, if you do not take advantage of a clear day to hand it in early, hoping to postpone it until later, what will you do if it rains or snows for days on end? The provincial and prefectural government often show no consideration for such problems among the people.

In paying the autumn tax of rice, in the beginning, not only do the authorities want dry plump grain, but they increase the weights they use for measures; later even if you pay in rice that is wet and spoiled, they decrease the weights used; moreover, later they convert the tax to cash payments at a discount.

In paying the silk tax, at first the authorities want thick, close-woven goods; later as the number being paid in reduces, they carelessly accept lightweight, coarse goods. Moreover, later they also discount the conversion rates.

[60] See 2.53 for further advice on budgeting.
[61] On tax brokers, see McKnight, *Village and Bureaucracy*, pp. 55–56.

Taxpayers and tax brokers often compare the difference in the measures used early and late and are not willing to pay their taxes until necessary. This can reach the point where they get pursued or pressured by the county or circuit.

In rural areas only the wise, wishing to save themselves trouble, do not wait until after the due date for the sake of some piddling difference. (1, 2)

3.71   BRIDGE AND ROAD PROJECTS

When your fellow residents are collecting money or goods to build a bridge, repair a road, or construct a ferry boat, you should assist them in accordance with your means. Do not refuse to take part on the grounds that you will be getting no return for your money. After all, once the road is done, you will enjoy its benefits; you will not have to worry about how carefully your coachman or horses are on your daily trips out and back or about taking your carriage or horse across a bridge or ferry. (1, 4, 5, 6)

3.72   RESPONSIBLE ENTREPRENEURS

Those whose enterprises lead to substantial profit, with the result that they become rich, usually got that way because of the good luck of the Creator blessing them in an unapparent way.[62] Yet some people who notice that others are making great profits and becoming wealthy quickly wish to usurp the prerogatives of Heaven and manage this by human efforts. If they sell rice, they add water to it; if they sell salt, they mix it with ashes; if they sell lacquer, they add oil to it; if they sell medicine, they substitute other things for it; their ploys are innumerable. Since before their eyes they are gain-

[62] For a successful entrepreneur who was a contemporary of Yüan Ts'ai's, see Wolfram Eberhard, "Wang Ko, An Early Industrialist."

ing a lot, they are happy. They do not realize that the Creator will take away what they have on some other occasion and they will end up in poverty. And think of the many who lose their capital because they substituted the fake for the genuine! This is what is meant by the saying, "Men cannot win over Heaven."

In general, in trade and manufacture, the first thing is to be conscientious. The goods must be genuine and they must be handled with respectful care, as if you wished to offer them to the gods. You also should not dare to covet great profits but accept whatever the workings of Heaven produce. Although what you have before your eyes may be meager, you will escape calamities later on. This is especially true if you buy state monopoly rights for marketing or manufacturing.[63] In making wine, you must be extremely clean and pure. Then the families who illegally sell private wine naturally will have difficulty competing. If some of them brew privately, you should carefully consider ways to put a stop to it, but you should not press them and force them to go bankrupt. Morning and evening you should give all your attention to paying the government taxes and supporting your offspring and dependents. You should not foolishly seek to accumulate a lot, or get involved with the accounting office, or delay paying funds due the government. Then, if you meet good luck you can become rich, and if you do not at least you won't be left impoverished. Those who manage businesses should observe these principles.   (1, 5)

3.73   CONSTRUCTION PROJECTS

To build a house is a very difficult project for a family. Even those in their middle years and familiar with the ways of the

[63] There were government monopolies in salt, tea, and wine. Licenses to deal in these goods under government regulations were sold to merchants.

world are not experts in construction. Naturally it is even worse with those of little experience! Very few of them escape ruining their families.

When a man begins to build, he starts by discussing his plans with a master builder. The master builder's primary fear is that the man will decide not to build when he hears the price, so he keeps the scale small and the cost low. The owner considers the project within his means and decides to go ahead. The master builder then gradually enlarges the scale until the cost has increased several-fold before the house is half done. The owner cannot halt the project in the middle, so he borrows money or sells land elsewhere. The master builder, delighted, goes on with more construction, increasing the charges for labor even higher.

I have advised people to build houses gradually over a decade or longer. That way, when the house is done the family will still be as rich as before. First consider the foundation; level the high spots and build up the low ones. Perhaps build the walls and dig out the ponds. Do this in stages, planning to take over ten years. Next consider the scale and the quantity of materials needed, down to details such as the number of logs for beams and the bamboo for fences. Each year buy some according to the numbers needed and have them hewn right away. Plan to have them all ready in ten odd years. Again, calculate how many tiles and stones you will need; plan to use whatever resources you have left to gradually store them up. Even the wages should not be handled on the spur of the moment. With this method the house can be finished with the family as rich as before.

(1, 2, 4, 5)

Editions of the Precepts for Social Life and Their Transmission

After many hand-copied versions had been made, Yüan Ts'ai first printed the *Precepts for Social Life* in 1179 while he was a magistrate in Le-ch'ing. He reissued it at least once, apparently from entirely new blocks, in 1190 while magistrate of Wu-yüan. Neither of these Sung editions survives. The book was mentioned in the early thirteenth-century bibliography, *Chih-chai shu-lu chieh-t'i*, and several subsequent ones, without mention of editions.[1]

During the Yüan dynasty, large parts of the *Precepts* were copied into two surviving "encyclopedias" for household reference, the *Chü-chia pi-yung shih-lei* and the *Shih-lin kuang-chi*.[2] The *Chü-chia pi-yung shih-lei* selections were clearly based on the 1179 version, but one with many differences in wording from later complete versions. The *Shih-lin kuang-chi* selections present a different case and may even have been based on the 1190 edition. In this encyclopedia Yüan Ts'ai's work was plagiarized to make up a full *chüan*; the work was retitled, as was each chapter, and the chapters and sections were rearranged. Moreover, wording was changed, often to make it simpler, passages were abridged,

---

[1] *Chih-chai shu-lu chieh-t'i*, 10, p. 303; *SS* 205, p. 5211; *Wen-hsien t'ung-k'ao*, 204, p. 1753A.

[2] These are both very interesting guides to what was considered useful knowledge in the thirteenth and fourteenth century; they cover subjects from family rituals and letter-writing etiquette to agriculture and medicine.

and the endings of passages were often cut to avoid starting a new line of text. Every item begins with a title six characters long. There is no way to know now whether the anonymous editor of the encyclopedia did the plagiarizing himself, or whether he made use of an altered and unattributed version. It is quite possible that through the Yüan dynasty hand-copied versions of the *Precepts* continued to circulate and were the source for one or both of these reference books.

Complete versions of the *Precepts* must have also been in circulation in the Yüan, for in the early Ming the text was copied, apparently in its entirety, into the *Yung-le ta-tien*, the enormous collectanea compiled at imperial command in 1407. Unfortunately, the section that included the *Precepts* is not among the small portion that survives today.

The earliest surviving complete versions of the *Precepts* are from the late Ming. The three earliest dated ones are 1596, 1603, and 1620–22, each of which is a distinct text, but all based on the 1179 edition. The 1596 text is in the *Yu-ch'un lu* (*YCL*), a series of books of value in moral instruction, published by Shen Chieh-fu (1533–1601) between 1573 and 1619. This is the best surviving transmission of the 1179 edition. The 1603 one is in the *Po-chia ming-shu* ("Famous books by a Hundred Authors," *PCMS*), a collectanea published by Hu Wen-huan. The text of the *Precepts* in this collectanea is said to have been "edited" or "collated" (*chiao*) by Hu Wen-huan, implying that he had more than one version available to him. Hu Wen-huan also published the *Precepts* in another collectanea, the *Ko-chih ts'ung-shu*, of uncertain date. He used the same printing blocks as for the *PCMS*, the only difference being that he omitted Yüan Ts'ai's preface. The *PCMS* edition is inferior to the *YCL* because it omits two passages (1.47 and 3.41) as well as Liu Chen's preface and the note Yüan Ts'ai added to it.

The 1620–1622 text is found in another collectanea, the

Pao-yen t'ang pi-chi (*PYT*), published by Ch'en Chi-ju (1558–1669) and Li Jih-hua (1565–1637). This edition of the *Precepts* is also said to have been "edited" (*chiao*), this time by six people, two for each chapter. Ch'en Chi-ju is listed as one of the editors. Apparently the main text they used was either the *PCMS* version, or an ancestor to it, for passages 1.47 and 3.41 are omitted here as well, as are Liu Chen's preface and Yüan Ts'ai's note. Another text, however, was definitely also used, for in four cases extra sentences were added at the end of items, found in no other surviving editions. In addition, this "edited" text has a great many misprints and is generally an inferior one. Unfortunately, the *PYT* had a wide circulation, and the *Precepts* as edited by Ch'en Chi-ju was also copied into another collectanea (a late Ming version of the *Po-ch'uan hsüeh-hai*) and even circulated separately as an independent text. The *Po-ch'uan hsüeh-hai* version (or one nearly identical to it) became the basis for several Japanese editions as well.

Also in the late Ming a condensed version of the *Precepts* was prepared, consisting of thirty-seven passages, first for inclusion in the *T'ang-Sung ts'ung-shu*, compiled by Chung Jen-chieh and Chang Sui-ch'en. In most cases where the wording of the editions edited by Ch'en Chi-ju (*PYT* and *Po-ch'uan hsüeh-hai*) differed from all the other editions, the *T'ang-Sung ts'ung-shu* wording is the same as the Ch'en Chi-ju ones. Either the compilers of the *T'ang-Sung ts'ung-shu* used a Ch'en Chi-ju text to make their excerpts, or they used a closely related version. In 1646–1647 an "enlarged" (Ch'ung-chiao) version of the *Shuo-fu* (a Yüan collectanea, compiled by T'ao T'ing) included this condensed, one-chapter version of the *Precepts*, copied directly from the *T'ang-Sung ts'ung-shu*, apparently even using the same printing blocks.

In the early eighteenth century, over three-quarters of the

Precepts was copied into the enormous encyclopedia, the *Ku-chin t'u-shu chi-ch'eng*, presented to the throne in 1725. The text was not included as a whole, but passages were quoted where appropriate under twenty-four topics. Many passages were repeated, some being used three and four times. The edition used by the *Ku-chin t'u-shu chi-ch'eng* editors was the *PYT* or one closely related to it. A few years later, in 1742, Ch'en Hung-mou (1696–1771) copied over a third of the *Precepts* into his compilation of advice books, *Wu chung i-kuei*.

In the late eighteenth century three further editions of the *Precepts* were published. The editors of the imperially sponsored *Ssu-k'u ch'üan-shu* do not seem to have discovered in their searching for rare books any of the superior editions of the *Precepts*. They did have the *PYT* edition but recognized that it had a great many errors, and so they reconstructed a version using the *Yung-le ta-tien* and the *PYT* together. This was issued in 1780 (*SK* ed.). Today, with the *YCL* and *Po-chia ming-shu* editions, as well as the 1190 version discussed below, we can see that the Ssu-k'u editors were overly distrustful of the *PYT* edition. In numerous cases the division of the material was different from that in the *PYT* edition, probably because the editors thought it made more sense that way; but the *PYT*'s divisions match those of the other editions. The *SK* edition also omits three passages, probably the result of scribal errors by the copyists. In addition it omits passages that imply the acceptability of family members becoming monks. Whether this was an editorial decision of the *Yung-le ta-tien* editors or the *Ssu-k'u ch'üan-shu* editors is unclear, but most likely the latter. In almost no case does the *SK* edition offer advantages over the *YCL*, and it is generally not worth consulting.

All of the editons discussed so far were based on the 1179 edition, printed in Le-ch'ing without item titles. In 1785,

Yüan T'ing-t'ao (1764–1810), a scholar and book collector from Su-chou, while on a search for materials to revise his family genealogy, discovered a Sung edition of the *Precepts* in a bookstore. It had a postface dated 1190, item titles, and colophons added in the Ming, dated 1520. The two colophons were written by collateral ancestors of Yüan T'ing-t'ao, also well-known scholars. The edition they had found had a collection of didactic stories and poems attached to the end of it, which were also published after it in the *Ko-chih ts'ung-shu*.[3] In 1790 this Sung edition of the *Precepts* (with the 1190 postface) was published with a preface by Yang Fu-chi (1747–1820) dated 1788 and a postface by Yüan T'ing-t'ao dated 1790 in Pao T'ing-po's (1728–1814) *Chih-pu-tsu chai ts'ung-shu* (*CPTC*), fourteenth series. In 1794 Wu Te-yü reprinted it as an independent volume, adding a postface of his own.

All considered, it seems quite plausible that Yüan T'ing-t'ao had found a genuine Sung edition, published in 1190 from new plates. First, Yüan, Yang, and Pao were all bibliophiles, as likely as any to detect a false "Sung edition." Second, one of the Yüan encyclopedias included similar titles (though edited to a uniform six characters each). Third, most of the changes between the 1179 and the 1190 editions are plausible either as improvements made by the author (such as the addition of titles), or scribal errors in copying the text. (See Appendix B.) In most cases these differences are minor. The only one that affects our understanding of Yüan Ts'ai is the omission of 1.65 on endowing schools instead of establishing charitable estates. Was this purposely left out of the later edition or merely lost in transmission?

---

[3] These stories and poems by Fan Hsin, a Sung man from P'u-t'ien, also circulated separately. See *Ch'ien-ch'ing t'ang shu-mu*, 12/10b, which lists a Sung edition. They appear, however, to have been attached to the 1190 ed. found in 1785. When this attachment was made is unclear.

The *Precepts* continued to be reprinted in the nineteenth century, both in the "condensed" one-chapter version and in three-chapter versions. The *Ch'ing-chao t'ang ts'ung-shu*, compiled by Li Huan-ch'un in 1835, reprinted the *T'ang-Sung ts'ung-shu* selection. In addition a new selection of forty-four items was made for the supplement to the *Sung Yüan hsüeh-an*, compiled in 1841 by Wang Tzu-ts'ai.

Basic information on known three-chapter editions is given in the outline below.

THREE-CHAPTER EDITIONS OF THE
PRECEPTS FOR SOCIAL LIFE

I. EDITIONS AVAILABLE IN TWENTIETH-CENTURY REPRODUCTIONS

   A. With 1179 preface/postface

      1. *Yu-ch'un lu* 由醇錄 (1596), ed. Shen Chieh-fu 沈節甫 (1573–1619). Reprinted by the Library of Congress, Peiping Library Rare Books Microfilm, roll 530. Sixty-three discrepancies with *CPTC* 1190 ed., all but five of which are found also in one or both of the other two 1179 editions listed below. No omissions. Preface. A superior edition.

      2. *Pao-yen t'ang pi-chi, hui-chi* 寶顏堂秘笈, 彙集 (ca. 1620–1622) by Ch'en Chi-ju 陳繼儒 (1558–1669) and Li Jih-hua 李日華 (1565–1637). Reprinted by Shanghai, Wen-ming shu-chü, 1922. One hundred thirty-two discrepancies with *CPTC* 1190 ed. Two omitted passages. Liu Chen's preface and Yüan Ts'ai's note also omitted. Postface. Inferior edition.

      3. *Ssu-k'u ch'üan-shu chen-pen* 四庫全書珍本 (1780). Reprinted in Taipei, Commercial Press, 1975, Chen-pen pieh-chi series. One hundred

twenty-nine discrepancies with *CPTC* ed. Three omitted passages. Postface. Inferior edition.

    4. *Pi-chi hsiao-shuo ta kuan, ssu-pien* 筆記小說大觀 四編 (1979) Taipei, Hsin-hsing shu-chü. Reprint of *Pao-yen t'ang pi-chi* ed.

B. With 1190 postface, item titles

    1. *Chih-pu-tsu chai ts'ung-shu* 知不足齋叢書 fourteenth series (1790), ed., Pao T'ing-po 鮑廷博 (1728–1814). Omission of 1.65. Addition of passage to 2.68. Superior edition.

        a. Reprinted by Taipei, Hsing-chung shu-chü, 1964. (Includes Ming and Ch'ing colophons and prefaces.)

        b. Reprinted by Taipei, I-wen-shu-chü, Po-pu ts'ung-shu chi-ch'eng series, 1965. (Omits Ming and Ch'ing colophons and prefaces.)

    2. Punctuated ed. published by Shanghai, Commercial press, Ts'ung-shu chi-ch'eng series, 1939. Based on *Chih-pu-tsu chai ts'ung-shu* ed. Includes Ming and Ch'ing colophons but not Yang Fu-chi's preface. Only one typographical error in the typesetting. Suitable for most purposes.

II. OTHER EDITIONS SEEN, SURVIVING IN INDIVIDUAL COPIES

A. With the 1179 preface/postface, no titles

    1. *Po-chia ming-shu* 百家名書 (1603) ed. Hu Wen-huan 胡文煥. Called "newly carved." 1 *ts'e*. Includes Yüan Ts'ai's preface (but not Liu Chen's preface or Yüan Ts'ai's note). In Library of Congress, Washington D.C., and Naikaku bunko, Tokyo.

    2. *Ko-chih ts'ung-shu* 格致叢書 (late Ming) ed. Hu Wen-huan. Identical to above but without Yüan

Ts'ai's preface. In the Institute for Humanistic Research, Kyoto.

3. *Po-ch'uan hsüeh-hai* 百川學海 (Ch'ung-pien 重編) (late Ming). *Precepts* ed. by Ch'en Chi-ju. Apparently copied from the *Pao-yen t'ang* ed., or an independently circulated text "edited" by Ch'en Chi-ju. In the Institute for Humanistic Research, Kyoto, the Tōyō bunko, Tokyo, the National Central Library and the Taiwan Provincial Library, Taipei.

4. Japanese edition (1793), published by Osaka Shorin, ed. Ch'en Chi-ju. Based on *Po-ch'uan hsüeh-hai* or closely related text. In the Institute for Humanistic Research, Kyoto, and Tokyo University, Tokyo.

B. With the 1190 postface, titles

1. Yü-shan t'ang 與善堂 ed. of Wu Te-yü 吳德裕 (1794). Based on the *Chih-pu-tsu chai ts'ung-shu* ed. In the Institute for Humanistic Research, Kyoto.

2. Japanese edition (1850), based on Ch'en Chi-ju's 1179 ed. and the *CPTC* ed. With 1179 postface but titles of 1190 ed. Includes marginal notes by the editor, Katayama Shin 片山信 discussing textual differences and interlinear notes explaining perplexing passages. In Institute for Humanistic Research, Kyoto, Naikaku bunko and Tokyo University, Tokyo.

III. RECORDED EDITIONS, EXTANT BUT NOT SEEN

1. Ming, Wan-li (1573–1619), printed ed. In Library of the National Palace Museum, Taiwan.

2. Ming ed., ed. Ch'en Chi-ju (I *ts'e*). In Naikaku bunko, Tokyo.

3. Japanese edition (1669), ed. Ch'en Chi-ju (3 *ts'e*). In Naikaku bunko, Tokyo.

4. *Hsi-ching ch'ing-lu ts'ung-shu* 西京清麓叢書 ed. Ho Jui-lin 賀瑞麟 *Yang-cheng ts'ung-pien* 養正叢編 section (1895). In Shanghai Library, Peking University Library, and Peking Normal University Library. Listed in *Ssu-k'u chien-ming mu-lu piao-chu* as *Chu Tzu i-shu*.

5. *Chin-ho kuang-jen t'ang so-k'o shu* 津可廣仁堂所刻書 (Kuang-hsü period, 1875–1907). In the Library of the Academy of Sciences, Peking, the Shanghai Library, and the Shantung Provincial Library.

IV. RECORDED EDITIONS, NOT KNOWN TO BE EXTANT

1. 1603 edition. Had the 1179 preface, also a preface by an official named Wu Hsien-t'ai 吳獻台 (*chin-shih* 1580). Recorded in *T'ien-lü lin-lang shu-mu, hsü-mu* (1798) 16/13a. Three *ts'e* in one *t'ao*. Listed also in *Ssu-k'u chien-pien mu-lu piao-chu*, so perhaps surviving.

2. *Cheng-i t'ang* 正誼堂 edition. Listed in *Ssu-k'u chien-ming mu-lu piao-chu*. Could be another title for the *Chu Tzu i-shu*, which in turn is an alternate title for *Hsi-ching ch'ing-lu ts'ung-shu*.

V. TRANSLATIONS

(Into Japanese) by Nishida Taiichiro. Osaka: Sogensha, 1941. Available in the Institute for Humanistic Research, Kyoto, and other Japanese academic libraries.

Discrepancies Between the
1179 and 1190 Editions

As explained in Appendix A, the two most valuable transmissions of the *Precepts* are the *YCL*, the best version of the
1179 edition, and *CPTC*, the only transmission of the 1190
edition. Three other transmissions, *PCMS*, *PYT*, and *SK*
have some value, however, in indicating which of the discrepancies between the *YCL* and *CPTC* editions are likely to
be due to differences between the original editions and which
are most likely to be copyists' errors.

Below is a list of all of the discrepancies between *YCL* and
CPTC in which *YCL* was matched by at least one of the
other three important 1179 versions. Possible reasons for the
discrepancies are numerous. Yüan Ts'ai may well have corrected some misprints in the first editions, and he may have
made some improvements, including some minor changes
in wording. He also seems to have added a lengthy passage
to one item. At the same time, the copyists may have mis-
copied characters, introducing new errors, most very minor.
Further minor errors could have resulted when the book was
copied in 1790. At the same time the *YCL* undoubtedly
differs in minor ways from the 1179 edition, since it also may
have been recopied several times in the interval between 1179
and 1596. Below, when the differences are trivial and could
have come from copyist errors in the transmission of either
text, nothing is listed under "better version." In other cases
the better reading is indicated.

Discrepancies Between 1179 and 1190 Editions of the *Precepts for Social Life*

Item	1179 edition	1190 edition	Better version
1.9.1	高年 *kao-nien*, "high years"	年高 *nien-kao*, "years high"	
1.19.8	可惡之時下無可愛之者 "after the youngest has reached the detestable stage, there is no one who is lovable"	當可愛之時不無可惡之者 "at his lovable stage he still has features that are detestable"	1179
1.19.12	—	可也 *k'o-yeh*, "can happen"	
1.22.6	金 "several tens of metal" (*XPYT*)	文 "several tens of coins"	1190
1.26.6	二年 "two years"	三年 "three years"	1190
1.29.1	宜各 "should each" (*XSK*)	各宜 "each should"	
1.30.2	辨 *pien*, "distinguished" (*XPYT, PCMS*)	辯 *pien*, "discuss"	1190
1.31.6	不自然愛 *pu-tzu-jan ai*, "unnaturally love" (*XSK, PYT*)	不然自愛 *pu-jan-tzu-ai*, "not so of themselves"	1190
1.32.4	我 *wo*, "self" (*XPYT, SK*)	己 *chi*, "self"	

Item	1179 edition	1190 edition	Better version
1.39.1	宦 *huan*, "official"	官 *kuan*, "official"	1190
1.39.16	陪 *p'ei*, "accompany" (*XPYT*, *SK*)	賠 *p'ei*, "repay"	1190
1.46.3	逐去 *chu-ch'ü*, "cast away"	逐出 *chu-ch'u*, "cast out"	
1.50.1	親姻 *ch'in-yin*, "relatives and marriage relations"	親戚 *ch'in-ch'i*, "relatives"	
1.53.2	破蕩家產 *p'o-t'ang chia-ch'an* (*XPYT*)	破家蕩產 *p'o-chia t'ang-ch'an*	
1.62.14	鑒 *chien*, "examine"	覽 *lan*, "observe"	
1.64.2	心中 *hsin-chung*, "in the mind"	中心 *chung-hsin*, "middle mind"	1179
1.65	whole item	omitted	1179
2.1.3	口 *k'ou*, "mouth" (*XPYT*)	舌 *she*, "tongue"	
2.5.1	榮 *jung*, "glory"	樂 *le*, "pleasure"	1179
2.7.2	設 *she*, "to suppose"	役 *i*, "to employ"	1190
2.7.11	爲 *wei*, "be"	做 *tso*, "be"	
2.26.5	侮 *wu*, "insult"	悔 *hui*, "regret"	1179
2.26.7	以此 *i-tz'u*, "with this"	—	1190

Item	*1179 edition*	*1190 edition*	*Better version*
2.29.7	爲 *wei*, "do, make, be" (*XPCMS*)	惟 *wei*, "be, only"	
2.30.1	有 *yu*, "have" (*XPYT*)	之 *chih* (particle)	1190
2.42.1	以 *i*, "because"	聞 *wen*, "hear"	
2.50.3	聞見 "hear and see"	見聞 "see and hear"	
2.52.2.	取 *ch'ü*, "take" (*XPYT*)	多 *to*, "much"	
2.53.5	省用速謀 "reduce expenditures and quickly plan"	省悟遠謀 "recognize their situation and make long-term plans"	1190
2.54.3	破壞 *p'o-huai* (*XSK*)	破敗 *p'o-pai*	
2.60.3	作謁 *tso-yeh*, "make visits" (*XPYT*)	干謁 *kan-yeh*, "visit for the purpose of seeking advantage"	1190
2.60.4	揮啞 *hui-ching*, "boisterous"	持便 *ch'ih-pien*, "slick"	1190
2.60.6	他 *t'a*, "other"	人 *jen*, "other"	
2.66.11	爲辱 *wei-ju*, "cause insults"	罵辱 *ma-ju*, "curse and insult"	1190
2.67.10	——	若 *jo*, "if"	1190
2.68.6	結託 *chieh-t'o* (*XSK*)	給託 *chi-t'o*, "send"	1190
2.68.9	客口券	客券	

Item	1179 edition	1190 edition	Better version
	"guest-mouth tallies" (*XSK*)	"guest tallies"	1179
2.68.18	備足 *pei-tsu*, "make up"	補足 *pu-tsu*, "make up"	1190
2.68.18	—	three paragraphs	1190
3.1.1	垣牆 *yüan-ch'iang*	牆垣 *ch'iang-yüan*	
3.8.3	long passage	garbled	1179
3.10.4	鄰里 *lin-li*, "neighbors"	鄰居 *lin-chü*, "neighbors"	
3.10.7	灰燼 *hui-chin*, "ashes" (*XPCMS*)	煨燼 *wei-chin*, "ashes"	
3.19.1	婢僕 "male and female servants"	—	1179
3.25.3	堂 *t'ang*, "room"	室 *shih*, "room"	
3.26.3	心欲 *hsin-yü*, "in his heart will want"	必欲 *pi-yü*, "will necessarily want"	1190
3.33.4	胡倅 Assistant Hu	胡氏 Mister Hu	1179
3.35.1	縊 *i*, "hang" (*XPYT, SK*)	經 *ching*, "hang"	
3.38.3	備 *pei*, "prepare"	見 *chien*, "see"	1190
3.39.10	言 *yen*, "say"	令 *ling*, "order"	1179
3.45.3	顧 *ku*, "look after" (*XSK*)	雇 *ku*, "hire"	1190
3.46.8	爲之祥	徉狂自恣	

Item	1179 edition	1190 edition	Better version
	"created omens"	"roamed wildly and acted with no restraint"	1190
3.46.9	人 *jen*, "man"	士 *shih*, "gentleman"	1190
3.47.1	簿書 *p'u-shu*, (*XSK*)	書簿 *shu-p'u*	
3.47.3	家累 *chia-lei*, "family and its dependents"	家業 *chia yeh*, "family estate"	1190
3.49.4	家 *chia*, "family"	家人知也 *chia-jen chih-yeh*, "family members know"	1190
3.54.4	墓 *mu*, "grave"	塋 *ying*, "grave"	
3.54.4	錄 *lu*, "record" (*XSK*)	叢 *ts'ung*, "thickset"	1190
3.56.4	弃 *ch'i*, "abandon"	充 *ch'ung*, "supply"	
3.57.5	可不 *k'o-pu*, "can you not"	可以 *k'o-i*, "you should"	1190
3.71.3	惴慄 *chui-Ii*, "worry"	惴惴 *chui-chui*, "worry"	
post. 17	終當 *chung-tang*, "in the end matched"	遂強 *sui-ch'iang*, "so, by force"	1190
post. 17	舊云 *chiu-yün*, "earlier said"	所云 *so-yün*, "what was said"	1190

Note. Item number gives the chapter, the item in the chapter, and the line, respectively, in *CPTC* (a or b). An "x" before the name of an edition indicates that that edition does not match *YCL*.

GLOSSARY

ch'a 察
ch'an 產
Chang An-kuo 張安國
Chang Chih-po 張知白
Chang Hsiao-hsiang 張孝祥
Chang Kung-i 張公藝
Chang Shih 張栻
Chang Tsai 張載
Chang Yung 張詠
Chao Ting 趙鼎
Ch'en Fu-liang 陳傅良
Ch'en Liang 陳亮
cheng-chih 正直
Cheng Ching-yüan 鄭景元
Ch'eng Hao 程顥
Cheng-ho tsa-chih 政和雜志
Ch'eng I 程頤
Cheng Po-ying 鄭伯英
chi (to give) 給
Chi (Viscount) 箕
ch'i 氣
ch'i-chia (to found a family)
  起家
ch'i-chia (to regulate a family)
  齊家
ch'i-nu 妻孥
ch'i-ts'ai 妻財
chia (family) 家
chia (a "stem") 甲
chia-ch'an 家產

chia-chang 家長
chia hsing-sheng 家興盛
chia-yeh 家業
chiao 校
ch'ieh 妾
Ch'ien-chin fang 千金方
Ch'ien Jo-ch'ung 錢若沖
Ch'ien-lü pi-shuo 千慮鄙說
chien-ping chih-chia 兼幷之家
chien-ping chih-jen 兼幷之人
chih chia 治家
chih-sheng 治生
chin 謹
chin-shih 進士
ching 敬
ch'ing 頃
Ching-chieh chieh-fa 經界捷法
Ching-ch'üan chung-hsing ts'e
  經權中興策
ch'ing-ta-fu 卿大夫
chiu-ku 舅姑
Chou-hou po-i fang 肘後百一方
Chou Mi 周密
chu 主
Chu Hsi 朱熹
chu-mu 主母
Chu Yü 朱彧
Ch'ü-chou 衢州
chün-i 均壹
chün-tzu 君子

chung (good faith) 忠

chung (group) 衆

chung-fen t'ien-yeh 衆分田業

chung-ts'ai 衆財

Chung yung 中庸

Fan Ch'eng-ta 范成大

Fan Chung-yen 范仲淹

Fan Ying-ling 范應鈴

fang 防

fen 分

fu-hsiung 父兄

fu-nü 婦女

fu-pu-jen chih jen 富不仁之人

fu-tsu 父祖

Hsi-hsü tzu 希歐子

hsiao-jen 小人

hsiao-min 小民

Hsieh Liang-tso 謝艮佐

Hsien-ling hsiao-lu 縣令小錄

hsin 信

Hsin-an 信安

hsing 性

hsiung-ti tzu-chih 兄弟子姪

hsü-k'ung 虛空

Hu Yen-t'e 胡彥特

Hu Ying 胡穎

Hu Yüan 胡瑗

Huang Kan 黃榦

Huang T'ing-chien 黃庭堅

Huang Tsung-hsi 黃宗羲

Hung-fan 洪範

Hung Mai 洪邁

i 義

I ching 易經

i-ts'ai 異財

jen (benevolence) 仁

jen (forbearance) 忍

jen-lun 人倫

jen-yü 人欲

ju-chia 儒家

Ko Hung 葛洪

ku 姑

kuan 管

k'uan 寬

kung 公

kung-p'ing 公平

kuo 國

Le-ch'ing 樂清

li (principle) 理

li (ritual, politeness) 禮

li (slave) 隸

Li Chao-yen 李昭言

Li Chih 李贄

Li Fang 李昉

Liu Chen 劉鎮

Liu K'ai 柳開

Liu K'o-chuang 劉克莊

Liu Tz'u 柳玭

lü 慮

Lu Chiu-shao 陸九韶

Lu Chiu-yüan 陸九淵

Lü-chu 綠珠

Lü Ta-fang 呂大防

Lü Tsu-ch'ien 呂祖謙

Lu Yu 陸游

mai nai-pi 買奶婢

ming 命

Mo Tzu 墨子

mou 畝

Nei-tse 內則

Ni Ssu 倪思

nu 奴

nu-li 奴隸

nu-pi 奴婢

nu-p'u 奴僕
Ou-yang Hsiu 歐陽修
pao 保
pi 婢
pi-ch'ieh 婢妾
pi-p'u 婢僕
p'o chia 破家
p'u 僕
pu-hsiao 不肖
San-ch'ü 三衢
Shang-shu 尚書
Shang-ti 上帝
Shen Chi-chung 申積中
shen chih ts'ung-ming 神之聰明
sheng 省
shih (gentleman) 士
shih (social world) 世
Shih Ch'ung 石崇
Shih fan 世範
shih-huan 失歡
shih-jen 士人
shih-ta-fu 士大夫
ssu (private, selfish, individual) 私
ssu (to think) 思
ssu-ai 私愛
ssu-hsin 私心
Ssu-k'u ch'üan-shu 四庫全書
Ssu-ma Kuang 司馬光
ssu-ts'ai 私財
Su I 蘇扱
Su Hsün 蘇洵
Su Shih 蘇軾
Sun Hsiu 孫秀
Sun Ssu-mo 孫思邈
Sun Wen-i 孫文懿
ta-hsüeh 大學

Tai Chen 戴震
T'ao Hung-ching 陶弘景
tien 典
tien-mai (buy an interest in, buy on a revocable contract) 典買
tien-mai (sell on a revocable contract, pawn) 典賣
t'ien-hsia 天下
t'ien-li 天理
ting-fen 定分
Ting Wei 丁維
ts'ai 財
Ts'ai Hang 蔡杭
tsao-wu che 造物者
tse-shan 責善
Tso-i tzu-chen 作邑自箴
tsu (ancestor) 祖
tsu (lineage) 族
tsu-chung ts'ai-ch'an 祖眾財產
tsu-tsung 祖宗
Ts'ui Yin 崔駰
tsung 宗
tsung-jen 宗人
tsung-tsu 宗族
tu 篤
t'ung-chü 同居
t'ung-chü chih-jen 同居之人
t'ung-chü kung-ts'ai 同居共財
t'ung-tsung 同宗
tzu-jan t'ien-shu 自然天屬
Tzu Kung 子貢
Tzu-ssu (name) 子思
tzu-ssu (selfish) 自私
tzu-ti 子弟
Wang Ch'ung 王充
Wang Huai-chung 汪懷忠

Wang Yang-ming 王陽明

Wen-kuo Kung 溫國公

Weng Fu 翁甫

Wu-p'o 梧坡

wu-ssu 無私

Wu-yüan 婺源

Yang Fu-chi 楊復吉

Yang Wan-li 楊萬里

yeh 業

Yeh Meng-te 葉夢得

Yen Chih-t'ui 顏之推

ying 營

ying-fen jen 應分人

yü 欲

yu-fen jen 有分人

yu-shih chih jen 有識之人

yu yüan-shih chih jen
 有遠識之人

Yüan Chün-tsai 袁君載

Yüan T'ing-t'ao 袁廷檮

Yüan Ts'ai 袁采

Yüeh-shih san-yao 閱史三要

Yung-le ta-tien 永樂大典

SOURCES CITED

For editions of the *Precepts for Social Life* used to prepare the translation, see "Editions available in twentieth-century reproductions," in Appendix A. The basic text used has been the 1190 version published in the *Chih-pu-tsu chai ts'ung-shu.*

Sources cited in the notes have been divided into three categories to make reference from the notes easier. Works in Chinese written before 1900 are arranged by title, as this is how they are best known. Since translations of these books have been cited by translator, they are listed here as a separate category, arranged by translator, with the original text indicated when it is not evident from the title. Secondary sources and other twentieth-century works come last, arranged by author.

WORKS IN CHINESE WRITTEN BEFORE 1900, BY TITLE

Ch'eng-chai chi 誠齋集, 133 ch., by Yang Wan-li 楊萬里 (1127–1206). *SPTK* ed.

Ch'i-tung yeh-yü 齊東野語, 20 ch., by Chou Mi 周密 (1232–1308). *TSCC* ed.

Chia-hsün pi-lu 家訓筆錄, 1 ch. (1144), by Chao Ting 趙鼎 (1084–1147). *TSCC* ed.

Chia fan 家範, 10 ch., by Ssu-ma Kuang 司馬光 (1019–1086). Chung-kuo tzu-hsüeh ming-chu chi-ch'eng ed.

Chia-yu chi 嘉祐集, 15 ch., by Su Hsün 蘇洵 (1009–1066). Wan-yu wen-k'u ed.

Chieh-tzu t'ung-lu 戒子通錄, 8 ch., by Liu Ch'ing-chih 劉清之 (1130–1195). *SKCP* ed.

Ch'ien-ch'ing t'ang shu-mu 千頃堂書目, 32 ch., by Huang Yü-chi 黃虞稷 (1629–1691). Taipei: Kuang-wen shu-chü's Shu-mu ts'ung-pien ed.

Chih-chai shu-lu chieh-t'i 直齋書錄解題, 22 ch., by Ch'en Chen-sun 陳振孫 (ca. 1190–1249+). *TSCC* ed.

Chin shu 晉書, 130 ch., by Fang Hsüan-ling 房玄齡 (578–648) et al. CHSC ed.

Chin-ssu lu 近思錄, 14 ch., by Chu Hsi 朱熹 (1130–1200) and Lü Tsu-ch'ien 呂祖謙 (1137–1181). Taipei: Kuo-hsüeh chi-pen ts'ung-shu ed.

Ching-ch'u-t'ang tsa-chih 經鉏堂雜志, 1 ch., by Ni Ssu 倪思 (1147–1220). In *Chü-chia pi-pei* (Ming).

Ch'ing-po tsa-chih 清波雜志, 12 ch. (1192), by Chou Hui 周煇 (1127–1198+). *TSCC* ed.

Ch'ing-yüan t'iao-fa shih-lei 慶元條法事類, 80 ch., by Hsieh Shen-fu 謝深甫. Tokyo: Koten kenkyūkai facsimile reprint of Sung ed., 1968.

Chiu T'ang shu 舊唐書 200 ch. (945), by Liu Hsü 劉昫 (887–946) et al. CHSC ed.

Chou-hsien t'i-kang 州縣提綱, 4 ch., anon. (twelfth century). *TSCC* ed.

Chü-chia pi-yung shih-lei 居家必用事類, 20 ch., anon. (fourteenth century). Kyoto: Chūmon 1979 facsimile reprint of Japanese 1673 ed.

Ch'ü-chou fu-chih 衢州府志, 15 ch. (1564), ed. Yang Chun 楊準 et al. Washington, D.C.: Library of Congress, Peiping Library Rare Books Microfilm, rolls 399–400.

Ch'ü-chou fu-chih 衢州府志, 16 ch. (1622), ed. Lin Ying-hsiang 林應翔 et al. Washington, D.C.: Library of Congress, Peiping Library Rare Books Microfilm, rolls 400–401.

Chu Tzu wen-chi 朱子文集, 18 ch., by Chu Hsi 朱熹 (1130–1200). *TSCC* ed.

Chu Wen-kung ch'üan-chi 朱文公全集, by Chu Hsi 朱熹 (1130–1200). *SPTK* ed.

Erh-lao t'ang tsa-chih 二老堂雜志, 5 ch., by Chou Pi-ta 周必大 (1126–1204). *TSCC* ed.

Fa yen 法言, by Yang Hsiung 揚雄 (53 B.C.–18A.D.). In *Fa yen i-shu* 20 ch., by Wang Jung-pao 汪榮寶 (1878–1933). Taipei: SCSC, 1962.

Fang-chou shih 方舟集, 24 ch., by Li shih 李石 (1108–1181). *SKCP* ed.

Han shu 漢書, 120 ch. (A.D. 76), by Pan Ku 班固 (32–92). CHSC ed.

Ho-nan Shao-shih wen-chien ch'ien-lu 河南邵氏聞見前錄, 20 ch. (1151), by Shao Po-wen 邵伯溫 (1057–1134). *TSCC* ed.

Hou te lu 厚德錄, by Li Yüan-kang 李元綱. In *Hsü po-ch'uan hsüeh-hai*. Taipei: Hsin-hsing shu-chü facsimile reproduction of Ming ed.

Hou-ts'un hsien-sheng ta-ch'üan chi 後村先生大全集, 196 ch., by Liu K'o-chuang 劉克莊 (1187–1269). Shanghai: Han-fen lou, 1929.

Hsiao-hsüeh 小學, 6 ch. (1187), by Chu Hsi 朱熹 (1130–1200). In *Hsiao-hsüeh chi-chieh* 集解, by Chang Po-hsing 張伯行 (1651–1725)). *TSCC* ed.

Hsin-pien shih-wen lei-yao ch'i-cha ch'ing-ch'ien 新編事文類要啓箚青錢 (Yüan). Tokyo: Koten kenkyūkai facsimile reprint of 1324 ed., 1963.

Hsü wen-hsien t'ung-k'ao 續文獻通考, 254 ch. (1586), by Wang Ch'i 王圻. Tsai-te t'ang ed., 1847.

Hsün Tzu 荀子, 20 ch., by Hsün Ch'ing 荀卿. In *Hsün Tzu chi-chieh* 集解 ed. Wang Hsien-ch'ien 王先謙. SCSC ed.

Hui-chu ch'ien-lu 揮麈前錄, 4 ch. (1166), by Wang Ming-ch'ing 王明清 (1127–1214+). *TSCC* ed.

Hui-chu hou-lu 揮麈後錄, 11 ch. (1194), by Wang Ming-ch'ing 王明清 (1127–1214+). *TSCC* ed.

I-chien chih 夷堅志, 207 ch., by Hung Mai 洪邁 (1123–1202). CHSC ed.

Ku-chin t'u-shu chi-ch'eng (ch'in-ting) 古今圖書集成, 欽定, 10,000 ch. (1725), ed. Ch'en Meng-lei 陳夢雷 et al. Peking: CHSC reprint of Palace ed., 1934.

Lo Yü-chang hsien-sheng wen-chi 羅豫章先生文集, 10 ch., by Lo Ts'ung-yen 羅從彥 (1072–1135). *TSCC* ed.

Lu Fang-weng ch'üan-chi 陸放翁全集, 186 ch., by Lu Yu 陸游 (1125–1210). Hong Kong: Kuang-chih shu-chü ed.

Lu Hsiang-shan ch'üan-chi 陸象山全集, 36 ch., by Lu Chiu-yüan 陸九淵 (1139–1192). SCSC punctuated ed., 1966.

Lü Tung-lai wen-chi 呂東萊文集, 20 ch., by Lü Tsu-ch'ien 呂祖謙 (1137–1181). *TSCC* ed.

Meng-liang lu 夢梁錄, 20 ch. (1274), by Wu Tzu-mu 吳自牧. *TSCC* ed.

Mien-chai chi 勉齋集, 40 ch., by Huang Kan 黃榦 (1152–1221). *SKCP* ed.

Ming-kung shu-p'an ch'ing-ming chi 名公書判清明集. Tokyo: Koten Kenkyūkai facsimile ed. of Seikado Bunko copy, 1964.

Nan-chien chia-i kao 南澗甲乙稿, 22 ch., by Han Yüan-chi 韓元吉, (1118–1187). *TSCC* ed.

O-chou hsiao-chi 鄂州小集, 5 ch., by Lo Yüan 羅願 (1136–1184). *TSCC* ed.

Ou-yang Hsiu ch'üan-chi 歐陽修全集, 158 ch., by Ou-yang Hsiu 歐陽修 (1007–1072). SCSC ed.

P'ing-chou k'o-t'an 萍州可談, 3 ch. (1119), by Chu Yü 朱彧. *TSCC* ed.

San-kuo chih 三國志, 65 ch., by Ch'en Shou 陳壽 (233–297). CHSC ed.

Sheng-hsin tsa-yen 省心雜言, 1 ch. (1160), by Li Pang-hsien 李邦獻. *SKCP* ed.

Shih chi 史記, 130 ch. (87 B.C.), by Ssu-ma Ch'ien 司馬遷 (145–86 B.C.). CHSC ed.

Shih-lin chia-hsün 石林家訓, 1 ch., by Yeh Meng-te 葉夢得 (1077–1148). In *Shih-lin i-shu*, Ch'ang-sha, 1911.

Shih-lin chih-sheng chia-hsün yao-lüeh 石林治生家訓要略, by Yeh Meng-te 葉夢得 (1077–1148). In *Shih-lin i-shu*, Ch'ang-sha, 1911.

Shih-lin kuang-chi (*Hsin-pien tsuan t'u tseng-lei ch'ün-shu lei-yao*) 事林廣記, 新編纂圖增類羣書類要, 50 ch., by Ch'en Yüan-ching 陳元靚 (thirteenth century). Unpublished photocopy of Naikaku bunko Yüan ed.

Shih-lin yen-yü 石林燕語, 10 ch. (1136), by Yeh Meng-te 葉夢得. *TSCC* ed.

Shuo-fu (*ch'ung-chiao*) 說郛, 重校, 120 *han*, ed. T'ao Tsung-i 陶宗儀 (Yüan). Reedited by T'ao T'ing 陶珽 (Ming). 1644–1646 ed. of Yüan-wei shan-t'ang.

Ssu-k'u chien-ming mu-lu piao-chu 四庫簡明目錄標注, 20 ch., ed.

Shao I-ch'en 邵懿辰 (1810–1860). Published with supplements, CHSC, 1959.

Ssu-k'u ch'üan-shu tsung-mu t'i-yao chi ssu-k'u wei-shou shu-mu chin-hui shu-mu 四庫全書總目提要及四庫未收書目禁燬書目. Taipei: Commercial Press ed.

Ssu-ma shih shu-i 司馬氏書儀, 10 ch., by Ssu-ma Kuang 司馬光 (1019–1086). *TSCC* ed.

Ssu-ma Wen-cheng kung ch'uan-chia chi 司馬文正公傳家集, 80 ch. by Ssu-ma Kuang 司馬光 (1019–1086). Taipei: Kuo-hsüeh chi-pen ts'ung-shu ed.

Su-k'ao 俗考, 1 ch., by Hung Mai 洪邁 (1123–1202). In *Chü-chia pi-pei* (Ming).

Sung hsing-t'ung 宋刑統, 30 ch., by Tou I 竇儀 (914–966) et al. Taipei: Wen-hai, 1964 reprint of 1918 ed.

Sung hui-yao chi-pen 宋會要輯本, 460 ch., ed. Hsü Sung 徐松 (1781–1848) et al. SCSC reprint, 1964.

Sung shih 宋史, 496 ch. (1345), ed. T'o T'o 脫脫 (1313–1355) et al. CHSC ed.

Sung Yüan hsüeh-an 宋元學案, 100 ch. (1846), by Huang Tsung-hsi 黃宗羲 (1610–1695) et al. Shanghai: Commercial Press, 1928.

Sung Yüan hsüeh-an pu-i 宋元學案補遺, 100 ch., ed. Wang Tzu-ts'ai 王梓材 (1792–1851). In *Ssu-ming ts'ung-shu*. Taipei: Chung-hua ta-tien reprint.

Ta Yüan sheng-cheng kuo-ch'ao tien-chang 大元聖政國朝典章, 60 ch. (1307). Taipei: Wen-hai ch'u-pan she facsimile reprint of 1908 ed.

T'ai-p'ing kuang-chi 太平廣記, 500 ch. (978), ed. Li Fang 李昉 (925–996). Peking: Jen-min wen-hsüeh ch'u-p'an she, 1959.

T'ang-Sung ts'ung-shu 唐宋叢書, 161 ch., ed. Chung Jen-chieh 鍾人傑 and Chang Sui-ch'en 張遂辰. Ming ed.

T'ien-lu lin-lang shu-mu (ch'in-ting) 天祿琳琅書目, 欽定, 10 ch. *hou-pien* 後編 20 ch., ed. Yü Min-chung 于敏中 and P'eng yüan-jui 彭元瑞 (1798). Taipei: Kuang-wen shu-chü's Shu-mu hsü-pien ed.

Tsa tsuan 雜纂, 3 ch., by Li Shang-yin 李商隱 (813–858), Wang Ch'i 王琪 (ca. 1020–1092), and Su Shih 蘇軾 (1036–1101). *TSCC* ed.

Tso-i tzu-chen 作邑自箴, 10 ch. (1117), by Li Yüan-pi 李元弼. *SPTK* ed.

Tung-ching meng-hua lu 東京夢華錄, 10 ch. (1147), by Meng Yüan-lao 孟元老. SCSC ed.

Tung-hsüan pi-lu 東軒筆錄, 15 ch., by Wei T'ai 魏泰 (ca. 1050–1110). *TSCC* ed.

T'ung tien 通典, 200 ch., by Tu Yu 杜佑 (735–812). Taipei: Hsin-hsing shu-chü reprint of Shih-t'ung ed.

Wen-hsien t'ung-k'ao 文獻通考, 348 ch., by Ma Tuan-lin 馬端臨 (ca. 1250–1325). Taipei: Hsin-hsing shu-chü reprint of Shih-t'ung ed.

Wen hsüan 文選, 60 ch., by Hsiao T'ung 蕭統 (501–531). Hong Kong: Commercial Press, 1965 ed.

Wu chung i-kuei 五種遺規, 13 ch., by Ch'en Hung-mou 陳宏謀 (1696–1771). Taipei: Ssu-pu pei-yao ed.

Yen-shih chia-hsün 顏氏家訓, 7 ch., by Yen Chih-t'ui 顏之推 (531–591＋). *TSCC* ed.

TRANSLATIONS OF WORKS WRITTEN IN CHINESE, BY TRANSLATOR OR EDITOR

Bauer, Wolfgang, and Herbert Franke, trans. *The Golden Casket: Chinese Novellas of Two Millenia.* Baltimore: Penguin Books, 1967.

Chan, Wing-tsit, trans. *Reflections on Things at Hand: The Neo-Confucian Anthology Compiled by Chu Hsi and Lü Tsu-ch'ien.* New York: Columbia University Press, 1967. (Translation of *Chin-ssu lu*)

———, trans. and comp. *A Source Book of Chinese Philosophy.* Princeton: Princeton University Press, 1963.

Chang, H. C., trans. *Chinese Literature: Popular Fiction and Drama.* Edinburgh: Edinburgh University Press, 1973.

Ch'en, Li-li, trans. *Master Tung's Western Chamber Romance (Tung Hsi-hsiang chu-kung-tiao).* Cambridge: Cambridge University Press, 1976.

Crump, J. I., Jr., trans. *Chan Kuo Ts'e.* Oxford: Clarendon Press, 1970.

————, trans. *Chinese Theater in the Days of Kublai Khan*. Tucson: University of Arizona Press, 1980.

Ebrey, Patricia Buckley, ed. *Chinese Civilization and Society: A Sourcebook*. New York: Free Press, 1981.

Egerton, Clement, trans. *The Golden Lotus*. 4 vols. New York: Grove Press, 1954. (Translation of *Chin P'ing Mei*)

Forke, Alfred, trans. *Lun-Heng: Philosophical Essays of Wang Ch'ung*. New York: Paragon Book Gallery reprint of 1907–1911 ed.

Hawkes, David. *The Story of the Stone*. 4 vols. Baltimore: Penguin Books, 1973—. (Translation of *Hung-lou meng*)

Lau, D. C., trans. *Mencius*. Middlesex: Penguin Books, 1970.

Legge, James, trans. *Li Chi, Book of Rites*. New York: University Books, 1967 reprint of Oxford, 1885 Sacred Books of the East ed.

————, trans. *The Chinese Classics*. Hong Kong: Hong Kong University Press, 1961 reprint of Oxford, 1865–1895 ed.

Vol. 1. *Confucian Analects, The Great Learning*, and *The Doctrine of the Mean*. (Translation of *Lun-yü, Ta hsüeh*, and *Chung-yung*)

Vol. 3. *The Shoo King*. (Translation of *Shang-shu*)

Vol. 5. *The Ch'un Ts'ew with the Tso Chuen*. (Translation of *Ch'un-ch'iu* and *Tso chuan*)

Liao, W. K., trans. *The Complete Works of Han Fei tzu*. London: Probsthain, 1939–1959.

Ma, Y. W., and Joseph S. M. Lau, eds. *Traditional Chinese Stories: Themes and Variations*. New York: Columbia University Press, 1978.

Makra, Mary Lelia, trans. *The Hsiao Ching*. New York: St. John's University Press, 1961.

McKnight, Brian E., trans. *The Washing Away of Wrongs* by Sung Tz'u. Ann Arbor: Center for Chinese Studies, University of Michigan, 1981. (Translation of *Hsi-yüan lu*)

Sun, E-tu Zen and Shiou-chuan Sun, trans. *T'ien-kung K'ai-wu: Chinese Technology in the Seventeenth Century* by Sung Ying-hsing. University Park: Pennsylvania State University Press, 1966.

Sung, Z. D., trans. *The Text of the Yi King (And Its Appendixes)*. New York: Paragon, 1969 reprint of Shanghai, 1935 ed. (Translation of *Chou I*.)

Teng, Ssu-yü, trans. *Family Instructions for the Yen Clan* by Yen Chih-t'ui. Leiden: Brill, 1968. (Translation of *Yen-shih chia-hsün*)

Waley, Arthur, trans. *The Analects of Confucius*. New York: Random House, 1938.

————, trans. *The Book of Songs*. London: Allen, 1937. (Translation of *Shih ching*.)

————, trans. *The Way and Its Power: A Study of the Tao Te Ching and Its Place in Chinese Thought*. New York: Macmillan, 1934.

Watson, Burton, trans. *The Basic Writings of Mo Tzu, Hsün Tzu, and Han Fei Tzu*. New York: Columbia University Press, 1967.

————, trans. *The Complete Works of Chuang Tzu*. New York: Columbia University Press, 1968.

————, trans. *Courtier and Commoner in Ancient China: Selections from the History of the Former Han by Pan Ku*. New York: Columbia University Press, 1974. (Translation of *Han shu*)

————, trans. *Records of the Grand Historian of China, Translated from the Shih chi of Ssu-ma Ch'ien*. New York: Columbia University Press, 1961.

————, trans. *Su Tung-p'o: Selections from a Sung Dynasty Poet*. New York: Columbia University Press, 1965.

Yang Hsien-yi, and Gladys Yang, trans. *The Courtesan's Jewel Box: Chinese Stories of the xth–xviith Centuries*. Peking: Foreign Languages Press, 1957.

————, trans. *The Dream of Red Mansions*. Peking: Foreign Languages Press, 1981.

————, trans. *Selected Plays of Guan Hanqing*. Peking: Foreign Languages Press, 1958.

SECONDARY SOURCES

Alitto, Guy S., H. D. Harootunian, Edward T. Ch'ien, Hao Chang, and Thomas A. Metzger. "Review Symposium: Thomas A. Metzger's *Escape from Predicament*." *Journal of Asian Studies* 39 (February 1980): 237–90.

Sources Cited

Aoyama Sadao 青山定雄. "HokuSō o chūshin to suru shidaifu no kika to seikatsu ronri" 北宋を中心とする士大夫の起家と生活倫理. *Tōyō gakuhō* 57 (1976): 35–63.

———. "The Newly-Risen Bureaucrats in Fukien at the Five-Dynasties-Sung Period, with Special Reference to their Genealogies." *Memoirs of the Research Department of the Toyo bunko* 21 (1962): 1–48.

———. "Sōdai ni okeru Kahoku kanryō no keifu no tsuite" 宋代における華北官僚の系譜について. *Seishin joshi daigaku ronsō* 21 (1963): 21–41; 25 (1965): 19–49; *Chūō daigaku bungakubu shigakuka kiyō* 12 (1967): 67–110.

———. "Sōdai ni okeru Kahoku kanryō no kon'in kankei" 宋代における華北官僚の婚姻関係. *Chūō daigaku hachijyūnen kinei ronbun shū* (1965): 362–88, *Uno Tetsujin sensei jijū shukuka kinen tōyō gaku ronsō* (1974): 21–34, *Egami Namio kyōgu koki kinen ronshū* (1977): 209–227.

———. "Sōdai ni okeru Ka'nan kanryō no keifu ni tsuite—toku ni Yosuko karyū iki o chūshin to shite" 宋代における華南官僚の系譜について — 特に揚子江下流域を中心として. *Chūō daigaku daigakuin bungakubu shigakuka kiyō* 19 (1974): 51–76.

———. "Sōdai ni okeru Kosei shusshin no kokan no kon'in kankei" 宋代における江西出身の高官の婚姻関係. *Seishin joshi daigaku ronsō* 29 (1967): 17–33.

Balazs, Etienne. *Chinese Civilization and Bureaucracy: Variations on a Theme.* Translated by H. M. Wright. New Haven: Yale University Press, 1964.

———. *Political Theory and Administrative Reality in Traditional China.* London: School of Oriental and African Studies, 1965.

Beattie, Hilary H. *Land and Lineage in China: A Study of T'ung-ch'eng County, Anhwei, in the Ming and Ch'ing Dynasties.* Cambridge: Cambridge University Press, 1979.

Berkhofer, Robert F., Jr. *A Behavioral Approach to Historical Analysis.* New York: Free Press, 1969.

Burns, Ian Robert. "Private Law in Traditional China (Sung Dynasty)." Ph.D. dissertation, Oxford University, 1973.

Cahill, James. *Hills Beyond a River: Chinese Painting of the Yüan Dynasty, 1279–1368*. Tokyo: Weatherhill, 1976.

———. *Parting at the Shore: Chinese Painting of the Early and Middle Ming Dynasty, 1368–1580*. Tokyo: Weatherhill, 1978.

Chaffee, John William. "Education and Examinations in Sung Society (960–1279)." Ph.D. dissertation, University of Chicago, 1979.

Chang, Carson. *The Development of Neo-Confucian Thought*. New York: Bookman, 1957.

Chang, Chung-li. *The Chinese Gentry: Studies on their Role in Nineteenth Century Chinese Society*. Seattle: University of Washington Press, 1955.

Chang Fu-jui. "Le *Yi-kien tche* et la Société des Song." *Journal Asiatique* 256 (1968): 55–93.

Ch'ang P'i-te 昌彼得 et al. *Sung-jen ch'uan-chi tzu-liao so-yin* 宋人傳記資料索引. Taipei: Ting-wen shu-chü, 1977.

Ch'ien Mu 錢穆. *Chu Tzu hsin hsüeh-an* 朱子新學案. 5 vols. Taipei: San-min shu-tien, 1971.

Chikusa Masaaki 竺沙雅章. "HokuSō shidaifu no shikyo to baiten—omo ni Tōba seki toku o shiryō to shite" 北宋士大夫の徙居と買田—主に東坡尺牘を資料として. *Shirin* 54, no. 2 (1971): 28–53.

Ch'ü, T'ung-tsu. *Han Social Structure*. Vol. 1 of *Han Dynasty China*. Edited by Jack L. Dull. Seattle: University of Washington Press, 1972.

———. *Law and Society in Traditional China*. Paris: Mouton, 1965.

———. *Local Government in China Under the Ch'ing*. Cambridge: Harvard University Press, 1962.

Cohen, Myron. *House United, House Divided: the Chinese Family in Taiwan*. New York: Columbia University Press, 1979.

Dardess, John W. "The Cheng Communal Family: Social Organization and Neo-Confucianism in Yüan and Early Ming China." *Harvard Journal of Asiatic Studies* 34 (1974): 7–52.

———. "Confucianism, Local Reform, and Centralization in Late Yüan Chekiang, 1342–1359." In *Yüan Thought: Chinese Thought and Religion under the Mongols*, edited by Wm. T. de Bary and Hoklam Chan. New York: Columbia University Press, 1982.

Sources Cited

Davis, Richard L. "'Protection,' Imperial Favor, and Family Fortunes in Sung China." Paper presented at the Conference on Family and Kinship in Chinese History, Asilomar, January 2–7, 1983.

de Bary, Wm. Theodore and Conference on Ming Thought. *Self and Society in Ming Thought*. New York: Columbia University Press, 1970.

———. "Some Common Tendencies in Neo-Confucianism." In *Confucianism in Action*, edited by David S. Nivison and Arthur F.Wright. Stanford: Stanford University Press, 1959.

——— and the Conference on Seventeenth-Century Chinese Thought. *The Unfolding of Neo-Confucianism*. New York: Columbia University Press, 1975.

———. *Neo-Confucian Orthodoxy and the Learning of the Heart-and-Mind*. New York: Columbia University Press, 1981.

Dennerline, Jerry. *The Chia-ting Loyalists: Confucian Leadership and Social Change in Seventeenth-Century China*. New Haven: Yale University Press, 1981.

Duke, Michael. *Lu You*. Boston: Twayne, 1977.

Eberhard, Wolfram. *Social Mobility in Traditional China*. Leiden: E. J. Brill, 1962.

———. "Wang Ko, an Early Industrialist." In his *Settlement and Social Change in Asia*. Hong Kong: Hong Kong University Press, 1967.

Ebrey, Patricia. *The Aristocratic Families of Early Imperial China: A Case Study of the Po-ling Ts'ui Family*. Cambridge: Cambridge University Press, 1978.

———. "Conceptions of the Family in the Sung Dynasty." *Journal of Asian Studies* 43 (February 1984): 219–45.

———. "The Early Stages of the Development of Kin Group Organization." Unpublished paper prepared for *Kinship Organization in Late Imperial China*, edited by P. B. Ebrey and J. L. Watson, forthcoming.

———. "Estate and Family Management in the Later Han as Seen in the *Monthly Instructions for the Four Classes of People*." *Journal of the Economic and Social History of the Orient* 17 (1974): 173–205.

———. "Women in the Kinship System of the Southern Song

Upper Class." In *Women in China*, edited by Richard Guisso and Stanley Johannesen. New York: Philo Press, 1981.

Elvin, Mark. *The Pattern of the Chinese Past*. Stanford: Stanford University Press, 1973.

Franke, Herbert, ed. *Sung Biographies*. Wiesbaden: Franz Steiner Verlag, 1976.

Geertz, Clifford. *The Interpretation of Cultures*. New York: Basic Books, 1973.

Gernet, Jacques. *Daily Life in China on the Eve of the Mongol Invasion, 1250–1276*. Translated by H. M. Wright. Stanford: Stanford University Press, 1970.

———. "La Vente en Chine d'Après les Contrats de Touen-houang (IXe–Xe Siecles)." *T'oung Pao* 45, nos. 4–5 (1957): 295–391.

Golas, Peter J. "Rural China in the Song." *Journal of Asian Studies* 39 (February 1980): 291–325.

Graham, A. C. *Two Chinese Philosophers, Ch'eng Ming-tao and Ch'eng Yi-ch'uan*. London: Lund Humphries, 1958.

Granet, Marcel. *The Religion of the Chinese People*. Translated by Maurice Freedman. New York: Harper and Row, 1975.

Gutman, Herbert G. *The Black Family in Slavery and Freedom, 1750–1925*. New York: Random House, 1976.

Haeger, John Winthrop, ed. *Crisis and Prosperity in Sung China*. Tucson: University of Arizona Press, 1975.

Hanan, Patrick. *The Chinese Vernacular Story*. Cambridge: Harvard University Press, 1981.

Hareven, Tamara K., ed. *Family and Kin in Urban Communities, 1700–1930*. New York: New Viewpoints, 1977.

Harrell, Stevan. *Ploughshare Village: Culture and Context in Taiwan*. Seattle: University of Washington Press, 1982.

Hartwell, Robert M. "Demographic, Political, and Social Transformations of China, 750–1550." *Harvard Journal of Asiatic Studies* 42 (1982): 365–442.

———. "Financial Expertise, Examinations and the Formulation of Economic Policy in Northern Sung China." *Journal of Asian Studies* 30 (February 1971): 281–314.

———. "Historical Analogism, Public Policy, and Social Science

Sources Cited

in Eleventh- and Twelfth-Century China." *American Historical Review* 76 (June 1971): 690–727.

Hatch, George. "Su Shih." In *Sung Biographies*, edited by Herbert Franke. Wiesbaden: Franz Steiner Verlag, 1976.

———. "The Thought of Su Hsün (1009–1066): An Essay in the Social Meaning of Intellectual Pluralism in Northern Sung." Ph.D. dissertation, University of Washington, 1972 (University Microfilms no. 73–13831).

Hegel, Robert E. *The Novel in Seventeenth-Century China*. New York: Columbia University Press, 1981.

Hervouet, Yves, ed. *A Sung Bibliography*. Initiated by Etienne Balazs. Hong Kong: Chinese University Press, 1978.

Ho, Ping-ti. "Early-Ripening Rice in Chinese History." *Economic History Review*, 2nd ser., 9 (1956): 200–218.

———. "An Estimate of the Total Population of Sung-Chin China." *Etudes Song, In Memoriam Etienne Balazs* 1, no. 1 (1970): 3–53.

———. *The Ladder of Success in Imperial China: Aspects of Social Mobility, 1368–1911*. New York: Columbia University Press, 1962.

Hsü, Francis. *Under the Ancestor's Shadow: Kinship, Personality, and Social Mobility in China*. Rev. ed. Stanford: Stanford University Press, 1971.

Huang, Ray. *1587, A Year of No Significance: The Ming Dynasty in Decline*. New Haven: Yale University Press, 1981.

Hymes, Robert Paul. "Prominence and Power in Sung China: The Local Elite of Fu-chou, Chiang-hsi." Ph.D. dissertation, University of Pennsylvania, 1979 (University Microfilms no. 80-09418).

Ihara Hiroshi 伊原弘. "Sōdai Minshū ni okeru kanko no kon'in kankei" 宋代明州における官戸の婚姻関係. *Chūō daigaku daigakuin kenkyū nenpō* 1 (1971): 157–168.

———. "Sōdai no Sessei ni okeru toshi shidaifu" 宋代の浙西における都市士大夫. *Tōyōgaku* 45 (1981): 44–62.

Johnson, David. "The Last Years of a Great Clan: The Li Family of Chao Chün in Late T'ang and Early Sung." *Harvard Journal of Asiatic Studies* 37 (1977): 5–102.

————. *The Medieval Chinese Oligarchy*. Boulder: Westview Press, 1977.

Kracke, E. A., Jr. *Civil Service in Early Sung China, 960–1067*. Cambridge: Harvard University Press, 1953.

————. "Region, Family and Individual in the Chinese Examination System." In *Chinese Thought and Institutions*, edited by John K. Fairbank. Chicago: University of Chicago Press, 1957.

————. "Sung Society: Change Within Tradition." *Far Eastern Quarterly* 14 (August 1955): 479–88.

Kroeber, A. L., and Clyde Kluckhohn. *Culture: A Critical Review of Concepts and Definitions*. New York: Random House, 1963.

Kryukov, M. V. "Hsing and Shih: On the Problem of Clan Name and Patronymic in Ancient China." *Archiv Orientalni* 34 (1966): 535–53.

Langlois, John D., Jr. "Authority in Family Legislation: The Cheng Family Rules." In *State and Law in East Asia: Festschrift Karl Bunger*, edited by Dieter Eikemeier and Herbert Franke. Weisbaden: Otto Harrassowitz, 1981.

Laslett, Peter. *The World We Have Lost: England Before the Industrial Age*. 2nd ed. New York: Scribner's, 1971.

Lee, Thomas H. C. "Life in the Schools of Sung China." *Journal of Asian Studies* 37 (November 1977): 45–60.

Levi-Strauss, Claude. "Social Structure." In his *Structural Anthropology*. New York: Basic Books, 1963.

Liang T'ai-chi 梁太濟. "Tu 'Yüan-shih shih fan' ping lun Sung tai feng-chien kuan-hsi ti jo-kan t'e-tien" 讀《袁氏世范》並論宋代封建關係的若干特點. *Nei-meng-ku ta-hsüeh hsüeh pao*, vol. 1978, no. 2, 35–44.

Liu, Hui-chen Wang. "An Analysis of Chinese Clan Rules: Confucian Theories in Action." In *Confucianism in Action*, edited by David S. Nivison and Arthur F. Wright. Stanford: Stanford University Press, 1959.

Liu, James T. C. "An Early Sung Reformer: Fan Chung-yen." In *Chinese Thought and Institutions*, edited by John K. Fairbank. Chicago: University of Chicago Press, 1957.

————. *Ou-yang Hsiu: An Eleventh-Century Neo-Confucianist.*

Stanford: Stanford University Press, 1967.

————. *Reform in Sung China: Wang An-shih (1021–1086) and His New Policies*. Cambridge: Harvard University Press, 1959.

Lo, Winston Wan. *The Life and Thought of Yeh Shih*. Hong Kong: Chinese University Press, 1974.

Ma, Laurence J. C. *Commercial Development and Urban Change in Sung China (960–1279)*. Ann Arbor: University of Michigan Press, 1971.

Maspero, Henri. *China in Antiquity*. Translated by Frank A. Kierman, Jr. Amherst: University of Massachusetts Press, 1978.

Makino Tatsumi 牧野巽. *Kinsei Chūgoku sōzoku no kenkyū* 近世中國宗族の研究. Tokyo: Nikko, 1949.

McDermott, J. P. "Land Tenure and Rural Control in the Liangche Region During the Southern Sung." Ph.D. dissertation, Cambridge University, 1979.

McKnight, Brian E. *Village and Bureaucracy in Southern Sung China*. Chicago: University of Chicago Press, 1971.

Metzger, Thomas A. *Escape from Predicament: Neo-Confucianism and China's Evolving Political Culture*. New York: Columbia University Press, 1977.

Munro, Donald J. *The Concept of Man in Early China*. Stanford: Stanford University Press, 1969.

Niida Noboru 仁井田陞. *Chūgoku hōseishi kenkyū: Dorei, nōdo hō, kazoku, sonraku hō* 中國法制史研究：奴隷農奴法, 家族村落法. Tokyo: Tokyo University Tōyō bunka kenkyūjo, 1962.

————. *Tōsō hōritsu monjo no kenkyū* 唐宋法律文書の研究. Tokyo: Daian, 1967 reprint of 1937 ed.

Polachek, James. "Gentry Hegemony: Soochow in the T'ung-chih Restoration." In *Conflict and Control in Late Imperial China*, edited by Frederic Wakeman, Jr., and Carolyn Grant. Berkeley: University of California Press, 1975.

Prusek, Jaroslav. *Chinese History and Literature: Collection of Studies*. Dordrecht-Holland: Reidel, 1970.

Saeki Tomi 佐伯富. *Chūgoku zuihitsu zaccho sakuin* 中國隨筆雜著索引. Kyoto: Society for Oriental Researches, 1960.

————. *Sōdai bunshū sakuin* 宋代文集索引. Kyoto: Society for Oriental Researches, 1970.

Sahlins, Marshall. *Culture and Practical Reason*. Chicago: University of Chicago Press, 1967.

Schirokauer, Conrad. "Neo-Confucians Under Attack: The Condemnation of Wei-hsüeh." In *Crisis and Prosperity in Sung China*, edited by John Winthrop Haeger. Tucson: University of Arizona Press, 1975.

Schumpeter, Joseph. *Imperialism, Social Classes: Two Essays*. Translated by Henz Norden. New York: New American Library, 1951.

Schurmann, H. F. "On Social Themes in Sung Tales." *Harvard Journal of Asiatic Studies* 20 (1957): 239–91.

———. "Traditional Property Concepts in China." *Far Eastern Quarterly* 15 (August 1956): 507–516.

Shiba, Yoshinobu. *Commerce and Society in Sung China*. Translated by Mark Elvin. Ann Arbor: Center for Chinese Studies, University of Michigan, 1970.

———. "Urbanization and the Development of Markets in the Lower Yangtze Valley." In *Crisis and Prosperity in Sung China*, edited by John Winthrop Haeger. Tucson: University of Arizona Press, 1975.

Shiga Shūzō 滋賀秀三. *Chūgoku kazoku hō no genri* 中國家族法の原理. Tokyo: Sōbunsha, 1967.

———. "Family Property and the Law of Inheritance in Traditional China." In *Chinese Family Law and Social Change in Historical and Comparative Perspective*, edited by David C. Buxbaum. Seattle: University of Washington Press, 1978.

Smith, Arthur H. *Proverbs and Common Sayings from the Chinese*. Shanghai: American Presbyterian Mission Press, 1914.

Soloman, Richard H. *Mao's Revolution and the Chinese Political Culture*. Berkeley: University of California Press, 1971.

Stone, Lawrence. *The Family, Sex and Marriage in England 1500–1800*. New York: Harper and Row, 1977.

Sung Hsi 宋晞. *Sung-shih yen-chiu lun-ts'ung* 宋史研究論叢. Taipei: Kuo-fang yen-chiu yüan, 1962.

Taga Akigoro 多賀秋五郎. *Sōfu no kenkyū* 宗譜の研究. Tokyo: Tōyō bunko, 1960.

Tillman, Hoyt Cleveland. *Utilitarian Confucianism: Ch'en Liang's*

Challenge to Chu Hsi. Cambridge: Harvard University Press, 1982.

Trauzettel, Rolf. "Sung Patriotism as a First Step Toward Chinese Nationalism." In *Crisis and Prosperity in Sung China*, edited by John Winthrop Haeger. Tucson: University of Arizona Press, 1975.

Twitchett, Denis, "The Composition of the T'ang Ruling Class: New Evidence from Tun-huang." In *Perspectives on the T'ang*, edited by Arthur F. Wright and Denis C. Twitchett. New Haven: Yale University Press, 1973.

———. "Documents of Clan Administration, I: Rules of Administration of the Charitable Estate of the Fan Clan." *Asia Major*, 3rd ser., 8(1960): 1–35.

———. "The Fan Clan's Charitable Estate, 1050–1760." In *Confucianism in Action*, edited by David S. Nivison and Arthur F. Wright. Stanford: Stanford University Press, 1959.

———. *Financial Administration Under the T'ang Dynasty.* Cambridge: Cambridge University Press, 1961.

Waley, Arthur. *The Life and Times of Po Chü-i 772–846 A.D.* London: George Allen and Unwin, 1949.

———. *Yüan Mei, Eighteenth Century Chinese Poet.* London: George Allen and Unwin, 1956.

Waltner, Ann Beth. "The Adoption of Children in Ming and Early Ch'ing China." Ph.D. dissertation, University of California, Berkeley, 1982 (University Microfilms no. 82-00301).

———. "Widows and Remarriage in Ming and Early Qing China." *Historical Reflections* 8 (1981): 129–46.

Wang Te-i 王德毅. *Sung hui-yao chi-kao jen-ming so-yin* 宋會要輯稿人名索引. Taipei: Hsin-wen-feng, 1978.

Ward, Barbara E. "Varieties of the Conscious Model: The Fishermen of South China." In *The Relevance of Models for Social Anthropology*, edited by Michael Banton. New York: Tavistock, 1965.

Watson, James L. "Chinese Kinship Reconsidered: Anthropological Perspectives on Historical Research." *China Quarterly* 92 (1982): 589–627.

Wolf, Margery. *Women and the Family in Rural Taiwan.* Stanford:

Stanford University Press, 1972.

Yang, Lien-sheng. "The Concept of 'Pao' as a Basis for Social Relations in China." In *Chinese Thought and Institutions*, edited by John K. Fairbank. Chicago: University of Chicago Press, 1957.

————. *Money and Credit in China: A Short History*. Cambridge: Harvard University Press, 1952.

Yang, Martin C. *A Chinese Village: Taitou, Shantung Province*. New York: Columbia University Press, 1945.

Zurndorfer, Harriet T. "The *Hsin-an ta-tsu-chih* and the Development of Chinese Gentry Society 800–1600." *T'oung Pao* 68 (1981): 154–215.

INDEX

Index

diligence, 78–79, 121, 123
discernment, 63
discord in families, 81, 86–87,
  90–92, 97–98, 181–84, 186–87,
  192–93, 196–97, 202–203,
  206–207, 223–24
division of property, 112–15, 127,
  132, 198–202, 227–29, 305,
  308–310
divorce, 98
doctors, 89
dowry, 94, 96, 102, 103, 116–18,
  133, 218, 224, 266, 308
Dream of Red Mansions, 170–71

education, 24, 88–89, 191–92; *see
  also* childrearing
Elementary Learning, 31, 34, 49
elites, 3n; see also *shih-ta-fu*
entrepreneurs, 319–20
envy, 69, 72–74, 146, 234, 238–39
epitaphs, 31, 41–42, 46, 49–50
equal inheritance, 34
Escape from Predicament, 22–24
etiquette, 36–37, 72–73, 90, 232
examinations, civil service, 12–13,
  15–17, 191, 234
extended family, 83

family (*chia*): classical views on,
  30–55; as a concept, 25; as a
  corporate unit, 37–51; ethics of,
  32–37; expenses of, 131–32;
  financial base of, 39–46,
  132–33; forms of, 83; head of,
  41–42, 102–103, 105–106, 121;
  management of, 46–50, 196–97,
  255; preservation of, 75–79,
  158–59; *see also* discord in
  families; family property.

"Family Forms," 31, 35–36,
  47–49, 103–104, 121
"family instructions," 42, 71, 77,
  88, 168
family property, 78–79, 101–120;
  concept of, 101–102; division
  of, 112–15, 127, 132, 198–202,
  227–29, 305, 308–310; management of, 121–31; *see also*
  common funds, dowry, individual funds, wills
family relationships: *see* brothers,
  daughters, daughters-in-law,
  father-son relationship, filial
  piety, mothers, sisters, uncle-
  nephew relationship, wives
Fan Ch'eng-ta, 20
Fan Chung-yen, 13, 54
Fan Ying-ling, 55
fate, 45–46, 67–68, 236
father-son relationship, 78–79,
  83–84, 86–92, 181–96; *see also*
  filial piety, unworthy sons
favors, 147, 268–70
filial piety, 30, 33, 35–36, 38–39,
  45–46, 92, 168, 183–85, 187–89
fire, 144–45, 283–84
Five Cardinal Relations, 32, 157
forbearance, 70–72, 146, 186,
  243–44
foster sons, 109, 217–18
friends, 260–61
frugality, 47, 121, 131, 168, 263,
  265
funerals, 266

gods, 65, 241, 242
gossip, 72, 85, 97, 205–208, 249
government, 152–53
grandchildren, 195

Index

Index

213–14, 229, 254, 271–74, 306–314
laziness, 78–79, 268
Le-ch'ing, 12n, 18, 19n, 176
legal writings, 55–56
li (principle), 63–64
li (ritual), 35–37, 47–49, 73, 77, 157, 169, 259–60
Li Fang, 105
Li Huan-ch'un, 327
Li Jih-hua, 324, 327
Li Pang-hsien, 58
lineage, 52–55, 149, 169, 229–30
Liu Chen, 19, 176
Liu, James, 6, 156
Liu K'ai, 85, 206n
Liu K'o-chuang, 55, 103, 215n
Liu Tz'u, 261n
Lo Ts'ung-yen, 88n
Lo, Winston, 156
loans, 124, 208–209
lot (*fen*), 67–68
"lot-books," 115, 307–310
Lu Chiu-shao, 43–44, 74, 78, 158, 193n
Lu Chiu-yüan, 43
Lü-chu, 288
Lu Ta-fang, 154
Lü Tsu-ch'ien, 20
Lu Yu, 98n
luxury, 131, 263–65

maids, 82, 84–85, 110–112, 135–37, 286–87, 298–300; *see also* servants
male-female relations, 84–86
managers, 124–25
manners, 36–37, 72–73, 90, 232
marriage, 97–99, 116, 122, 148–49, 221–25; *see also* remar-

riage, wives
matchmakers, 98, 223, 304
material interests, 23–26
McDermott, J. P., 12n
Mencius, 38, 39, 52, 68n, 70, 92, 178n, 181n, 183n, 185n, 246, 267n, 305n
merchants, 89
Metzger, Thomas, 22–24, 162n
Mo Tzu, 38n, 65
moneylending, 124, 303, 315–17
monks, 89, 216, 230, 267, 325
moral example, 73
moral values, 61–80
mothers, 84–85, 103, 112, 190, 220–21

National University, 18
Nei tse, 35–36, 47, 49, 103, 121, 220n
neighbors, 74, 150, 282–83, 306
Neo-Confucianism, 23–24, 61, 63–64, 73, 99, 129, 162n
Ni Ssu, 44n
Nishida Taiichiro, 218n, 330
nuclear family, 83
nuns, 304

occupations, 88–89, 190–92, 266–68
officials' families, 132, 209–211
old age, 84, 147, 187, 225–27, 245, 252, 287
oppressive officials, 272–77; *see also* corrupt officials
orphans, 204, 216–19
Ou-yang Hsiu, 13, 54, 63

Pao T'ing-po, 326
Pao-yen t'ang pi-chi, 324–25,

Index

self-defense, 145–46
self-indulgence, 88
self-interest, 7, 67, 92
self-sacrifice, 33
selfish desires, 44–45
selfishness, 93–94
servants, 278–79, 285–86, 289–96,
299–300, 303; beating, 49, 138,
140–41, 292–93; death of,
141–42, 293–94; gossip by,
207–208; management of,
48–49, 84–85, 134–44, 289–92;
purchase of, 136–37, 299–300;
supervising, 140, 291; suicide
by, 142–43, 293–94, 299; terms
for, 135; *see also* maids
sex as a basis of authority, 83
sexual segregation, 36–37, 47–48,
110
shame, 240–41
Shang shu, 65, 179n, 237
Shao Po-wen, 74
Shen Chi-chung, 213n
Sheng-hsin tsa-yen, 58–59
shih (lower officers), 38–39
shih (social world), 61
Shih chi, 212n, 315n
Shih ching, 241
Shih Ch'ung, 288n
Shih fan: see Precepts for Social Life
Shih-lin kuang-chi, 218n, 222n, 322
shih-ta-fu, 3–7, 12–15, 21–22,
66–67, 99–100, 130; culture of,
6–7, 9, 29, 60, 156–71; defined,
3–5; landownership of, 130n;
manners of, 7; representative,
11, 28; as a social class, 21–22
Shuo-fu, 324
sibling rivalry, 93
sisters, 96

small *tsung*, 53
social classes, 5; see also *shih-ta-fu*
social ethics, 69–75
social mobility, 3n, 4–5, 159, 165,
212, 261–64
social relations, 136–52, 231–32,
248, 252–53, 270, 306; *see also*
bullies, charity, class consciousness, neighbors, social ethics,
thieves
social status, 67–68, 231–36,
252–53
speech, 246, 248–49, 250–51, 258
spoiling children, 84, 88
ssu (private), 166
Ssu-k'u ch'üan-shu, 325, 327–28,
331–36
Ssu-ma family, 41–42, 95
Ssu-ma Kuang, 13, 31, 33–37,
40–42, 46–49, 53, 77–78, 82,
88, 89, 92, 97n, 103–104, 105,
121, 157, 158, 161, 165, 169,
179, 195n, 203n, 225n, 265n,
286, 297n
statecraft, 50, 165
stem family, 83
stepsons, 33, 91, 227
Su Hsün, 54, 157
Su Shih, 13, 59–60, 157, 188n
submission, 33
suicide, by servants, 142–43
Sun Ssu-mo, 257
Sung period, 12–14, 156–57,
164–65
Sung-Yüan hsüeh-an, 21, 327
superior men, 46, 139, 150–51,
175–76, 244–46, 254–55

T'ai-p'ing kuang-chi, 66
T'ang Chün-i, 6

(*365*)

Index

Index

Library of Congress Cataloging in Publication Data

Yüan, Ts'ai, chin shih 1163.
   Family and property in Sung China.

   (Princeton library of Asian translations)
   Includes index.
   1. Conduct of life—Early works to 1900.   2. Family—
China.   3. Property—China.   4. Upper classes—China.
5. China—Social life and customs.   I. Ebrey, Patricia
Buckley, 1947— . II. Title. III. Series.
BJ1558.C5Y8313   1984   646.7'8   84-42580
ISBN 0-691-05426-6 (alk. paper)